HELLSONG

HELLSONG

The Music of Hillsong

– In Praise of Folly –

"These things have I written unto you
concerning them that seduce you."

— 1 John 2:26

LANCE GOODALL

CONTENTS

To Phinehas, the grandson of Aaron who stopped the plague and stayed the hand of God,* and in memory of all those who have gone before, who have contended earnestly for the faith.[1]

[1] Num. 25:1–9, Ps. 106:28–30, 1Jude 3

FOREWORD

My sheep hear MY voice, and I know them, and they follow Me.

—Jn. 10:27.

I write this foreword to a highly critical book about Hillsong with a deep concern on two fronts.

Firstly, as a pastor of more than 55 years, I am always mindful of Peter the Apostle's clear enjoinder to church leaders (elders) in his time:

The elders who are among you I exhort, who am also an elder, and a witness of the sufferings of Christ, and also a partaker of the glory that shall be revealed: Feed the flock of God which is among you, taking the oversight thereof, not by constraint, but willingly; not for filthy lucre, but of a ready mind; neither as being lords over God's heritage, but being examples to the flock; and when the chief Shepherd shall appear, you shall receive a crown of glory that fades not away. (1 Pet. 5:1–4)

There are two things in this passage that stand out.

Firstly, those that are true pastors (elders) are NOT the head Shepherd. Jesus is. One of my catch cries throughout my ministry has been that I am only an unworthy errand boy for Jesus. The second thing that is emphasised by Peter is that reward for service is NOT now but later when Christ appears. In my opinion and that of the author of this book, these two things are where Hillsong and its modus operandi reveal their true nature, what Jesus calls the hireling (Jn.10:12,13). The pastor is to feed, care for, and be an example to the sheep and not look to the allure of money that comes with position. Therefore I say Hillsong and most so-called megachurches are NOT churches in the true sense. They are corporations, enterprises that pursue money and the control of people. They are thieves.

Secondly, I have a deep concern for the people, some of whom are my relations, who are not hearing and therefore not following the True Shepherd, whose voice is drowned out by the raucous, worldly sound of what the author of this book calls – Hellsong. These people deserve to be rescued before the Chief Shepherd appears.

Recently I preached a message based on Psalm 23 entitled 'A Day in the Life of a Sheep', being a title that dropped into my mind many years ago and formed the basis for a message that I have preached in various parts of the world. When I revisited the 'sermon', I came across the following anecdote which I found to be most moving.

During World War I, some Turkish soldiers tried to steal a flock of sheep from a hillside near Jerusalem. The shepherd, who had been sleeping, awoke to find his flock being driven off. He couldn't recapture them by force, so he called out to his flock with his distinctive call. The sheep listened and returned to their rightful owner. The soldiers couldn't stop the sheep from returning to their shepherd's voice.

I pray that this book will amplify the voice of the True Shepherd and that many will heed it and return from the fold of the corporate church to the fold of the Chief Shepherd before it is too late.

For the Record

In April 2009 Hillsong of Sydney took over Garden City Christian Church (GCCC) in Brisbane, Australia. This corporate-like "buyout" had never been done in quite this way before—one church completely swallowed up by another. Until the 'takeover', Garden City Christian Church had a sixty year history forged though the dedicated prayers and work of a membership that spanned two generations.

Hillsong was able to acquire the congregation's property through the stealth management of the board, in particular through the underhanded instigation of Pastor Steve and "Pastrix" Joyce Dixon, who were stand-in leaders of the congregation at the time. When the deal was done, Brian Houston stood as the preferred and only candidate for senior pastor. The membership had a choice: it could vote for Brian, or it could vote for Brian. Steve Dixon threatened the voters with the ultimatum that if Brian was not elected, he and his wife would leave and head off to China to minister.

It was during this protracted takeover of GCCC by Hillsong United that Lance Goodall first attended Christian Witness Ministries Fellowship (CWMF) where I pastor, most recently in association with Jeff Pitman; and ever since, Lance and his wife have been loyal members.

As part of Christian Witness Ministries, we have for over 20 years regularly produced a magazine with the title *Contending Earnestly for the Faith*, or CETF. For this publication, beginning in the autumn of 2011, Lance wrote a three part series of significant articles on the subject of Hellsong—The Music of Hillsong. These articles were the catalyst for his writing this book, and my hope and prayer is that Lance's book will introduce a measure of self-examination to and accountability for

Lance Goodall

individual Christians and congregations mesmerized by Hillsong's music, any discernment about which, until Lance's writing, has been sadly lacking.

Hillsong United is having their own feature documentary produced that will be filmed on five different continents. The production will tell the story of Hillsong's worldwide rise to fame and notoriety. It is most unlikely that information like what is outlined here will be covered in Hillsong's Hollywood production.

So for a prelude to 'the rest of the story', read this book. We should all be disturbed by the godless entertainment mode of worship that has now become entrenched in churches worldwide. The church needs to heed the message of this book NOW!

Philip L. Powell

Pastor

Christian Witness Ministries Fellowship.

Ephesians 5:18–19

17 Nov 2014

INTRODUCTION

Where upon the king took counsel, and made two calves of gold, and said unto them, It is too much for you to go up to Jerusalem: behold thy gods, O Israel, which brought thee up out of the land of Egypt. And he set the one in Beth-el, and the other put he in Dan.

—1 Kings 12:28, 29

We see early in his reign: a king in Israel happened upon the idea of providing another worship centre for the people. They no longer needed to make the long journey to Jerusalem. King Jereboam made two calves of gold and set up one in the city of Bethel and the other in the city of Dan.

It seemed such a simple concept. They could incorporate their religious practice into their daily lives—a religion of convenience with little to no adjustment or change to their existing lifestyle. He even made a house of high places and made priests who were not of the sons of Levi (1 Kings 12:31). Jereboam brought a dynasty of departure throughout Israel and successive kings followed in his disastrous footsteps. Proud, aspiring men ruin one another, and involve others in the ruin.

In the Exodus, there in the wilderness, the children of Israel provoked Aaron to make them an idol made like the golden calf in Egypt. He cried out: 'These be your gods, O Israel, that brought you out of the land of Egypt' (Exod. 32:7,8)

What begins as a work of God can quickly become the work of man, which ends up corrupted and confounded. Leaders who consult human wisdom fail to put God first; instead give in to the desires of the people and fall into convenience, compromise, and contempt.

Therefore, our concept of God is important not only to our theology but also to our mode of living. Our failure in applying true Christian doctrine is based on a low and subjugated opinion of God. Our view of God, whether lofty or base, is the fountainhead from which all springs have their source. Perverted and twisted notions of God will by necessity mean a perverted religion. The deception in all this is we may have an orthodoxy that complies with the truth but, outworked practically, betrays an unworthy view of God.

Like Jereboam, a new breed of ministers has given rise to an alternative form of worship. This delight in the downgrade is justified by the need to maintain interest in religion in an ever-changing contemporary world.

The long history of the children of Israel shows this gradual decline away from God, which always began with the apostasy in her vision of God.

This book shows the modern-day Christian church has taken this very same path.

1

BUILD IT AND THEY WILL COME

And they said, Go to, let us build us a city and a tower, whose top may reach unto heaven; and let us make us a name.

—Gen. 11:4

After almost a century, the Anglican church of St Mary Magdalene in Brisbane, Australia, is closing its doors because of an ongoing decline in parishioners.[1] There are just a few faithful members left. God is dead and church is boring, right?

But, only suburbs away, Hillsong's Brisbane congregation is flourishing!

Every Sunday, this modern church, full of hand-raising, heart-thumping, hipster-style Christianity, packs the house. As the rock concert begins, words are displayed on the large multi-media screens. The lights are dimmed, the excited crowd stand to their feet, all clapping along in time to the music. The hi-tech laser lights fan the auditorium, the fog machines spread their mist, and the lead singer shouts 'let's lift up the name of Jesus'. The pounding force of the music, and the crescendo of

Lance Goodall

cymbals fills the room and intensifies the atmosphere. At Hillsong Church, you come for the Rock Concert, and soak in the sermon.

An article in the *Courier Mail* in November 2014 gave a glowing report of the incredible growth of Hillsong. Pastor Steve Dixon in Mt Gravatt, Brisbane, said Hillsong's attendance rate has grown exponentially over the last four or five years. Hillsong Church is part of the megachurch phenomenon exploding across the globe.

'Our church is alive and full, and we've got momentum going where people want to come and check it out,' Pastor Dixon said.

'The life in the church, the size of the church, and the momentum—people find it all very attractive.'[2] Parking is at such a premium that two traffic officers are paid by the Brisbane Campus to direct traffic between Sunday services.[3]

This is the new gospel revolution—God is now made glamorous!

Hillsong has packaged together what other churches only dream of. While many grapple with a simple name change, Hillsong continues to climb the charts with success, numbers, and revenue. They have an uncanny ability to produce catchy Christian rock 'worship', year in and year out, charismatic energy, and a global expansion programme, which engulfs and swallows up many a church. This all-embracing "we don't condemn" approach has brought worldwide appeal, a winning combination in major cities around the globe.

On any given Sunday, children and adults are assisted to make church that much easier with a crèche or breakout area, coffee stations for the adults to 'mix and mingle', and enumerable volunteers in their uniform T-shirt who welcome you with broad smiles, 'welcome home' packs, and directions to the best seats.

The church has just celebrated a milestone of 30 years, one of the most globally successful and influential churches.[4]

On the surface, Hillsong appears similar to any evangelical megachurch, but this Pentecostal phenomenon has grown into a global sensation.

The church has established locations in key cities across the globe, including London, Cape Town, Paris, Kiev, Stockholm, Amsterdam, Barcelona, Copenhagen, New York, and in recent months, cities in Argentina. And Ben Houston, the son of founders Brian and Bobbie Houston, now makes Los Angeles his home. Few churches in the U.S. could boast such global influence.

The New York location, co-founded by Brian's son Joel Houston, is one of the city's fastest-growing churches, attracting celebrities like singer Justin Bieber and Oklahoma City Thunder forward Kevin Durant.

Hillsong Church takes in $100 million a year from its tax-exempt Australian operations as its weekly flock of 34,000 hands over their hard-earned cash.[5]

Having said all that, Hillsong is never far from controversy. With their 'trending on Twitter' theology, their vast financial tax-free stash, and child abuse rumours involving Brian Houston's father, Frank, the organisation is always in the spotlight. Even during their Hillsong Conference in July 2015, their guest Mark Driscoll was interviewed, a man of controversy who has made it his trademark to make 'off' comments about women. Since then his leadership style has brought an implosion to his ministry at Mar's Hill Church. However, Hillsong, this 'Jesus Juggernaut', keeps ploughing on regardless, mostly through the mass marketing of its music. The church was originally known as Hills Christian Life Centre back in early 80s, but the music became so popular they took on the Hillsong name. Senior pastor Brian Houston founded

Lance Goodall

Hillsong 30 years ago in Australia.

"To be honest, when we started we had no idea that one day we would have campuses and churches all around the globe like we do today," Houston said.[6]

Young people are drawn to Hillsong's music. What once was a music ministry has become a music industry.

To date, the Hillsong United label has sold over 16 million albums. Its album *Zion* debuted at number one on iTunes overall albums chart in the United States and in seven other countries and was listed at number five on the Billboard 200. They also have *Hillsong Worship* which is the congregational expression of worship from Hillsong Church— a local church with global influence. More recently, they have a new arm to capture the tweens under the label *Young and Free*.

It has the largest Twitter following among any faith-based artists with more than 680,000 followers and more than 4 million Facebook fans.[7]

In the opening narration of the movie *Field of Dreams*, Ray (Kevin Costner) explains how he had a troubled relationship with his father, who was a devoted baseball fan. While walking through his cornfield one evening, he hears a voice that whispers, 'If you build it, he will come.'[8]

Hillsong's secret appears to be a combination of music, casual charismatic theology, and this kind of 'build it' philosophy. Hillsong frankly relies on its music, money, and marketing.

This success mantra is echoed by Marcia McFee, a worship consultant who coaches various churches on enhancing their services with light, sound, and motion. The idea is that today's modern worshippers can't sit still in the presence of God. This restless mob, must be doing something, whether it be responding with dancing or drumming or raising hands.[9]

What wonderful drawcards. Church filled with excitement, momentum, dancing, drumming, and rich visuals—what more could one want?

But the question must be seriously asked. Do we blindly follow this success? Do we just sit back and accept the giddy heights that Hillsong Church has reached and put it all down to God? Do we put it down to God's blessing or perhaps something else? We see that many are coming, but coming to what?

As we shall discover, not all that glitters is gold.

2

BAD BLOOD

Their feet run to evil, and they are swift to shed innocent blood: their thoughts are thoughts of iniquity; wasting and destruction are in their paths.

— Isa. 59:7

Taylor Swift opened up the 2014 American Music Awards with her song 'Blank Space'.[1]

The 2015's award ceremonies just happened to fall on the 22 November, a perfect Masonic number sequence (22 + 11 = 33) to show much is hidden in plain view. More about that later. Only weeks before at the Video Music Awards (MTV), she showed off her talent with her debut single 'Shake it off' where she danced with a troop of guys in tuxes as she moved around three large figure sixes, which were ramps or aisle walkways, giving a clear triumphant shout out to the Satanic number 666 and her vile master.[2]

Although the young Australian hip-hop artist Iggy Azalea received the most nominations at the AMA Awards, it was Swift who gave the crowd- pleasing opening to the night's awards.

The AMA performance started off with Taylor Swift and her 'date', seated end to end at a long dining table, floating inside a large gilded frame in the form of a portrait. The frame lowered, and then Swift walked over and poisoned her date. Then she lit a rose on fire and moved the flame across to her fingertips. Moving on to another part of the set, she found another date. His movements seemed to defy gravity, with Swift sending him skyward he goes flying off stage, with a just flurry of her hands. The stage covered with picture frames and fire.[3]

Multichannel News reported that Swift had been recognised for her historical album sales as the only artist in history to have three albums— *Speak Now*, *Red*, and *1989*, each debuting with more than 1 million sold in their very first week.[4]

But hold the phone!

Taylor Swift (born 13 December 1989) was raised in Wyomissing, Pennsylvania. Taylor moved to Nashville, Tennessee, at the age of 14 to pursue a career in Country music.[5] But now, some years later, Swift's music now contains elements of country, pop, and pop rock. But she still self-identifies herself as a country artist.[6]

At the 2013 CMT Music Awards, a fan-voted awards show for country music videos and television performances, Swift's live rendition of her song 'Red' was with crimson red dress, red guitar, red mic, laser light show, and large flashing red pyramids dominating the stage, the crowd lapping up every twirl and toss of her hair.[7]

No one could be more appealing at the present time than this alluring angelic pop/country princess. But the gritty sound of Swift's music and the success factor that comes with it, oozes the darkness and the blackness of the occult. Taylor Swift opened the 2014 American Music Awards show ceremony with pure Illuminati pageantry.[8]

Swift's performance was themed around witchcraft, fire, magic, ritual sacrifice, sex, lust, and the shedding of innocent blood.

At the same award show, in the Contemporary Inspirational Artist category, Hillsong United was nominated along with Casting Crowns, and Newsboys.

Why is this ghastly Satanic sacrifice being offered up in the same breath as nominations for Christian artists? Do we blame Swift or those that drive the industry? Should the world's music industry be recognising the music of Christians? Should Christians be thinking that being recognised by the world scene is somehow to have made it?

It's now public knowledge that MK ULTRA mind control is real and that psychiatrists working for the CIA have used various mind control techniques on individuals. This destroyed the lives of many of the victims. These experiments continue to this day.

These same mind control techniques are being used in the music industry, in particular in grunge, gangsta rap, hip-hop, or any new genre. These are the same old techniques just with new labels.[9]

I am convinced that the enemy of our souls has trained up Hillsong Church as his number one tool to bring the church into his grip, at the very pinnacle of this age.

As shocking as this is, the story of Hillsong is one of the greatest conspiracies of our time!

I do not say this to be intentionally controversial. The point of this book is to show this is true. But due to the fact that their 'craft' and the occult influence behind it are even more subtle than first realised and because it is under the guise of good clean Christian lyrics and church 'worship', it is often difficult to recognise.

Most are oblivious to the end game, but the goal is still the same: to shed the blood of the innocent.

3

EVERYBODY'S FREE TO FEEL GOOD

But thou didst trust in thine own beauty, and played the harlot because of thy renown, and poured out thy fornications on every one that passed by.

—Ezek. 16:15

A throbbing beat washes over the cavernous nightclub in Crown Heights, Brooklyn. 'Feel the Holy Ghost vibe,' chanted out the DJ, urging on the audience, 'If you have a problem, and no one else can help!' he shouted. The audience thundered back, 'Call Jesus!'

On the first Saturday of every month the Omni goes through a 'conversion'. The Omni founded in New York becomes the Gospel Lighthouse, a club suited to the sensibilities of evangelical Christians.

Duane Knight, the founder of the Gospel Lighthouse and a disk jockey and master of ceremonies known as Dr D said, 'I knew there was a need in the body of Christ for more social events, a clean atmosphere where there was no smoking, no drinking and no cursing.'[1]

Back in 2003, *Time* magazine ran the story on a new phenomenon called the Christian nightclub. Club 3 Degrees in Minneapolis, Minnesota, boasts all the nightlife staples, like pool tables, DJs, and live bands. But a few things are missing, like alcohol, cigarette smoke, and music with racy lyrics. That's because the club was the city's first downtown Christian nightclub. 'We see this as a mission,' said the Rev Nancy Aleksuk, who has managed the club's move to its new $3 million venue with a capacity of 1,700.[2]

Russell David Hobbs—founder of The Door, Christian nightclubs in Dallas and Fort Worth, Texas—says his clubs have done so well he is opening a third in Plano, Texas. In Hallandale Beach, Florida, Club Mighty opens as a once-a-month Christian nightclub created by an insurance agent Sheldon Bland. 'We get believers and nonbelievers,' said Bland. 'People are looking for an alternative to the typical club scene.'[3]

The controversial Hobbs describes how he took some time out, spending three years in the wilderness, and received a greater revelation of God's character and a vision to 'bridge' the gap between the church and the 'secular' world.[4]

The church has slid so far from the truth that we now have Christian Halloween, Christian tattoos, and Christian trance parties.

Hobb's message to find a way to bridge the gap between the church and the world is much like a business merger: there can only be one winner.

4

YOU'VE GOTTA RIGHT TO PARTY

Love not the world, neither the things that are in the world. If any man love the world, the love of the Father is not in him. [16] *For all that is in the world, the lust of the flesh, and the lust of the eyes, and the pride of life, is not of the Father, but is of the world.*

—1 Jn. 2:15,16

The Difference, a Christian nightclub located in the metropolis of Houston, is catering to a new kind of clubber; and, for many, it's exactly what they have been looking for.

The Difference, or Club Manhattan as it's known the other days of the week, offers gospel, jazz, Christian comedy, and hip-hop.

The new philosophy is that people who still want some kind of sophisticated pleasure can do so without having to go to hell as a result. For these believers, the Difference offers a compromise between the godlessness of a typical nightclub and the puritan idea that no one should be caught up in such rioting and revelry. But can I ask how this facility can be a replacement for church as it is known in the traditional sense?

The owner suggests people don't want the scene in a standard nightclub, but they don't want to be obligated too much beyond attending the Sunday morning service either.[1]

This is a place where church folks can turn up. A blend of the Holy Ghost and dancing, singing, rapping, poetry, praying, crying, kneeling, preaching, and altar calls?

There is a different kind of convert today, and they seem to express their faith and lifestyle by no longer doing anything too worldly or too questionable. You see, God wants Christians to have a good time. This is the new kind of thinking. This is the new breed of religious convert. Give us just enough religion to ease our conscience but not too much to kill our fun.

The new creed is primarily concerned with reforming but continuing on in the old life. We simply add Jesus to our life. The world's pleasures are eventually added to the church.

The world in the background goes around with the idea that God offers universal forgiveness, regardless of our lifestyles. As long as we don't wander or stray too far from the path, then all is well. The root of our problem is we love our sin. So we construct a god for ourselves who will allow us to do what we want, when we want. The Lord Jesus rides around shotgun with us in our Christian convertible. God is to conform to our ideals, our standards, and our judgement of what is right or wrong. We use God's goodness as a license, liberty, and excuse for sin.

As Charles Finney, the 19th-century Evangelist, explains, we cannot just live having a mental ascent to the Law:

"Nothing is innocent unless it proceeds from supreme love to God and equal love to man, unless the supreme and ultimate motive be to please and honour God. In other words, to be innocent, any amusement must be engaged in, because it is believed to be at the time, most pleasing to

God, and is intended to be a service rendered to him, as that which, upon the whole, will honour him more than anything else that we can engage in for the time being. I take this to be self-evident." [2]

Sadly, all of us would fail this simple test. The world is what it is today, with all its pain and misery, as a direct result of sin and man's selfishness. We end up with all sorts of diseases, disasters, droughts, fires and famines, which we put down to climate change, failing to read the signs of God's impending wrath on sin in these types of calamities.

This is manipulating the character of God to our own ends. Man is in the centre. Man wants to be in control. What man wants to do, what man conceives, he will achieve is the modern motto. Yet this is the primary thinking for book sales of Christian leaders worldwide.

Man then is made supreme, and God is modified to fit in with our worldly viewpoint.

For men shall be lovers of their own selves, covetous, boasters, proud, blasphemers, disobedient to parents, unthankful, unholy. (2 Tim. 3:2).

In other words, modern theology, liberalism, and what we call humanism. It starts with man and ends with man.

We live this hedonistic heresy that 'everybody's free to feel good' and 'you've gotta right to party'.

We desire God's righteousness but not his rulership. We are happy with a Saviour but not a Sovereign

His favour but not his firmness. We want his pardon but not his preeminence. We desire His righteousness but not His rulership. We acknowledge the Lordship of Christ but we remain outlaws in God's kingdom. We have a belief that incorporates the treason and deceit of

Absalom and Joab (See 2 Sam. 14:1–20; 2 Sam. 18:2,11–15; 2 Sam. 20: 9–12).

We cannot manipulate God. We must follow Him rather than expect Him to follow us. Had the Israelites learned this lesson, they probably would not have demanded a king like the other nations but instead waited for God to provide His choice for them.

Our treason is our marketing departments and enterprise. Promotion is reasoned as the new pragmatism.

The modern believer acknowledges the need of salvation. Yes, but please don't talk to us about the cost of salvation.

'Today's church wants to be raptured from responsibility.' — Leonard Ravenhill.

We are called to separation, from the world's ways, the world's pleasures, and the world's lifestyle. Have they forgotten that Christ and Belial have no agreement (cf. 2 Cor. 6:14–15)?

The fact is, there is no difference anymore!

A. W. Tozer, (1897–1963)—who was an American Christian pastor, preacher, author, magazine editor, and spiritual mentor—wrote in his book *Tozer on Christian Leadership*, referring to the church:

Her power lies in her being different, rises with the degree in which she differs and sinks as the difference diminishes.[3]

Tozer argues that despite the clear examples of history and from scripture, we still repeat the same mistakes.

5

GIVE ME THE NIGHT

*We grope for the wall like the blind, and we grope as if
we had no eyes: we stumble at noonday as in the night;
we are in desolate places as dead men.*

—Isa. 59:10

The room is black, the coloured lights flash all around. The atmosphere is electric, laser lights glide through the room. The youth are pumping! There is noise and hollering. The MC onstage shouts out (just being heard) over the beat, the clamour, and cymbals, 'Oh yeah . . . this is good. You're dancing crazy. I'm excited to be here.' That was crazy!! The place was awash with youthful exuberance. What was he saying? I don't think he even knew what was coming next. What I just described to you was not on the Sunset Strip, LA, or in a discotheque in Manhattan, New York.

This was an in-house event on August 2010, held at Hillsong Brisbane City Campus for the young adults at Powerhouse, just 18 months after Hillsong, Sydney, took over the church there.[1]

Now the nightclub has been brought right into the House of God!

It is only because of the Lord's mercies that we are not consumed. (Lam. 3:22). There is no longer any difference between the Church and the world. The devil has won! Youth being led by youth! This type of ministry is appalling! These same young people come to church with alcohol on their breath from the night before, while the little ones are allowed to dress up in Halloween costumes during the October vigil.

Meanwhile, the adults are making sure they are catered to with a romantic dinner called "Wine-Night Stand"? Themes linked to drunkenness and debauchery. The Bible says not to even *name* such things among you (cf. Eph. 5:3).

People object to the statement that the devil has won! But just stop for a moment. When God's children are just reformed but not transformed, when we are attracted to what the world esteems, when the Lord Jesus is nothing more than a fashion accessory, or T-shirt then the gospel has fallen in the streets.

Such carnality is unacceptable to God and, as we shall see, is totally incongruous with the true worship of God.

The sins of the world are now wholly approved by a shocking number of professing Christians. Tozer declared, 'Young Christians take as their models from the rankest kind of worldlings, and try to be like them as much as possible.'[2]

To show how significant the downgrade is, the walls have been painted dark or black. And I know from my own experience they placed black paper over the windows of the doors of the main entrance as part of this transition. I remember coming into the auditorium one Sunday morning just before 10:30 am. The bizarre aspect was the auditorium was so dark (like low mood lighting or a nightclub)! As I walking down one of the aisles, I was saying to myself, *What have they done? Why is it so dark in here?* Two minutes before, I had been walking in the car park in beautiful, bright sunshine! We have gone back to black.

A new 'Plague of darkness' is being promoted and copied from church to church and from state to state. Church after church has blackened their walls. They have bought into the godless world of entertainment. This 'franchise of folly' is the staple diet of churchgoers in these metropolitan churches up and down the country. And they think God isn't angry! They even think he's pleased!

This is soulish religion based on buildings, buses, programmes, pizza nights, coffee and conferences.

This is totally wrong thinking! We are being slowly poisoned. Like the lobster in the pot, the water temperature is slowly increased till it's all too late. This tidal wave of profanity and corruption, is seeking to carry away every hint of genuine Christian community. These men are swayed by the fashion of Hollywood, and not the inner life of Christ. Modern Christian faith is nothing more than a label, a surface religion that has less depth than a tattoo. We stoop to society's moral standard and congratulate ourselves on receiving applause and approval from the world on social media.

This is a most grievous thing to contemplate—the blind are leading the blind!

6
DANCING IN THE DARK

*Therefore night shall be unto you, that ye shall not have
a vision; and it shall be dark unto you, that ye shall not
divine; and the sun shall go down over the prophets,
and the day shall be dark over them.*

—Micah 3:6

In the last two years, Hillsong has opened an additional church campus
in Brisbane, Australia, in a precinct colloquially called 'The Valley', a
campus location they are calling Brisbane City, now a hub of flashy
apartments, niche shopping, eateries, expensive European sports cars, all-
night clubbing, drunkenness, and vice.[1]

The venue for church is a regular nightclub. One review of the Met club
tells of Friday and Saturday night's with girls in cages and a smoky haze.[2]

Although this should be enough, the idea, according to Brian Houston
is, by taking over a rented facility in this nightclub, any revellers who
wake up from their drunken state the next morning will find themselves
in church is sheer, spiritual, Laodicean lunacy.[3]

Clever stuff, but does a church use a nightclub as a common facility for worship where dancing and revelry occurred the night before? And have we sunk so low that this is the only way to get sinners inside 'our' walls? Is this the new evangelism? The new theology is we will meet the sinner where they are, and both will fall into the ditch.

By the way, the new logo for the Met nightclub is a fiery dragon in a form like the one slain by St George during the Middle Ages, telling us who really owns this facility.[4] Since the initial setting up of this campus (May 2014) they have moved into a performing arts studio in the area.[5] Its seems according to their website all this is designed to reveal Jesus through music, creativity and innovation, to present the gospel in a fresh way. It just so happens that one of the building tenants, an Asian food café down on street level, displays a red dragon as it's signage.

At the same time Ben, Brian Houston's younger son, is spreading his wings and embarking on a 'church' plant in downtown Los Angeles. Admittedly, it's taken just a little bit of organising; but with a few keen youth and a mosh pit band, they have managed to kick off in a nightclub, bar, and burlesque theatre called The Belasco in 1050 S Hill Street, Los Angeles.[6]

As I take a breath, Hillsong has launched a new church plant (or takeover) of local congregations in the Gold Coast region, the beach and glitter strip of Queensland, some 50 minutes from Brisbane, Australia. The previous pastors caved in to Hillsong. Hillsong Brisbane Pastor Steve Dixon said the opportunity was too good to ignore.[7]

The change, according to the young couple, came as a complete 'suddenly'.[8] Do they mean a complete redundancy? In fact there are three sites on the Gold Coast now, which means the surfers and clubbers are spoilt for choice.[9] Hillsong is hoping to reform the 'sin city' stereotype. These Gold Coast campuses join 149 other venues around the globe to incorporate live sermons and televised content from the church's Sydney headquarters.

In the heart of the desert, the city of Grace church, Arizona, co-pastored by Terry and Judith Crist, has acquiesced to the appeal of the failsafe formula that Hillsong employs.[10] And not satisfied with just one plant on the California coast, Ben Houston and his wife, Lucille, are 'spying out the land' in the Bay Area of San Francisco, looking to 'expand their territory'.[11] It may be great for business, but it has nothing to do with preaching the gospel.

But wait, there's more. If you still haven't had enough, you can grab the remote and turn to Hillsong's very own TV channel 24/7, courtesy of a partnership with Trinity Broadcasting Network.[12] Hillsong's new channel could be Christianity's version of MTV?! Then in New York, 'Pastor of Cool' Carl Lentz has been holding Hillsong services at Irving Plaza, near Union Square, since September 2010.[13]

Irving Plaza is a 1,025 person ballroom-style music venue at 17 Irving Place and East 15th Street in the Union Square neighbourhood of Manhattan, New York City. The three-level auditorium has served as a Polish Army veterans' headquarters, a swing music ballroom,* and a rock venue and has hosted church services as well. It is featured on a list of '50 Best Concert Venues of America'.[14]

In 1978, the hall was converted to a rock music venue by future Peppermint Lounge promoters Tom Goodkind and Frank Roccio, who, after a year, began to share promotional efforts with a Club 57. They brought in acts such as the B-52s, Talking Heads, the Ramones, with Friedman and Tropia, a wealth of British bands, establishing the venue as a premier American location for punk and new wave music.[15]

So can you see where I'm going with all this?

The rock club called Irving Plaza has had some 30 years of history as a rock and alternate rock venue, and this is the home of modern church services?

Although Irving has a seedy and questionable past, as the new headquarters for Hillsong NYC, I can see this is a perfect fit!

We think that if our church services are not sufficiently a 'Holy Ghost' party, we are not offering anything that will appeal to anyone.

Have the people ever stopped to ask what is church for, and for whom is the service for?

It matters little to have won 5 ARIAs (Australian Recording Industry Association Music Awards) or achieved platinum sales but rather that we have gladdened the heart of God, with our consecration and our worship!

There is a difference between worship and entertainment!

'But ye *are* a chosen generation, a royal priesthood, an holy nation, a peculiar people; that ye should show forth the praises of Him who hath *called you out of darkness* into his marvelous light' (italics added) (1 Pet. 2:9).

It seems clear to me that churchgoers these days are happy to have a 'sanctified party'. 'And this is the condemnation, that light is come into the world, and men loved darkness rather than light, because their deeds were evil.' (Jn. 3:19)

In an interview with CBS news Lentz said, 'you don't have to sell a party.'[16]

It seems we are comfortable with convenient compromise, and conformity to the world. Indeed, we are happy dancing in the dark! **

**Footnote Swing music, or simply Swing, is a form of American music that developed in the early 1930s and became a distinctive style by 1940. Swing uses a strong rhythm section of double bass and drums as the anchor for a lead section of brass instruments such as trumpets and trombones, woodwinds, saxophones, and clarinets, etc.

The Peppermint Lounge was a popular discotheque located at 128 West 45th Street in New York City that was open from 1958 to 1965. It was the launchpad for the global Twist craze in the early 1960s. Many claim The Peppermint Lounge was also where go-go dancing originated, although this claim is subject to dispute.[1]

7

CALIFORNIA DREAMIN'

I hate, I despise your feast days, and I will not smell in your solemn assemblies.

—Amos 5:21

Located in downtown Los Angeles, the Belasco is the new home of Ben Houston and the leadership team from Hillsong, otherwise- known as Hillsong LA. They have been renting the space since May 2014. The first service was on the 11th.[1*]

As the Twist craze hit in 1960–1961, celebrities swarmed into the Peppermint Lounge - Audrey Hepburn, Truman Capote, Marilyn Monroe, Judy Garland, Liberace, Noël Coward, Frank Sinatra, Norman Mailer, Annette Funicello, even the elusive Greta Garbo - to dance to the house band, Joey Dee and the Starliters. Jackie Kennedy was such an enthusiast that she arranged for a temporary "Peppermint Lounge" to be mounted in the White House. A sister club was opened in Miami Beach. The 128 West 45th Street venue reopened as a gay bar called "Hollywood", most notable for the 1970s DJ residency of Richie Kaczor, who went on to great success at Studio 54. [6] The 45 th Street space reopened as G. G. Barnum's Room on July 20, 1978, and continued until November 1980. [7] Male go-go dancers performed on trapezes over a net above the dance floor. [8] G. G. Barnum's Room was a popular meeting place for transsexuals, drag queens and homosexuals. The "G.G." was a reference to the Ianniello-owned Gilded Grape located at 719 8th Avenue, a notorious gay bar which operated from the early 1970s until 1977.

Right in the heart of entertainment central, The Belasco is a multipurpose event and entertainment venue. Opening in 1904, this historical landmark of the 1920s, completed in 1926, was renamed the Follies and became a popular burlesque destination. Its opening night in 1926 featured the play "*Gentlemen Prefer Blondes*". The Belasco has made a comeback in 2011 and is now one of the city's premier multi-purpose complex, with a long and rich history serving as a theatre, burlesque venue, church, and filming location.[2]

The theatre houses the Belasco Nightclub, Bar, Lounge and Vintage 10 Fifty Wine Bar. The theatre has sophisticated lighting and sound equipment, a venue with a vast event space, and dance club.[3]

Past performers at the Belasco include 2 Chains, deadmau5, and Tyga.[4]

So is this the venue for the work of God? Is this God's modern-day equivalent to Azusa Street?

Here in this well-established venue, every Thursday, Friday, and Saturday night are the compressed sounds of techno, excessive booze, modern-day burlesque girls in their 'Victoria Secrets', shaking their booty on stage. But a sweep of the floor, a switching on of the lights, the curtains are drawn, a tap on the microphone, and, hey, it's Sunday morning church folks. Let's give all our praise and worship to Jesus!

Yet just hours before, this pleasure palace was crowded with a myriad floodlights, synthesiser and bass, risqué dance moves, the sweat of bodies, hormones, and lime and tequila shots.

Now we mix a strange cocktail of Bibles, booze, bass and burlesque. This is spiritual suicide!

Hillsong's motto is championing the cause of the local church everywhere, a church growing in stature, innovation and most importantly, Godly influence.[5]

Yet how do they possibly think the holy God of Heaven will be comfortable to manifest His presence here? Where, can I ask, is the godly influence? It seems nothing more than a marketing idea, such as the concept of adding the word organic on the front of food packaging, or trying to reduce the sugar content to a cola by adding stevia. We have confused the world of media and harlotry with the God who says, 'I change not.'

Reviews of Hillsong LA suggest that church at Belasco theatre is fun while others comment that the surroundings are dark, the music too loud, and you have to have broad smiles and fake being happy.[6]

They hold baptisms at Hillsong LA with everyone in black T-shirts. This 'doctrine of darkness' has made even the aspect of white robes (the righteous acts of the saints) look outdated. This is a mockery of the scriptural reference to the saints robed in white washed clean (Rev 7:9,13,14).

Coincidentally, as I mentioned earlier, Hillsong Brisbane City campus moved out of a nightclub into a local performing arts studio in 2015.

Now like kissin' cousins Hillsong LA has made venue changes as well and has 'worked a miracle' and purchased a performing arts theatre in their neighbourhood. It hasn't been used in a long time, and it needs a lot of work and renovations. But Ben Houston is excited that after months of hard work and diligence, they signed a 15-year lease with two 5-year options in October 2015. This means Hillsong LA has a stake in the ground in downtown Los Angeles for the next 25 years![7] Hillsong is looking to move into the building by the beginning of 2017.

The Variety Arts Centre was originally built for the Friday Morning Club, a women's social and activism organisation founded in 1891 by suffragist Caroline Severance.

Later the women decided to demolish the building and raise a five- story stone structure suitable for large theatre performances, meetings, and more. The centre opened in 1924 and has had guests such as Charlie Chaplin, Cecil B. DeMille, and Eleanor Roosevelt.[8] Its two auditoriums and seating for almost 2,000 made it suitable for popular arts and theatre programs in the 1920s and 1930s. The venue was used for live plays, cabarets, meals, and revivals of early stage and radio dramas, as well as film shoots and special events rentals.[9]

In 1977, the women's club sold the building to the Society for the Preservation of the Variety Arts for theatre and other artistic uses. It hosted occasional dance nights and concerts with bands such as the costumed, fake-blood-spewing punk-act Gwar. The building has even been used twice by horror film producer Jason Blum as a Halloween haunted house.[10]

For Hillsong, this is nothing they can't fix. They will just reform the venue from heavy metal gore and horror-film blood to Jesus blood.

Ben says, "The Belasco will always hold a special place in our heart and we will continue to love people, love our city, and point people to Jesus from this great place."

It seems Hillsong is picking up from where historically, the Roman Catholic Church has always been, Christianising pagan temples and other structures into churches. A notable strategy called *interpretatio christiana* was the practice of converting pagan practices and culture, pagan religious imagery, pagan sites, and pagan calendar to Christian uses as a form of proselytization (evangelism). The idea was to take a non-Christian cultural element or historical fact with a view to adapting it to Christianity by means of appropriate interpretation and morphing it into the world view of Christianity.[11]

In Buenos Aires, Argentina they are doing the same thing, Church held in a rented downtown theatre where heavy metal bands like Slash, Sabaton and Megadeth have held concerts. I also note that all these church plants are in cities and areas of money and affluence, never in a slum district, where the Lord Jesus would willingly go.

"I do not think the devil cares how many churches you build, if only you have lukewarm preachers and people in them."— Charles Spurgeon

As the Mama and Papas song *California Dreamin'* narrates, one of them stopped by a church he passed along the way. Maybe this is Brian's hope as well.

But, to keep filling these ever-expanding venues, Brian's false gospel of accepting Jesus as 'Lord of your heart' provides the necessary splash of holy water, and keeps the flock coming back for the 'atmosphere'.[12]

So is this the way God builds His church? I wonder.

8
I WANT TO BREAK FREE

Who do I have in heaven but You? And I desire nothing on earth but You.

—Ps. 73:25

Though many can't seem to resist the excitement and vibe at Hillsong, I left Hillsong some six years ago. I was an active member of Garden City Christian Church (GCCC) for nine years from March 2001 to October 2009 under the leadership of Bruce Hills, pastor. I was part of the choir and for a short period was one of their backing vocalists.

It was a great surprise to me, and a great many others for that matter, that there was about to be a takeover by Hillsong.

After his return from three months' leave, Pastor Hills was told by the board of GCCC in November 2008 that they wanted a pastor who was more of a CEO to run the church.[1] By his own confession and recounting of the story, Bruce was told to resign.[2] Money talks! This is exactly what they got in Brian Houston, a CEO rather than a pastor to run a corporation and not the church of God.

This begs the questions, 'How long had the board been thinking of changing the leadership?' And who contacted whom? Did Brian Houston contact GCCC, or did the current assistant pastor Steve Dixon pick up the phone and raise the matter with Hillsong?

Brian Houston became Brisbane's senior pastor, under the guidance, leadership, and affirmation of assistant pastor Dixon and the board of GCCC. So-called campus pastor Steve Dixon, according to various reports, was unsure just how long he would remain part of the pastoral team.[3]

Another question that begs an answer is 'Why did the elders and board members of GCCC unanimously endorse the "takeover" by Hillsong, and Brian Houston as senior pastor without investigating Hillsong for themselves?' On the day of the members' vote, a number of the elders stood onstage and testified that they had never ventured south to attend even ONE Hillsong conference in Sydney, yet they were backing this change all the way! Once source clarified that i

t wasn't unanimous, it was a tie. Steve Dixon casted the last and deciding vote (perhaps that explains the reason why he became so strongly committed to the new Hillsong system in order to make sure it works and that it was the right decision endorsed by him – coupled with personal gain of course!).

Members and adherents of GCCC weren't given any opportunity to make any suggestions or participate in any open discussion of leadership alternatives. The decision had been made. GCCC members were simply presented with one leadership appointment and asked to vote.

There had been only one side of the story. The promo was always presented in a positive light, with little opportunity to question or linger on doubts. Any questions raised were screened and well managed. I have since learnt this is a technique used by the business world to manage change. There had been more spin over the pulpit in God's name during these months than found in your average toothpaste commercial.

Once the decision was made, GCCC became an instant 'franchise' of Hillsong. The church is now market driven under the guise of being 'purpose driven'.

GCCC totally lost its identity!

Without a moment to breathe, the leadership from Sydney suddenly arrived, putting their stamp on this new way to 'do church'. We were presented with a spokesman for this and a spokesman for that. We even had a special 'money preacher' to encourage and remind us of the need to tithe and give generously. Such coercion from a 'church' vis-à-vis Hillsong, which is a juggernaut financially with a turnover of $90 million plus a year, is neither godly nor, in my opinion, acceptable.[4]

GCCC was no longer just affiliated with strong ties to Hillsong—we became Hillsong!

From day one, everything had to change, and it did. For example, there was a fairly new coat of paint on the 'church' walls from previous renovations, painted to a modern grey. Yet within days of the signs and the optic fibre going in the carpark, the auditorium was repainted to the colour of the other Hillsong churches. Why spend the money?

As part of the takeover, we had the celebrity gala feast from Hillsong Sydney, all of them given top billing, visiting to give their counsel, and ideas. All the rich and famous were given a place of honour. For those who couldn't get enough of their Hillsong idols, they could now have them visit here in Queensland. With every guest appearance, Brian Houston became more like an Amway Diamond than a pastor.

Hillsong, when it is all said and done, is run as a corporation, not a church.

There is no New Testament precedent for this model and certainly not for its duplication.

The church has taken its cue from Wall Street. It has been offered the kingdoms of this world; and yet instead of denying the flesh, it has embraced the path of least resistance and, in so doing, has denied the cross and the One who bought us. By love for the world, we make ourselves an enemy of the cross: "Do not love the world or the things in the world. If anyone loves the world, the love of the Father is not in him." (1 John 2:15)

- Edwin Orr pointed out that 'seldom does God call one who ministers the Word to the ministry of money making. They are two separate callings'.[5]

Ambition and success are the new golden calf.

Warren W Wiersbe comments, 'Few things taint our goodness like covetousness; a desire to be popular, and the ecstatic feeling that comes when we exercise power over the people who give us their idolatrous adoration. When our motives are wrong; our ministry is wrong; and the consequences are tragic for us, for those who follow us and for the whole church.'[6]

This is now playing itself out at Hillsong.

The Hillsong way actually follows to the letter what is known as the seeker-sensitive or church-growth movement model. This model is to help bring 'unchurched' sinners into the meetings and to make them as comfortable as possible with the experience:

- Dress down in clothing and style.

- Jeans are the new formal wear.

- Low mood lighting similar to a bar or nightclub.

In Brisbane campus, it is so dimly lit it appears like night-time, yet it's 10.30am. Quite a contrast especially in Queensland when the sun is up as early as 5.30am.

Secular music is played as background music prior to the start of the service e.g. The Verve - 'Bitter sweet Symphony'.

Worship – now accommodates the excitability of the young and the unchurched. Music is now more about entertainment than the sole purpose of lifting up our God above all other gods.

The lyrics (words) of the songs have progressively become 'I, me, my' focused instead of Christ Jesus focused, e.g. 'In Your Freedom I Will Live'.

Worship is now limited to 20 to 30 minutes. Big screens are not there for the glory of God. It's not pictures of creation but the names and faces of those onstage that are lifted up.

Hillsong relies on the quality of programmes, not the power of the Holy Spirit, for transformed lives. Preaching is often a simple 30-minute sermonette. Preaching on the whole is 'relevant' and topical. It is now a people-based message to 'help' the hearer with their felt needs, e.g. happiness, family, finances, relationships, job, career etc.

What it boils down to is a type of pop spirituality that effectively teaches that every human being is divine or basically good, God's Word is not really the final authority but is still useful as a moral guide, the goal of my life is centred on me, and what I desire determines what happens in my life.

What this type of church model does is nothing more than increase the numbers of adherents and leaves the sinner in his sins.

The church now has a flock of deceived sheep, or are they in reality misguided goats? Hillsong's messages lack any mention of sin, repentance, prayer, obedience, death to self, holiness, sacrifice, suffering, hell, even God himself. Preaching lacks sound doctrine. Closer analysis reveals it is more based around pop psychology than biblical truth.

I left Hillsong for some of the following reasons:

- The Hillsong way actually follows to the letter what is known as the seeker-sensitive or church-growth movement model, which is walking away from biblical principles.

- Preaching lacks sound doctrine. Messages often fail to mention sin, repentance, prayer, obedience, death to self, holiness, sacrifice, suffering, hell, even God himself.

. Closer analysis reveals it is more based around pop psychology, than biblical truth e.g. purpose.

The message has little challenge or need for personal self-assessment. The scripture exhorts us to examine ourselves (cf. 2 Cor. 13:5).

- The music and worship is man centred.

- Brian Houston's preaching could be termed heterodox humanism.

- The preaching frequently includes different Bible versions but mainly the use of The Message, which is a New Age interpretation, and not a true translation.

Often this is quoted in church to expound or reveal a greater truth. It is normally thrown up on the big screen for everyone to read. The Message Bible was produced by Eugene Peterson, not as a translation from the original texts but as one man's version in a form of paraphrase. Yet, without fail, not a Sunday will go by without this Bible version being quoted.

Brian Houston frequently preaches a message that is a watered-down gospel. He teaches from Bible verses that were never meant to say what he teaches. This is known as eisegesis. Eisegesis (from the Greek root εις, meaning *into, in, among*) is the process of misinterpreting a text in such a way that it introduces one's own ideas by reading into the text. While exegesis draws out the meaning from the text, eisegesis occurs when a reader reads his/ her interpretation into the text. As a result, exegesis tends to be objective while eisegesis is regarded as highly subjective. Verses are used just because they have a certain word or contain a truth that fits with the message.

To highlight this, in 2011 in a sermon *The Power of the Risk – Part 1*, Brian Houston outlined that life was a risk, and Hillsong was a risky church. He suggested that by Jesus going to the cross, He took a risk!?

Houston will say anything to make a point. Jesus was sent of the Father and was as part of the divine plan to die on the cross, He was able to say, 'It is finished', (Jn.19:30), and by doing so, remove the debt of our individual sin that was so offensive to God.

He knew the awfulness of the cross, and declared to his disciples that he could if he chose, have the Father send him twelve legions of angels (Matt.26:53). But the cross was his determined will. In fact, he qualified this prior in his prayer to the Father in the garden, that his mission was finished. (Jn. 17:4).

Christians are to live by faith, and wisdom, not by risk. If you want risk, join a rock climbing club.

A few minutes later, Brian embarks on this crusade again suggesting that Jesus was a risk taker turning up at the tomb of Lazarus, with a crowd gathering. He said 'Jesus risked failing, he risked looking stupid!'

To develop his message further he quotes;

> 41 "Then they took away the stone *from the place* where the dead man was lying. And Jesus lifted up *His* eyes and said, 'Father, I thank You that You have heard Me'. 42 And I know that You always hear Me, but because of the people who are standing by I said *this,* that they may believe that You sent Me." – Jn. 11:41,42 NKJV

He stops short and fails to quote the key part of verse 42, *'that they may believe that You sent Me'*, the very reason that Jesus was there at Lazarus' tomb in the first place. Jesus' whole point for being there was to raise Lazarus from the dead. This was so that they would believe on him as the son of God, not to show that he was a risk taker.[7]

Jesus said, 'Father, I thank You that You have heard Me', therefore risk is totally absurd, as Jesus then went on and raised Lazarus from the dead.

Houston's message to help his hearers embrace life and risk, at the same time demeans the Lord Jesus, undermines his divinity and over emphasises his humanity.

This is a ruthless disregard for biblical accuracy to say the least. This then is Eisegesis: A verse used like an evangelical fortune cookie, plucked out of its context to make a point irrespective of the flow, and the text's obvious message.

Let's overlook the obvious that Jesus was God come in flesh to deal with our sin, and instead talk about life lessons and taking risks.

Yes, Jesus is our example, but it has nothing to do with risks, but obedience and suffering; he humbled himself, and became obedient unto death, even the death of the cross. (Phil 2:8, 1 Pet. 2:21).

The shocking reality about modern preaching is more about what is NOT said, than what is said.

Martyn Lloyd-Jones brings this out when he states 'There is one invariable characteristic of the false teaching, which is, that it always takes from and detracts from the glory of the Lord Jesus Christ'. (D.M. Lloyd-Jones, Christian Unity, Ephesians Series, Banner of Truth, Eph. 4:14, P. 239)

He writes that they don't deny the Lord Jesus outright; they are too clever for that. But their false teaching always detracts from His glory by bringing prominence to man.

This then is doctrine on the downgrade. This departure has bred a pedigree of dumbed-down disciples. The scriptures are to make us wise unto salvation through faith which is in Christ Jesus. The bible is for doctrine, for reproof, for correction, for instruction in righteousness: not risk taking (2 Tim 3:16,17). The Lord Jesus is being portrayed in pulpits as one who helps us to live our lives, to help solve our problems. The church can no longer stomach sound doctrine.

Brian Houston was asked by a reporter why his church is so prosperous in a country like Australia, which is decidedly *not* the Bible belt. He replied, 'We are scratching people where they are itching' ('The Lord's Profits',

Sydney Morning Herald, January 30 2003). Brian is literally fulfilling prophecy.

"For the time will come when they will not endure sound doctrine; but after their own lusts shall they heap to themselves teachers, having itching ears" (2 Timothy 4:3).

A whole generation of illiterate believers brought up 'drinking the kool-aid' will only end in disaster.

Apart from such examples of biblical violence outlined here and in other parts of this book;

- Hillsong lacks discernment on a number of levels.

- From my own visits, I saw only the ministries, books and products Hillsong promotes available in the Hillsong Resource Centres (bookshop), along with Houston material of course.

- Houston happily accepts and promotes the following teachers, most of whom have personally been at Hillsong conference.

Those who have made an appearance at Hillsong conferences over the years are the following:

- Joyce Meyer, prosperity teacher/preacher (cf. Paul's instruction about women teachers (1 Tim. 2:12).

- Joel Osteen, prosperity preacher and denier of the true gospel

- Jerry Saville, prosperity preacher

- T D Jakes, prosperity preacher and denier of the Trinity, guest speaker at the 2010 Hillsong Conference

- Rick Warren, member of the Council of Foreign Relations (CFR) trained under Robert H Schuller (a.k.a the *Hour of Power*)

- Bill Hybels, pastor of Willow Creek Church who has admitted getting it wrong with the seeker-sensitive model. Hybels trained under Robert H Schuller and is good friends with Rick

Warren.

- In recent conferences, Steven Furtick from Elevation church in North Carolina.

- Joseph Prince from Singapore.

Darlene Zschech and Hillsong United band played for the Pope Benedict during his visit to Sydney in 2008.[9]

Sisterhood (a term widely used by Hillsong) is a concept borrowed from the women's liberation movement and the new age.

Finally, one of the worst instances of spiritual bankruptcy I've experienced was the live performance of the "Hillsong Creation story", featured at Hillsong Brisbane on 11 October 2009.[10] Aspects can only be touched on here. The play was done in humour and obviously aimed at a young audience. However, the fun and humour ended very quickly, where the creation narrative turned into a sham. Plants and animals were various members of the congregation and pastoral team, dressed in costumes. Somehow we were meant to make the mental leap, as a congregation, from the bouncing chicken and the freckle-faced rat to God's act of creating our world and the universe out of nothing!

The seven days of creation were played out by various actors, and God even created for us superheroes like Batman and the Incredible Hulk. God is so great that He invented superheroes, can openers, and cars!

At one point the Holy Spirit was taking too long to come 'hovering over the waters'. Towards the end, Adam and Eve appeared clothed (minus the fall, sin, Satan, and God's provision). The story (skit) ended. The point here is the gravity of creation was belittled and undermined.

Steve Dixon then expounded for about twenty minutes the creation story as found in Genesis chapters 1 and 2. He touched on a few points, expressing the view that we are not able to know the exact time frame of God's creation, whether it was a literal seven days or a certain period of time. Darwin would have been proud on the 150th anniversary of his *Origin of Species*, and Richard Dawkins would be more than bemused.

It must be said that they who began well have turned aside to follow a shepherd who is no shepherd. The hireling has crept in unawares.

Paul complained in his day, 'For I have no man like-minded, who will naturally care for your state. For all seek their own, not the things which are Jesus Christ's' (Phil. 2:20,21).

The evangelical bus has lurched, swerved, and veered way off track. But where are we heading? The way, once narrow but now abandoned, has become a broadened highway, opening up to the verdant plains leading on to the gates of a city that arises in the distance. It is that great city, clothed in fine linen and purple and scarlet, decked with gold and precious stones and pearls! It is a city proud, that grand and ancient city founded upon seven hills —mystery Babylon, papal Rome! (Rev. 17:3.4).

9

AND THE BEAT GOES ON

That at what time ye hear the sound of the cornet, flute, harp, sackbut, psaltery, dulcimer, and all kinds of music, ye shall fall down and worship the golden image.

—Dan. 3:5

It's 1967. Sonny and Cher released the song 'The Beat Goes On'.

The song was a satire or metaphor of the fashion and cultural trends of their day. The song mentioned sexual overtone and the reference to the new religion (last line). Nowadays, our beat is the sound of rock music in all its shades, pounding away in our iPods, shopping centres, online, and in every kind of church service. The beat is still going on, and 'drums keep pounding a rhythm to the brain'.

Hard rock (or heavy rock), according to Wikipedia, is a loosely defined genre of rock music that has its earliest roots in mid-1960s garage rock, blues rock, and psychedelic rock. It is typified by a heavy use of distorted electric guitars, bass guitar, drums, and often accompanied with pianos and keyboards.

Hard rock developed into a major form of popular music in the 1970s, with bands such as Led Zeppelin, Deep Purple, Aerosmith, AC/DC, and Van Halen and reached a commercial peak in the mid-to-late 1980s. The glam metal of bands like Bon Jovi and Def Leppard and the rawer sounds of Guns N' Roses followed up with great success in the later part of that decade before losing popularity in the face of grunge.

Despite this, many post-grunge bands adopted a hard rock sound; and in the 2000s there came a renewed interest in established bands, attempts at a revival, and new hard rock bands that emerged from the garage rock and post-punk revivals. Hard rock is a form of loud, aggressive rock music.

The instruments of choice for the modern-day adolescent are the electric guitar, a strong bass drum, and a backbeat on snare, sometimes using cymbals for emphasis. The bass guitar works in conjunction with the drums, providing a backing for the rhythm and lead guitars.[1]

Vocals are often growling, raspy, or involve screaming or wailing, sometimes in a high range or even falsetto voice.

In the late 1960s, the term *heavy metal* was used interchangeably with *hard rock*. Heavy metal took on 'darker' characteristics after Black Sabbath's breakthrough at the beginning of the 70s and the 1980s. It developed a number of subgenres, but, despite this differentiation, hard rock and heavy metal have existed side by side.[2]

With the ascendance of rock and roll, a watershed moment occurred between 1962 and 1964 when the Surfaris released 'Wipe Out' and when Ringo Starr of The Beatles played his Ludwig kit on American television—events that motivated legions to take up the drums.

Irwin Silber, a communist who desired to see social degeneration that would overthrow the 'old order', observed that rock music has this power

and it lies in its backbeat rhythm. He wrote, 'The great strength of rock
& roll lies in its beat. It is a music that is basically sexual, unpuritan'
(*Sing Out*, May 1965).[3]

As we close out this chapter, I want to make reference to the verse used
as the header from Daniel 3:5–7. Nebuchadnezzar wanted to be
worshipped, but he knew that he was just a man; so he needed an image
of some 90-feet tall of pure gold to magnify himself. The gold speaks of
Babylon. Today various groups want to return us to this golden age. The
Antichrist will just be a man, but he will magnify himself through a
similar image.(Rev. 13:15).

The scriptures make it clear that the King was declaring himself to be a
god and demanding worship. But the worship was to be directed at the
statue. And even the numbers are clues: A statue 60 cubits tall, 6 cubits
wide and celebrated with 6 instruments. And we know from the book of
Revelation that 666 is the number of the Antichrist. Here is a
foreshadowing of the religious system of the future Antichrist. He will
have power over all people and his religious system will be based on the
worship of him.[4] Notice that Nebuchadnezzar's image in Daniel 3:1 has
the **exact same 10:1 size ratio as the obelisk,** known as the Washington
Monument in Washington DC.

In the coming days (and soon), those who refuse to worship the Beast's
image will be killed just as Nebuchadnezzar proclaimed death to anyone
who didn't bow to worship his IMAGE. Satan is using the Masonic
pyramid and All-seeing Eye to recruit followers to the New World
Order. Notice that the same thing will happen when the Antichrist
comes. Those who refuse to worship the Beast's image will be killed.
Satan is using worldly music to captivate the end times church, now
given over to the 'modern' sound, heavy beat, syncopation, back beat, etc.
Interestingly there are four lists of these instruments in Daniel 3. And of

these, six instruments are named three times.[5]

Contemporary Christian music (CCM) will take on the same purpose as all worldly music today. It wasn't about singing or lyrics but THE MUSIC.

Likewise, in these last days, Satan is conditioning the world to worship the Beast and the image of the Beast through the medium of music. Just look at concerts and festivals like Rock am Ring in Germany, and

Tomorrow land for example, and you see this culture of Satan worship. As we continue to investigate this further, it will not be hard to see that Hillsong this Christian, rock-powered mega-church, plays into this same culture. As we shall see has similarities between Nebuchadnezzar's image and the coming Antichrist's image are more than coincidental.[6]

Satan's methods haven't changed.

10
WORSHIP WARS

David again brought together all the able young men of Israel—thirty thousand.² He and all his men went to Baalah in Judah to bring up from there the ark of God. . . . They set the ark of God on a new cart and brought it from the house of Abinadab.

—2 Sam. 6:1–3

How easy it is for God's people to do the wrong thing. Left to ourselves, we will naturally choose the way that ends in failure.

Here is the story of David, with all his zeal and enthusiasm, desiring to bring back the long-awaited ark of God. But it was one of David's great mistakes, as the ark ought not to have been put upon a cart, old or new. The ark had never been carried on the back of a wooden wagon.

The law gave instruction for it to be carried by the Levites and those specifically of the family of Kohath (see Num. 7:9). Everything used in the worship of God was to be *set apart* for that purpose: a new cart may have been made out of respect, a cart that had never been used for anything profane or common, but this was not sufficient, for the ark should have been carried on the shoulders of the priests; and the neglect of this was the cause of the terrible death of Uzzah.

David should have known, and so too should the priests and Levites, who were well-versed in the law of God. They should have stopped, taken a breath, and at least referred to the sacred book. Instead, they were led by the example of the Philistines who put it on a new cart and set it off towards Bethshemesh and were not punished for it.

How many Christians use this very concept as a rule for life and living? Because God hasn't punished me straightaway, he must be okay with it, not knowing that the goodness of God, his patience, and his kindness are to lead us to repentance and to correct our ways (see Rom. 2:5,6).

Church leaders run whole organisations on this same premise that, if God seems to be silent on an issue, then He must be okay with our programmes. Like David, these leaders run around with a bunch of young people, caught up in youthful enthusiasm.

Thirty thousand young men? This has a corresponding reflection in our day. Young men are appointed to leadership to bring growth but, in fact, drive away the presence of God and quench the Spirit in our midst.

But it should have been considered that the men of Gath were an ignorant heathen who had no proper understanding of the nature of the precious furniture they had in their possession, and, of course, the Philistines had no such thing as a Levite. The lesson here is Christian worship is God-initiated. God himself provides the clear and specific guidelines for communion with him, and his people should respond accordingly. Uzzah was too familiar with holy things. He thought that because they were all worshipping God and bringing back the ark with all the excitement and jubilation around it, God wouldn't care about His law. We don't know what Uzzah knew of the law, but of course, the

Levites should have, and David also.

If we break one of the commandments, we tend then to break them all. Uzzah was standing too close to the ark and then felt it his responsibility to steady it from falling. In Numbers 4:15–20, the Levites are forbidden to touch the ark *on pain of death*. This penalty was inflicted upon Uzzah. He was the first to suffer for this breach of the law. Here, we see the dangers of following the Lord through good intentions, running with something that works or doing anything based on general principles and not the direct patterns of scripture.

'God, we are saving our young people', but how are you saving them? 'God, we are here and praying for revival', but what are you doing right now that either hinders or stops revival? Uzzah sinned through ignorance and impulse. The oxen stumbled. The ark was falling. He did what he thought was right and stretched out his hand to prevent it. It was the natural thing to do. Uzzah touched the ark with impunity, thinking that as a Levite, he was free from any form of punishment.

But, even in things that may seem small and trivial, and though your effort may be done with good intention, as this was, it does not excuse the sin; ignorance of the Law, therefore, is not sufficient for sinner or saint. Neither are those who are the most zealous in religious matters exempted from marks of God's displeasure when things go wrong.

Human initiative is not necessarily the work of God. Uzzah was not the first to make this error. Abraham, generations before, had sought to have a child through a surrogate birth. Yes he obtained a child, but not the one God had promised.

Notice Uzzah died by the hand of God as the token of his displeasure, and this shows that it is dangerous in matters of worship to act contrary to the command of God. He did not leave the ark of God to the hand of

God but chose to influence and steady the direction of the ark by the hand of man. When a pastor participates in something, he gives it a type of divine sanction. Pastors then have an important role in the direction of a church. The role of a modern pastor is often busy, leading to a failure to seek God and to obtain direct guidance and a proper mandate.

Their agenda then becomes their own preservation, their own gain, and their own importance. Pastors fall into the trap of maintaining the equilibrium, making sure that no one 'rocks the boat', and that everyone 'toes the line' and the ark is steadied. The preaching in the pulpit in turn becomes a place of pleasantries and philanthropic philosophy. Commonly, the style of the leadership is lording it over the flock.

Therefore, one of the most dangerous places to stand in the church are in positions of leadership and, in particular those in worship or music ministry who fail to minister under divine ordinance. David chose a certain 'style' of worship to bring back the presence of God to Jerusalem, and Uzzah made sure it stayed on track, 'making it happen' according to man-made agendas. Both men saw God's displeasure.

We have all heard the anachronistic argument that new styles of music when introduced have always brought a certain amount of controversy. What's the big deal?

You see, if it was wrong, God wouldn't bless it. But just to make sure, these modernists bring the argument sufficient to silence the dissenters by dragging in the likes of Christian composer Isaac Watts. What has Isaac Watts got to do with modern worship? And why was he so controversial?

The argument goes something like this. Isaac Watts brought something new to the church, and it caused all sorts of controversy and debate. Modern worship music has been breaking 'new ground' and, in like manner, has had its fair share of critics; so, in the same way, although misunderstood, modern worship is bringing the gospel to the world.

So is this a valid argument? What was the setting?

Isaac Watts was born in Southampton, England, on July 17, 1674. According to encyclopedia.com, his parents were Dissenters—Non-Conformist, who were not members of the Church of England.

Non-conformist – tended to refer to a Protestant Christian who did not 'conform' to the governance and usages of the established church. That was a serious matter at the time; Dissenters were allowed to worship freely but were often denied certain civil rights. Isaac Watts, was the oldest of nine children, and was born while his father, (also named Isaac), was in prison. [1]

Watts had a classical education, learning Latin, Greek and Hebrew.[2]

"From an early age, Watts displayed a propensity for rhyme. As a precocious child, he once responded when asked why he had his eyes open during prayers:

'A little mouse for want of stairs

Ran up a rope to say its prayers.'

On receiving corporal punishment for this, he cried:

'O father, father, pity take

And I will no more verses make.'[3]

Complaining of the current hymns one day to his father, he was encouraged, 'Well then, give us something better, young man!'[4]

The United Reformed Church of the United Kingdom's website states, 'Isaac Watts was the man who, virtually single-handed, introduced, developed, invented the hymn as we know it today.'[5]

Psalm singing, or psalmody, was the main form of congregational musical involvement in services when Watts came on the scene.

Psalms and hymns at the time were sung to tunes that would be well-known to most members of a congregation or choir and that fitted the rhythm and meter of the words. Even so, Watts created a musical revolution.

A hymn, in the most general sense, is a song of praise to God; but it is distinguished from a psalm, a lyrical expression of devotion drawn from the book of Psalms in the Bible.

Sacred music scholar Stephen Marini (2003) describes the ways in which Watts contributed to hymnody.[6] "Notably, Watts led by including new poetry for 'original songs of Christian experience' to be used in worship. The Psalms, had been developed by 16th century reformer John Calvin, who initiated the practice of creating verse translations of the psalms in the vernacular for congregational singing.[7] Watts' introduction of extra-biblical poetry opened up a new era of Protestant hymnody as other poets followed in his path."[8]

As Paul said, 'Speaking to yourselves in psalms and hymns and spiritual songs, singing and making melody in your heart to the Lord' (Eph. 5:19). They were 'spiritual' hymns. In other words, doctrine put with melody.

Watts also introduced a new way of rendering the psalms in verse for church services. The psalms were originally written in biblical Hebrew within Judaism, which one can assume most people in England couldn't speak.

Marini sees two aspects to Watts' verses, which he calls 'emotional subjectivity and doctrinal objectivity'. Watts achieved an axiomatic quality that 'presented Christian doctrinal content with the explicit confidence that befits affirmations of faith'.[9]

So having said all that, does the comparison hold up? Are the controversies of Watts' day comparable to contemporary worship today?

Scott Aniol, founder and executive director of Religious Affections Ministries, makes a sound argument that such a comparison is not tenable today for the following reasons.

In Watts' day, the controversy was not over any particular musical style. 'Watts wasn't a composer; he did not write music. He wrote texts or poems to be put to music.' Watts wasn't out to create a new form of 'pop music'. The tunes used for the metrical psalmody that were common in churches in that day were then adapted for use with the new hymn texts once Watts and others began writing them.[10]

'The controversy then wasn't really over old style versus new.' At the time they were singing English paraphrases of the psalms. Age had nothing to do with it. 'Rather, the controversy was over whether it was permissible to sing texts written by mere humans, rather than to sing only the Psalms written under the inspiration of the Holy Spirit'. John Calvin taught that only inspired songs should be sung—that is, the psalms.

Watts (and others) argued that we should be permitted to sing non-inspired texts as long as the truth was accurate and compatible with the Bible truths. Many of the Watts hymns that we sing today are actually psalm paraphrases. ('O God, Our Help in Ages Past' is from Psalm 90, 'Jesus Shall Reign' is from Psalm 72, 'Joy to the World' is from Psalm 98; etc.)

So, yes, Watts was controversial! But not based on modern ideas of hymnody. He did not have to resort to sentimental words and sloppy tunes to help bring a deep experience of the love of God. He was arguing that we should be allowed to summarise scriptural truth in our hymns rather than limit ourselves to inspired psalms and that we should aim for a higher quality of English grammar and poetry in our sacred songs that doesn't water down biblical truth.[11]

So history doesn't always repeat. Nor are the reasons for controversy in previous times necessarily the same as the arguments for promoting today's music.

Again, it's the argument 'those songs were new then, and our songs are new now'. Many have bought into this fable, that hymns are old and outdated!

Please don't misunderstand me. I'm not against the 'modern' in Christian music. But it just seems that the modern music mutilates the gospel message. This contemporary genre, unfortunately even from its early days, tended to deviate a lot from well-established constructs. A lot of, not all, but MOST modern worship is 'lite' on doctrine and has become 7/11 choruses: seven lines sung eleven times.

'John MacArthur commented on worship at a recent conference;

"Low understanding of God — superficial, shallow, understanding of God — leads to shallow superficial content-less hysteria. You can whip that up, you can create that kind of frenzy, it has nothing to do with worship, it isn't worship….You've been singing hymns this week. Why? Because there's rich theology in hymns. We don't have to go hysterical; we want your mind fully engaged."[12]

We don't want the dirge, but we don't want the doctrine either.

Even Brian Houston seeks to jump on the bandwagon and stand up for the ideal of modern worship. In his 2014 vision message, he affirms that 'when God is moving, a pioneer [church] sings a song that is music to the uninitiated, but sounding brass to the establishment, in other words stepping forward into new ground, not everyone who represents the statuesque, or the establishment gets excited about the new thing that God is doing'.[13]

The lesson here is, modern mass media cannot replace the divine work of prayer and the power of the Holy Spirit.

Once more, Brian's argument is a thin veneer because a new cart won't get the move of God going too far before the oxen eventually stumble!

11

THE DEVIL HAS ALL
THE GOOD MUSIC

Thou art the anointed cherub that covers; and I have set thee so: thou wast upon the holy mountain of God. . . .[15] *Thou was perfect in thy ways from the day that thou was created, till iniquity was found in thee.*

—Ezek. 28:14,15

Larry Norman's name is synonymous with the beginnings of Christian rock. His gospel was 'Why should the devil have all the good music?'

His importance to the fledgling Christian rock music scene is hard to underestimate. Although now largely forgotten, in the late 60s and early 70s, as the Jesus people movement brought thousands of young people back to the church, Norman's music was a reflection of the radical changes taking place.[1]

Norman was born on 8 April 1947 in Corpus Christi, Texas. At the age of 3, he relocated to San Francisco, California, with his family and, in the mid-50s, became fascinated with the music of Elvis Presley.[2]

Elvis Presley, who was raised in the Mississippi delta, is a story of two worlds, of the present and the eternal. A fight went on for his soul, in a search for truth, in a world of lies and deceit, money and affairs, vice and Vallium. Presley was forever pulled and challenged by an undercurrent of gospel tradition, Southern charm, and generous heart. But Presley never found what he was searching for and subsequently never found Christ.

Norman was saved at the age of 5 and started singing at 9.[3]

During this time, he also frequently accompanied his father on Christian missions to prisons and hospitals. At the age of nine, Larry began writing and performing original rock-and-roll songs at school, experimenting and incorporating a spiritual message into his music.

Pop music had the Beatles, Stones, and Dylan; Norman seemed to represent a sanctified version of all three—a 'righteous rocker' to use the title of one of his songs. The 1972's *Only Visiting This Planet* topped lists as the single best Christian album of all time; and songs like 'I Wish We'd All Been Ready', 'Why Should the Devil Have All the Good Music', and 'Why Don't You Look into Jesus' captured perfectly the fervent last- generation mindset that typified those times.[4]

The 60s saw a great spiritual emphasis in rock music. Eastern ideals made regular appearances in music. Out of this climate came the Jesus movement and Larry Norman's first solo release, 'Upon This Rock', in 1969. This is considered by many to be the first Christian rock album.

After graduating from high school, Norman, with the band People became involved in the local rock music scene. He played big rock palaces of the 60s with people like The Doors, Jimi Hendrix, Janis Joplin, the Jefferson Airplane, the Grateful Dead, Bob Dylan, and others. It was in the late 60s that Larry, the nonconformist, began to attempt to combine the message of the gospel with the music of the drug culture. He called it Jesus Rock, and it became the sound of the Jesus movement.[5]

Norman worked and 'played' with these icons of music in his early career. Norman had been brought up in a Christian home, but this young man was hanging out with the most influential musicians of a generation, at a period where 'Jesus is just all right with me'. But these musicians were anti-god, and anti-religion. They were their own god, and, eventually, the thorns of success and celebrity came to choke and stifle the Holy Spirit and bring great compromise to Norman's religious life.

By the time Norman joined People, a San Jose sextet who hit the top 40 with a cover of the Zombies' 'I Love You' in the summer of 1968, his propensity for spinning stories was, apparently, already evident.

Band members maintain they were never even aware he was a Christian. They were, however, frustrated by a tendency towards secrecy and apparent self-centredness and eventually fired him from the group. Norman turned this incident around, claiming he had quit, foregoing sure-fire commercial success in order to stand up for his faith.

The following year, he recorded his debut solo release, 'Upon This Rock'. Despite claims to the contrary, it was not the first album of Christian rock music. A number of bands were already playing the style, significantly, the Hard Rock band Agape, who Norman had seen performing in Hollywood the year before.[6]

For an audience eager to hear the gospel message combined with rock sensuality, it was a match made in 'heaven.'

Larry was an assimilator. He was good at looking at the culture and saying, 'What is it that they want? They need a song, an apologetic for Christian rock music.' Okay, 'Why Should the Devil Have All the Good Music.' A line that was taken from the back of a Randy Matthews album.[7]

Yet with all this fanfare of taking a rock genre and making it palatable for Christian ears, it was still banned by the Christian music industry. Norman received his early kudos from mainstream audiences. The *Billboard* magazine named him 'the most important writer since Paul Simon'. Norman was loved, mostly overseas. He performed across the globe in Australia, Italy and Japan. He sold out the Royal Albert Hall in London six times.[8]

The years 1971 and '72 were banner years for Christian music.

Maranatha! music began with its release of the Everlastin' Livin' Jesus Concert in 1971. Maranatha! is a praise and worship production house, still releasing albums today.

That same year Love Song recorded their self-titled debut album, now considered a CCM classic. A kind of Christian answer to Woodstock, it was a great success. The year 1972 also saw the beginning of Myrrh Records, an exclusively Christian label. Several new records were released that year, including rock band Petra's first release.

Donald Nelson writes, 'Between 12 and 17 June 1972 more than 75,000 high school and college students met in Dallas, Texas, for EXPLO 72. During the day they attended classes on evangelism and Bible study. In the evening they gathered at the Cotton Bowl to hear messages by famous preachers and for 'Christian' rock concerts. Explo was the 'first major trans-denominational endorsement of the rock beat as an acceptable Christian music form' (Donald E Nelson, *Explo '72 Biblically Examined*, p. 10). 'This was a tragic sin! They had taken 'strange fire' from the pagan altar and offered it to God' (Donald E Nelson, Explo '72 *Biblically Examined*, p. 10,27).

'After Explo 72, when Billy Graham preached on the same stage that Jesus rock groups such as Love Song, Children of the Day, and Larry Norman performed on, the former music of the devil was given his imprimatur' (*Jesus Rocks the World: The Definitive History of Contemporary Christian Music*, vol. 1, p. 3).

Even though it was decades ago, throughout the beginnings of CCM, it was criticised both within and without the Christian community. Some felt this Christian music was too much like secular music and would only lead young people astray. Others thought it lacked theological depth. Some just considered it inferior to its secular counterpart. Despite these often harsh criticisms, the 70s saw significant growth for the CCM scene, with its gradually being accepted by the Christian Church.

In 1974 production quality improved, as seen on *With Footnotes* by the 2nd Chapter of Acts and *White Horse* by Michael Omartian. The year 1975 saw the emergence of radio stations with a CCM format. The year 1976 saw the beginning of celebrity conversions, beginning with B. J. Thomas releasing his first Christian album *Home Where I Belong*. Sparrow Records began that same year, signing Barry Macguire, Annie Herring, John Michael Talbot, and Keith Green, who is particularly noteworthy for his huge influence on Christian music. He debuted in 1977 with *For Him Who Has Ears to Hear*. Due to anger at the commercial aspects of Christian music, in 1980 Green began to give his albums away for free. In 1978 Amy Grant released her debut album. This album was only marketed to Christians, with her crossover success only coming several years later.[9]

'Why Should the Devil Have All the Good Music?' is one of the 'rally cries' of the CCM community.

Paul Baker titled his book on the History of Contemporary Christian music, *Why Should the Devil Have All the Good Music?*

Webster's dictionary defines *all* as 'every; the whole quantity of, everything; the total'.

The simple conclusion then is, if the devil has all the good music, then we must conclude that the Holy, Almighty, Omnipotent God has little to no such music?

CCM claims everyone from the Protestant founder Martin Luther, General William Booth and even John Newton in order to justify their disobedience to the word of God and their love for rock music. All these are supposed to have made the infamous statement, 'Why should the devil have all the good music?'

But where did 'Why should the devil have all the good music?' *actually* come from?

A well-known quote shows that Martin Luther knew the power of music for good or evil and was not naive to its wantonness.

'I have no use for cranks who despise music because it is a gift of God. Music drives away the devil, it makes people gay. . . . Experience proves that, next to the Word of God, only music deserves to be extolled as the mistress and governess of the feeling of the human heart. We know that to the devil music is distasteful and insufferable. My heart bubbles up, and overflows in response to music which so often refreshed me and delivered me from dire plagues.'[10]

Note that Luther describes music as 'a mistress and governess' of human emotions. Luther did not hold to the CCM philosophy that music is neutral and without inherent moral qualities and is in agreement with such philosophers as Plato on its effects.

Others have attributed to William Booth of the Salvation Army the statement about the 'devil's best tunes'; however, it is quite probable that

Booth was quoting the late Rev. Rowland Hill (1744–1833).[11]

The 'mis-quote' was taken from a message Reverend Rowland Hill, pastor of Surrey Chapel in London, preached in 1844. Reverend Hill did NOT say the actual phrase, 'Why should the devil have all the good music?' What he actually said was, 'The devil should not have all the best tunes.' Reverend Hill's message was not a 'call' to copy the culture or a desire to bring the 'devil's' music into the church. During the time Reverend Hill preached his message, in England, church music had fallen in both quantity and quality, which is certainly not the case today. His was a call for Christians to write, compose, and produce quality Christian music. It was NOT an appeal for Christians to sing the devil's music for the Lord (Lowell Hart, *Satan's Music Exposed*, p. 169–170, V. J. Charlesworth, *Rowland Hill*, p. 156).[12]

It seems that CCM have conveniently failed to get the facts straight. After all, what's the truth got to do with rock 'n' roll?

Fanny Crosby is a well-known hymn writer of over 9,000 hymns (research this for yourself on the web)! There was a time before she was saved when she wrote secular music, but after being saved, she sang a whole different tune! Here is a quote from her as a Christian: 'Sometimes I need to reject the music proposed for my songs because the musicians misunderstand that the Fanny Crosby who once wrote for the people in the saloons has merely changed the lyrics. Oh my no. The church must never sing it's songs to the melodies of the world.'[13]

Larry Norman, the father of Christian rock, shows his thinking in the following song. This is from the man who changed a generation's taste in music: 'I want the people to know/ that he saved my soul/ But I still like to listen to the radio/ they say rock n roll is wrong/ well give you one more chance/ I say I feel so good/ **I gotta get up and dance. I know** what's right/ I know what's wrong/ I don't confuse it/ All I'm really trying to say/ **Is why should the Devil have all the good music . . . /** I ain't knocking the hymns/ **just give me a song that has a beat/** I ain't knocking the hymns/ Just give me a song that moves my feet/ **I don't like none of those funeral marches/** I ain't dead yet!' (emphasis mine)[14]

This song embodies the spirit behind the CCM movement: I'll do what pleases me!

These men, though not preachers, have a pulpit. Rock is okay. Heavy beat is okay. No matter what anyone says, we're going to rock 'n' roll. We'll dress as WE please, we'll live as WE please, and nobody is going to tell us what to do, and nobody has the right to judge us. This is their doctrine.

Is the song's message one of grace, peace, and godliness—or is it a subtle expression of rebellion?

There has been much concern voiced over the dangers and errors of contemporary Christian music and its refusal to separate from secular music.

One last thing, Larry Norman, sang on the TV show *The Rock Gospel Show*, 'Why don't you look into Jesus?' The show's two hosts were Cliff Richard and Sheila Walsh.

On this particular set, the props were large stage screens where soft lighting was shone through the back of them. The screens were embossed with silhouettes of various-sized pyramids. The significance of this will be explained in future chapters.[15]

12

RIGHTEOUS ROCKER
HOLY ROLLER

Even from the days of your fathers ye are gone away from mine ordinances, and have not kept them. Return unto me, and I will return unto you, saith the Lord of hosts. But ye said, How shall we return?

—Mal. 3:7

The Christian embrace of hip youth scenes can be traced, like so much, to the cultural ferment of the 1960s.

The mystic hippies of that era sparked the mass Jesus people movement, which injected a distinctly Christian feeling for love and apocalypse into a counterculture already caught up in 'free love' and Vietnam. It was an easy fit, man!

By the early 1970s, a new Jesus had hit the American mainstream. This 'hippie' or 'psychedelic' Jesus transformed American worship through the broad medium of folk music and rock 'n' roll. Today's suburban megachurches owe their soul to the Jesus movement, and the contemporary Christian music industry owes its billions to the early Jesus freaks. [1]

Although I have wanted to write more here at this point, the book needs to remain to the core focus; nevertheless, a small history lesson from the early days of the hippies and Calvary Chapel is necessary.

One of the first hard-rock Jesus music bands formed around the talent of Fred Caban. All Saved Freak Band's website recounts the early days of Caban. He was born and raised in California. The counterculture's music scene offered an intimate glimpse into rock 'n' roll lifestyles of such guitar phenomena as Jimi Hendrix, after whom the budding musician patterned his style.

Caban was evangelised one night down at a Huntington Beach coffeehouse called The Lightclub run by the infamous David Berg and family, the genesis point of what would eventually become the cult group the Children of God, who that night gave him the gospel of John.

Months after his conversion, Caban formed another band, naming it Agape, the Greek word for God's love. The band was to have an evangelistic focus. Caban stated, 'We'd play one or two songs. We'd jam. We'd blow them away. And then boom, we'd start preaching, and people would actually stick around and listen.'[2]

Within six months, a group of 50 young converts gathered for Bible studies and strategy sessions to promote the band's concerts.

As a musical entity, Agape's hard rock gained a large following throughout the West Coast, sharing stages with other Jesus music bands like Love Song and JC Power Outlet, playing the popular Gazzari's Hollywood- A-Go-Go, and were invited to share the bill at the first California Jesus Festivals held at the Hollywood Palladium in 1971.

Though some believed their music was a compromise as a close imitation of other 'worldly' rock bands, none of the members backed down from their vision. Caban states, 'We were basically a secular rock band that became Christians. When we got on stage *we played it as hard as we did before.* But where we had previously been selfish and desiring fortune and fame, we now sang about our faith in Jesus Christ. Nothing on the outside changed. We had been transformed from within.'[3]

Agape played at a number of venues throughout the California area. They ran concurrent with the ascendancy of another premier Jesus musician Larry Norman. Both Agape and Norman blossomed as Jesus music forces at the same time.

A devout follower of both Jesus Christ and Elvis Presley, Norman appeared on the CBS television variety series *The Original Amateur Hour* in 1959. In 1965 Norman co-founded the Bay Area psychedelic group People but later left the group late in 1968 over differences relative to the album's title *3* and their new interest in Scientology.[4]

Love Song was one of the other main Jesus music bands and one of the first Christian rock bands. It was founded in 1970 by Chuck Girard, Tommy Coomes, Jay Truax, and Fred Field. They were a part of the Jesus movement of the late 60s and early 70s, coming out of Chuck Smith's Calvary Chapel.

Their classic debut album, *Love Song* (1972), is considered one of the greatest Christian music albums of all time.[5]

In 1969, Calvary Chapel became a hub in what later became known as the Jesus movement. John Higgins the boyfriend of Chuck Smith's daughter introduced Smith to Lonnie Frisbee, the 'hippie evangelist' who became a key figure in the both the Jesus movement and in Calvary Chapel.[6]

While pastoring there in the early years, Pastor Chuck considered young people with long hair as 'dirty hippies'. But over time, God gave Chuck Smith a heart for the hippie generation. These 'Jesus freaks' brought a mass movement that swept through the West Coast. The move of God on this generation through Chuck Smith's ministry was seen as a great revival.[7]

Many of the hippies and other troubled youth who came to Christ in their dirty jeans and bare feet later became pastors as well.[8]

'He was an American hero who loved the Boomers when the Generation Gap was at its height. He was the first to be seeker friendly'— Pastor Dave Holden, Saddleback Church.[9]

Chuck Smith also paved the way for contemporary worship music. It all started with Chuck Girard and Love Song, the hippie band who sang the now-historic songs 'Welcome Back' and 'Little Country Church'. The little country church was none other than Calvary Chapel of Costa Mesa, California, in its very humble beginnings. Many more Christian bands sprang up, welcomed with open arms by Chuck Smith. He offered them all a chance and a platform to sing God's praises in this new genre.

The famed Maranatha Music came from Smith's ministry, and they graced believers everywhere with their new contemporary praise music. They were much like Hillsong today. They made countless records of their praise and worship songs and travelled the world to carry the 'good news'.[10]

But the Jesus people movement was a mixed bag.

According to Kent Philpott who ministered for years among the hippies on San Francisco's Bayside, although God was moving, there was still what he refers to as dark sides and wildfire during the awakening

(*Memoirs of a Jesus Freak*, p. 118).

During this influx of new converts, the concern was that a naive euphoria accompanied the movement. An all-embracing 'God is saving everyone' was the prevailing thinking at the time. This is readily seen in the way Chuck Smith allowed his new converts of the group Love Song to perform on live television on the *Kathryn Kuhlman Show*.[11]

The common presumption among the Jesus People was anyone who claimed to be a Christian was one. There was virtually no understanding or comprehension that someone could be falsely converted (*Memoirs of a Jesus Freak*, pp. 121,146).

In fact, this was the case with leaders such as Chuck Smith. His all-embracing heart meant that a great deal of the church services at Costa Mesa were run and carried along by the fervour of these new converts.

Among the converts were musicians who now were writing music for praise and worship. This became the genesis for Jesus music and Christian rock concerts. Maranatha Music was eventually formed to publish and promote the music. The services usually resembled rock concerts more than worship services. By the early 1970s, Calvary Chapel was home to ten or more musical groups that were representative of the Jesus people movement.[12]

In 1982, John Wimber, one of the Calvary Chapel pastors, and the Calvary Chapel leadership mutually agreed to part ways over Wimber's overemphasis on spiritual manifestations. On 3 October 2013, Pastor Chuck Smith died after a long battle with lung cancer.

Although Chuck Smith stood against this dangerous and unholy interest in the 'gifts', nevertheless, Maranatha Music failed on this point. In those days, at least, Calvary Chapel was quick to accept many and wasn't careful to try to ascertain whether the hippies were truly born again.

They an encouraged open platform for the newest babes in Christ to perform their new music.[13]

In 1997, Love Song band member Chuck Girard described how things were back in the early days at Calvary Chapel. At the suggestion of hippie youth Pastor Lonnie Frisbee, Girard and his three buddies were allowed to play a few of their songs for Chuck Smith. They had turned their lives over to the Lord only days before. The songs they played were *before* they met the Lord, but they just happened to be about God and Jesus.

'It was early 1970 when three of my buddies and I walked into a church called Calvary Chapel in Costa Mesa. . . . We had a few songs that we had written before we met the Lord that were about God and Jesus. The pastor thought the songs were of God, invited us to play at one of the weekly Bible studies and we accepted the invitation. . . . We didn't know much about what people called 'gospel music,' we were just writing the same kind of songs we would write if we weren't Christians but now we had Jesus to sing about' (Girard, foreword to *History of the Jesus Movement* by David DiSabatino).

Note that the members of Love Song started out by playing songs they had written even before they were converted. And when they started writing 'Christian' songs, all they did was add 'Jesus' to their old style of music. And they were encouraged to do so by the leadership of Calvary Chapel even though the Love Song hippies were the merest babes in Christ (at best) (see 1 Tim. 3:6).

These new Christians were novices and therefore should have been discipled and given a biblical foundation before any thought of them being allowed to minister in church. The Bible's wise counsel is not to elevate new converts or novices (see 1 Tim. 3:10).

Another young man who came to faith describes the religious scene of the early 70s at Calvary:

Saturday nights, we carpooled the 50 miles to Costa Mesa for intensely emotional, jam-packed rock concerts— featuring such classic Jesus-rock groups as Maranatha, Mustard Seed Faith, Petra, and One Truth— whipping ourselves into imagining that Calvary Chapel was ground zero in the 'great war' against the devil. We sang, 'Amazing Grace, how sweet the sound that saved a wretch like me'—but we sang it to the bouncy tune of 'The Happy Wanderer.' 'This is not religion,' we were told, and quickly parroted to our wide-eyed friends and family, 'this is a relationship!'[14]

They all wore the now-recognisable Calvary logo of the dove on T-shirts and, dangling it from chains around their necks, an oddly misshapen outline of a descending dove in a suicide dive. Coincidentally, this dove shape is the same as the one the German-based religious occult fraternity Ordo Templi Orientis (OTO) uses. It appears the cross was replaced by the dove after a few years of it being out the front of the church.

Kent Philpott observed that at his church, the focus changed from teaching and preaching to music and more music. 'The "worship" was relegated to only when the praise and worship band was on stage' (*Memoirs of a Jesus Freak*, p. 176).

One of the songs of Love Song was called 'Welcome Back' that appeared on their 1972 self-titled album.

This song, like many others, was limited to just a few enchanting words with blended harmonies reminiscent of the Beach Boys. Besides the plagiarised hard rock brought into the church world by Agape and Larry Norman, the flavour of this new music was pure mysticism. It created an emotional experience associated with a vague spirituality not solidly Bible based. There was no clear gospel message. There is nothing about sin, the cross, repentance, or biblical faith.[15]

In one night meeting back in '71, the drummer of Love Song performed a drum solo with no apparent reason except show off his talent, to entertain, and to hold an audience. What was the leadership thinking?[16]

The concept of Christian pop/rock music for some is seen as an unusual phenomenon since rock music has historically been associated with various themes such as sexual promiscuity, rebellion, and drug and alcohol use. This controversy caused by evangelical pop music was explored by Gerald Clarke in his *Time* magazine article 'New Lyrics for the Devil's Music'.[17]

Many studies on church growth show that churches have grown in size after changing the style of music. Criticism from others suggest that it is 'only about numbers', 'slick' and 'success' oriented.[18]

Incredibly, in 1984 heavy metal 'Jesus' band Stryper was allowed to perform centre stage at Calvary chapel!

Like Stryper converts like Lonnie Frisbee (1949–1993) illustrate the shallow nature of many of the Jesus People 'conversions'. Frisbee turned to Jesus at a time when he was gripped by LSD trips and began to receive 'prophecies' while high on drugs. In the video documentary on Frisbee, David Di Sabatino observes, 'One of the ironic twists of the 60s was that many openly stated that drugs, LSD in particular, played a large part of their experience in Christian salvation' (*Frisbee: The Life and Death of a Hippy Preacher*).

Sandy Heefner, for example, describes her salvation, 'I took my LSD, laid down on the floor a couple of hours and when I could get together to get up, I got up as a Christian. It's just that simple.'

False conversions seem to be frequent rather than a rarity. By 1971, Chuck Smith parted company with Frisbee because of their different perspectives on Pentecostal signs and Smith's desire to focus more on the teaching of scripture.

Frisbee was divorced in 1973. His ex-wife says, 'At the end of the marriage he told me that he had been staying late in some gay bars' (Connie Bremer-Murray, *Frisbee: The Life and Death of a Hippy Preacher*).

The devil reacted to the move of God that began among a confused generation of hippies, which spilled over into the long-established denominations. He sowed tares that resembled the wheat on the outside and brought in the unholy spirit, resulting in all types of corresponding outcomes. Although Maranatha! gave us precious songs like, Psalm 5, and 'As the deer' this never excuses mixture.

What Chuck Smith failed to renounce was Christian rock itself.

The field of Christian rock in general has been *rife* with spiritual shipwreck, heresy, and such things as divorce, adultery, and homosexuality since its inception, as any honest history of the movement will acknowledge.[19]

Unfortunately, the hero of the faith Larry Norman had an affair with the wife of his friend and confident Randy Stonehill, which meant divorce for both of their marriages.[20]

Larry Norman, when asked by *Buzz* magazine what church he attended, refused to answer the question except to say, 'I think it's unimportant' and 'I don't like the question.' He said that he believes it is an 'obsessive compulsion' to meet at regular times for church, which flies in the face of Hebrews 10:25 and the example of the early Christians (see Acts 2:42; 20:7).[21]

In spite of Maranatha's more 'conservative' image, Christian rock continued side by side with the softer sound. Over time Maranatha Music acted as a means to broaden support for Christian rock in that early period.[22]

Chuck Girard of Love Song says, 'We were amazed to see and hear the album *Upon This Rock* by Larry Norman.' Even the softer rock was commonly rejected by churches in the 1970s, but the resistance was gradually broken over time.[23]

The role played by Calvary Chapel and Maranatha Music in the 1970s (whether by design or not) was similar to what Dick Clark's *American Bandstand* did in the 1950s in broadening the popularity of rock 'n' roll by cleaning up the 'bad boy' images of the likes of the Beatles.

Maranatha Music ran workshops that have a large influence in cross-denominational churches. Church leaders from 'all denominations' are welcome (maranathamusic.com). Unfortunately Maranatha tends to spread the heresies of non-judgmentalism, ecumenism, and 'cultural liberalism'.[24]

So how do we review the Jesus movement with true biblical discernment? I have had to spend hours looking at articles, references, and Calvary Chapels background and history, which included YouTube clips of this period before I could answer this vital question.

A way of testing this period is to ask some questions:

- Did these believers love of worldly pleasure progressively die?

- Were they convicted of the ugliness and guilt of sin, and of God's holiness?

- Was there an understanding of the need of prayer?

- Was there power to live righteous lives?

- Was there the importance and authority of the Word of God?

- Did they earnestly begin to seek God's kingdom and righteousness?

- Did they develop a greater knowledge of God?

If yes, then the Spirit of God must have been at work during this period. We may learn another way to judge between spirits from 1 John 4:6: one is a spirit of truth and the other a spirit of error.

In a counterfeit revival, people flock to something that makes them feel good without truly turning from sin. Those with a counterfeit conversion think Jesus saved them *in* their sin instead of *from* their sin. Their newfound faith tends to be an excuse for sin. Church ends up a place of blessing rather than a place to reach out to the lost in evangelism. Are they gathering unto Him or gathering for entertainment? The focus changes to numbers and not the purity of truth and the life changed. It becomes a movement but not necessarily a move of God. True revival then can be discerned by the way it promotes righteousness and holiness, restores relationships, and purifies individual hearts and attitudes and motives. It changes one's focus from living for self to making Jesus the Lord of the life.

The question then is, can this period of church history be considered a true work of God and therefore included with other revivals of history as a spiritual awakening?

Philpott suggests that there were definitely tares amongst the wheat. He acknowledged that the work of the Jesus movement 'was tarnished, which should not be unexpected' (Kent Philpott, *Memoir of a Jesus Freak*, p.189).

While I agree there was an ingathering of the elect at this time, one other man was less generous. The controversial John Todd, an ex-Satanist and former Illuminati occult member, said that Jesus Rock was specifically brought into the church to stop a major mass revival that would have swept across the country at the time.[25]

In pondering this, and the subsequent history since, I have to reluctantly agree with Todd's statement. It leaves a deep sense of regret of what might have been.

13
PURPLE HAZE

Therefore they say unto God, Depart from us; for we desire not the knowledge of thy ways. What is the Almighty, that we should serve Him? And what profit should we have, if we pray unto him?

—Job 21:14,15

A myriad of music styles and liberal theology are self-evident at Rick Warren's Saddleback Church in Southern California.

In chapter 8 of *The Purpose-Driven Life*, Warren writes: "God loves all kinds of music because he invented it all--fast and slow, loud and soft, old and new. You probably don't like it all, but God does! . . . Christians often disagree over the style of music used in worship. . . . But there is no biblical style! . . . God likes variety and enjoys it all. There is no such thing as "Christian" music; there are only Christian lyrics. It is the words that make a song sacred, not the tune. There are no spiritual tunes" (pp. 65,66).

In chapter 15 of his other book *The Purpose-Driven Church*, he says a similar thing—that churches need to admit that there is no particular style of music that's sacred. In his usual simplistic manner, Warren states music is nothing more than an arrangement of notes and rhythms; it's the words that make the song spiritual. All you need to do to reach out to your neighbourhood is to 'match your music to the kind of people God wants your church to reach'. [1]

This is more of Rick's rock rhetoric!

Yet listen to these men that echo their wisdom down through the ages.

'Music directly represents the passions or states of the soul—gentleness anger, courage, temperance. If a person habitually listens to the kind of music that rouses ignoble passions, his whole character will be shaped to an ignoble form. In short, if one listens to the wrong kind of music he will become the wrong kind of person; but conversely, if he listens to the right kind of music he will tend to become the right kind of person' (Aristotle, *Republic*, Politics, 8, 1340, quoted in Donald J Grout, *A History of Western Music*, 1980, p. 8).

'Music is the most powerful stimulus known among the perceptive senses. The medical, psychiatric and other evidence for the non-neutrality of music is so overwhelming that it frankly amazes me that anyone should seriously say otherwise' (Dr Max Schoen, *The Psychology of Music*, 1940).

'Rock is communication without words, regardless of what ideology is inserted into the music' (Dr William J. Shafer, *Rock Music*, 1972).

Warren did some more biblical gymnastics in his book and used Paul to endorse his wanderings. He states, 'The point Paul is making is that we must be willing to adjust our worship practices when unbelievers are present (1 Cor. 14:23). God tells us to be sensitive to the hang-ups of unbelievers in our services. Although Paul never used the term "Seeker Sensitive," he definitely pioneered the idea' (*Purpose-Driven Church*, p.

243).

When Warren says that God loves all kinds of music, well, he means ALL kinds.

In the past Saddleback Church has featured eight to nine different 'worship venues on the property'. There is a worship style to suit every worldly taste.

On 17 April 2005, Warren announced his PEACE program to Saddleback Church at Angel Baseball Stadium. He began the conference by singing part of Jimi Hendrix's drug-drenched song 'Purple Haze' to the congregation, accompanied by his 'praise and worship' band. He said he had wanted to do that for a long time.[2]

Though he is long dead, Jimi Hendrix's influence lives on, but it is an evil influence that should be reproved rather than encouraged. His music and his life epitomised the rock-and-roll philosophy, which is live as you please. Music was Jimi Hendrix's god. He attended church in his youth, but later he testified, 'I used to go to Sunday School, but the only thing i believe in now is music' (Curtis Knight, *Jimi*).

Hendrix understood the mystical and hypnotic power of rock music. He said, 'Once you have some type of **rhythm**, like it can get **hypnotic** if you keep **repeating** it over and over again. . . . **It releases a certain thing in there so you can put anything you want right inside that**, you know. I always like to take people on trips. **That's why music is magic**' (emphasis added) (Hendrix, David Henderson, p. 356).[3]

'**Atmospheres are going to come through music, because the music is a spiritual thing of its own.** . . . I can explain everything better through music. You **hypnotize** people to where they go right back to their natural state, . . . you **can preach into the subconscious what we want to say**' (emphasis added) (Robin Richman, 'An Infinity of Jimis', *Life*, 3 Oct. 1969).

Our friends over at Planetshakers have been having 'awakening' conferences. They describe these events where 'God has set in motion an unstoppable move of His Spirit intended to shift the **spiritual atmospheres** of our cities and awaken individuals to their identities and purposes in Christ'[3] (emphasis mine).

Hendrix said, 'We're making our music into Electric Church Music; a new kind of Bible, not like in a hotel, but a Bible you carry in your hearts, one that will give you a physical feeling. We try to make our music so loose and hard hitting so that it hits your soul hard enough to make it open. It's like shock therapy or a can opener.'

Hendrix knew what he was talking about. He continued, 'If parents really want to love their kids, they should be aware of their music.'[4]

Music has an awesome power to mould the thinking of the masses and particularly the youth, and rock musicians know it. Crosby of Crosby, Stills & Nash made that plain enough when he bragged, 'I figured that the only thing to do was steal their kids. I still think it's the only thing to do. . . . I'm not talking about kidnapping . . . but about changing young people's value system' (*Rolling Stone*, vol 1, p. 410).

Warren inadvertently agrees with Hendrix on the construct of music when he says, 'A song can often touch people in ways a sermon can't. Music can bypass intellectual barriers, and take the message straight to the heart. It's a potent tool for evangelism' (*The Purpose-Driven Church*, p. 279)

This is occult influence to the core!

According to their previous worship leader Rick Muchow, 'the target at

Saddleback's weekend seeker services is the adult seeker. The target determines the musical style, lyric content, presentation [congregational/special music], length of service and "stage look" of the event'.[5]

'Being seeker sensitive in our worship is a biblical command' – Rick Warren[6]

That's just a religious way of saying that the guy from the neighbourhood who is used to playing Motley Crew at home comes along to your church, not makes sure he served up a similar style of 'worship'. Sheer insanity!

These observations and warnings should be taken seriously by Christians. Those who think that there is no spiritual danger in rock music are deceiving themselves and are leading others down the primrose path of delusion.

Observe that Hendrix was referring to the power of the music itself without the words.

David Bowie said, 'Rock has always been the devil's music. . . . I believe rock and roll is dangerous. . . . I feel we're only heralding something even darker than ourselves' (David Bowie, *Rolling Stone*, 12 Feb 1976, p. 83).

Dr Steven Halpern, a new age musician, makes it clear if we still want to hold to our position, 'Words are incidental at best, or monotonous and moronic as usual. But the point is, that they don't matter. What you dance to is the beat, the bass and drums. And with this mix and volume, not only is the beat sensed, but literally felt, as this aspect of the rhythm section takes precedence over melody and harmony' (*Tuning the Human Instrument*, 1978, p. 14).

Angus Young, lead guitarist for AC/DC, is called the guitar demon, and he admitted that something takes control of the band during their concerts, 'It's like I'm on automatic pilot.

By the time we're halfway through the first number someone else is steering me. I'm just along for the ride. I become possessed when I get on stage' (*Hit Parader*, July 1985, p. 60).

Robert Fripp guitarist in the band King Crimson affirms the words of Hendrix when he said 'that certain feeling happened to me in a big way quite often with the first King Crimson. Amazing things would happen—I mean, telepathy, qualities of energy, things that I had never experienced before with music. . . . You can't tell whether the music is playing the musician, or the musician is playing the music' (*Down Beat*, June 1985, p. 61).

Robert Plant and Jimmy Page of Led Zeppelin both claim that *they don't know* who wrote their occultic song 'Stairway to Heaven'. Plant testified, 'Pagey had written the chords and played them for me. I was holding the paper and pencil, and for some reason, I was in a very bad mood. Then all of a sudden my hand was writing out words. I just sat there and looked at the words and then I almost leaped out of my seat' (Stephen Davis, *Hammer of the Gods*, p. 164).

Jimi Hendrix's girlfrien Fayne Pridgon said, '**He used to always talk about some devil or something was in him**, you know. He didn't know what made him act the way he acted ...It seems to me he was so tormented and just torn apart and like he really was obsessed, you know, with something really evil' (*Heartbeat of the Dragon*, p. 50). (emphasis added)

Based on these men's personal testimonies, it is therefore inexcusable for Rick Warren and his 'worship' team to perform any Jimi Hendrix song on any occasion whatsoever. The use of the song was inappropriate and says a lot about Warren on a number of levels.

Like Hendrix, the church's spiritual vision though promised light has been blinded by a cloud of 'purple haze' (Jer. 13:16, Jer. 18:15).

14
LOVE YOURSELF

Ye shall be as gods, knowing good and evil.

—Gen. 3:5

Just a stone's throw from Rick Warren's Saddleback Church, nestled near Disneyland in Anaheim, California, is a towering glass structure known as the Crystal Cathedral in Garden Grove, California. It's right on two main intersections, where traffic comes under the shadow of this impressive architectural monolith. It is literally a sea of glass with over 10,000 panes. This has been the pastoral enterprise of Robert H Schuller for over 60 years.[1]

In his early days, Schuller went door to door, inviting people to come to his church and asking them what type of church they would like to attend. He began to see his church as a mission, a place where non-Christians would feel comfortable enough to come in and then later 'accept Jesus'.[2]

How would he do this? By preaching only positive things! Schuller credits close friend Norman Vincent Peale, a 33 degree Mason whose 'grandfather was a Mason for 50 years, my father for 50 years' who was fine-tuning his own positive faith message and laying the foundation for his own *Possibility Thinking* that was to come.[3]

Schuller a universalist, and probably a mason himself, believes that all people are the children of God. His goal is to help each person understand and enjoy this 'fact'.[4]

I make this point in this chapter: why? Because all of this has had a profound influence on what is going on within 'Christendom' this very moment, including the Australian brand of it.

For example, at the 2006 Hillsong Conference in Sydney, Rick Warren was a guest speaker. That year along, with Warren, were Bill Hybels, Reinhard Bonnke, Jentezen Franklin, and Rick Godwin.[5]

Hybels was back for the 2014 Hillsong Conference.[6]

The Purpose-Driven Church, (1995), written by Rick Warren, is a development of Robert Schuller's church-growth marketing methods.

The first pastor to 'make it big' using modern church-growth techniques was, in fact, Robert Schuller! Schuller says proudly, 'An undisputed fact is that I am the founder, really, of the church-growth movement in this country. . . . I advocated and launched what has become known as the marketing approach in Christianity.' [7]

Schuller, applauding Warren, said in his *Hour of Power* sermon on 4 April 2004, 'And there's Rick Warren, a pastor who today is phenomenal. He came to our institute time after time.'

Schuller's landmark 1975 book *Your Church Has Real Possibilities* impressed Warren and Hybels who both visited Schuller often to learn more.

Hybels called his first meeting with Schuller a 'divine encounter'. Kay

Warren, Rick's wife, said that Schuller had a 'profound influence' on Rick, who was 'captivated by his positive appeal to unbelievers'.[8]

Warren has since shared the platform at several of Schuller's leadership conferences, and an endorsement by Schuller appears at the beginning of his book: 'I'm praying that every pastor will read this book. . . . Rick Warren is the one all of us should listen to and learn from' (*The Purpose-Driven Church*).

Rick Warren's message and methodology has been taught in countless numbers of churches worldwide, including Hillsong. The theories and principles of that book were born in the bowels of the Crystal Cathedral.

Warren has merely made them more palatable. And in so doing, he has achieved a place of prominence by repackaging the gospel into a glib and dumbed-down marketing book.

What we have now, throughout Christendom, is pastors believing that if Warren has achieved this kind of growth and success, then 'God' must be blessing it. It's the blind leading the blind.

The church of Christ should be God directed, not purpose driven.

Rick Warren held a Building a Purpose-Driven Church seminar at Saddleback Church way back in January, 1998, a seminar that was taped, transcribed, and reported on by Dennis Costella in his article 'The Church Growth Movement'.

Rick Warren taught that all sort of aspects of church had to change to transform a traditional church into a growing purpose-driven church. Such radical sharp turns were necessary in the areas of dress, making church more contemporary styled, non-threatening. The music needed to be contemporary, the kind that people listen and hear every day on their radio. The message must be only positive, a mix of pop psychology and inspirational 'feel good'. The church was to be more about meeting needs and all this in a spirit of pragmatism.

Dennis Costella reported that Warren's Saddleback Community Church sound system, band, singers, and presentation would rival any secular rock concert.

Warren suggested throwing out the organ and replacing it with a band who would play 'loud, raucous music with a driving beat'. He said, 'We are really, really loud on a weekend service. . . . I say, 'We're not gonna turn it down.' Now the reason why is baby boomers want to feel the music, not just hear it.'"[9]

In the worst piece of twisting and mocking of the scriptures. Warren suggested the following, 'I believe that one of the major church issues [of the future] will be how we're going to reach the next generation with our music.'

Did he say 'reach' the lost with 'our music'? That's what record companies and rock stars do! Is that what Jesus sent US to do? Is that what transforms sinners from the old life into the new?[10]

Did Jesus carry a band around with Him to help draw a crowd so He could 'reach' His generation with the gospel?

But some would say, well Jesus didn't have our music and technology back then. The truth is churches like saddleback want to be attractive by entertaining, and not evangelising the lost. The principle which remains true to this day is God commands we preach the gospel. The gospels tell us that the guards said of Jesus that 'none spoke like this man', not none sang like this man (John 7:46). Only lukewarm believers would come up with this non-sense (Rev 3:15,16).

In one fell swoop, Rick Warren changed the whole church landscape! Hymns ditched, music as you hear it on the radio, preaching watered down to positive uplifting messages, and evangelism are put away in the back closet for another day.

Rick Warren has become a modern-day Larry Norman, saying, 'Why should the devil have all the good music?' but just in a more sophisticated way; and pastors around the world have bought it hook, line and sinker!

'For the time will come when they will not endure sound doctrine; but after their own lusts shall they heap to themselves teachers, having itching ears' (2 Tim. 4:3).

Prophecy is being fulfilled right before our eyes!

'Discernment is not knowing the difference between right and wrong. It is knowing the difference between right, and almost right' — Charles H. Spurgeon.

Government agents don't learn to spot counterfeit money by studying the counterfeits. They spend most of their time studying genuine bills until they master the look of the real thing. They recognise the counterfeit money by knowing the genuine thing. Yet we have a whole generation with a brand of Christianity which is nothing more than a counterfeit, and have been duped into believing it's the true. This current generation has been tossed into a sea of religious forgetfulness, so that we know little or nothing of the foundations. Our great need is to know God's character, God's ways, and his Word, otherwise we remain blind to what is truth and what is error.

Just to make quite clear which side he is on, Rick Warren is a member of the Council of Foreign Relations (CFR) and for many years trained under Robert H Schuller (a.k.a. The Hour of Power).[11]

There is a long history of no separation from the world at Saddleback Church. Any sorry piece of rock or rap music is fine as long as it is accompanied by a thin veneer of religiosity.

If you have always wanted to be in a band then saddleback is the place for you. Saddleback Church is where you can learn to play in a band. The best way to learn is to play with other 'rockers' like you! This is worship, Rick Warren style.[12]

Hillsong's pastor Brian Houston follows, to the letter, the ideas of Warren and Hybels. Its' kingdom now replacing the kingdom of God within. It's the visible in the form of carnal goals and objectives instead of seeking 'first the kingdom of God, and His righteousness'. Brian Houston gives us his version of 'purpose'. It's his take on Warren's *The Purpose-Driven Life*.

Having studied Houston's messages, it seems that for him purpose is an enduring theme. Warren made another of a number of previous guest appearances in Sydney (1 July 2015).[13]

According to Warren's bio on *Wikipedia*, he has been invited to speak at various national and international forums, including the United Nations, the World Economic Forum in Davos, the African Union, the Council on Foreign Relations, Harvard's Kennedy School of Government, TED, and *Time*'s Global Health Summit. He has been a member of the Council on Foreign Relations (CFR) since 2005.[14]

Brian Houston's purpose for himself is to be a carbon copy of Rick Warren. Yet Warren has been under the mentorship of Robert Schuller and business guru Peter Drucker for over 20 years. Unwittingly or with knowledge, each of these men has branded what turns out to be a new form of Christian existentialism.

Søren Kierkegaard, posthumously regardedas the fatherof existentialism, maintained that the individual is solely responsible for giving his or her own life meaning.[15]

Sounds familiar?

Speaking of self, we have no better example than the Lakewood Church pastors: the Osteens.

Joel Osteen's other half, Victoria, spoke out one Sunday morning. Joel was standing next to her (in seeming approval). These are her words:

So I just want to encourage every one of us to realize when we obey God, we're NOT doing it for God. That's one way to look at it, we're doing it for OURSELVES. Because God takes pleasure when we're happy. . . . Do good because God wants you to be happy. When you come to church, when you worship Him, you're NOT doing it for God really! You're doing it for YOURSELF! Because that's what makes God happy, amen? [16]

This appalling garbage is nothing but a gospel of man. This gospel of self is pushing God to the sidelines. Man is the centre of the universe. Sheer blasphemy! As we are warned, in the last days, men will be lovers of self, but these false teachers make it part of their very religion (see 2 Tim 3:2).

"When you worship Him, you're NOT doing it for God really! You're doing it for YOURSELF" — Victoria Osteen

The cross is and will always be God's instrument to save. The cross means death to self.

However, Robert Schuller has little qualms in offering a different idea.

Schuller says: 'Is there any possibility of a person being "saved" without accepting Jesus Christ in a way evangelicals preach it today? My answer is, I don't know. That's the honest-to-God truth. But I believe in the sovereignty of God and the sovereignty of Jesus Christ. I hope so. Is it possible to be saved without making public repentance? I think so. On the cross, Jesus said, "Father, forgive them for they know not what they do"' (from *O' Timothy*).

The church has been seduced on self-esteem. Then to top it all off, Schuller and Billy Graham spoke in a video conference in 2007 of the wideness of God's mercy.[17]

Robert H Schuller died on 2 April 2015. He never held to the truth of the gospel or God's actual way of salvation.

15
IT'S THE RHYTHM OF THE NIGHT

Seek ye the Lord while he may be found, call ye upon him while he is near: Let the wicked forsake his way, and the unrighteous man his thoughts: and let him return unto the Lord, and he will have mercy upon him; and to our God, for he will abundantly pardon.

—Isa. 55:6

As I have shown, rhythm is pulse of music, 'the sexuality of music is usually referred to in terms of rhythm it is the beat that commands a directly physical response'.1

In 1952, Alan Freed, a disc jockey from Cleveland, came up with the term *rock and roll* from the juke joints, which is a bar with a jukebox and usually an area for dancing.2 He decided to name it after a ghetto term that black people used for premarital sex in the back seat of a car—hence, the term *rock 'n' roll* was coined.3

'The rock beat is Satan's sound of lawlessness. The rock beat is musical perversion. Every knowledgeable musician knows that the term "rock" essentially means a shameful act of lust'.4

But that is not the only problem! The beat of rock is nothing new.

Pagan, animistic tribes had the 'rock beat' long before it came to America. They use the driving beat to get high and bring them into an altered state of consciousness. Ancient drumming in particular developed techniques that are designed to alter your brainwaves into more mediative states. If you research YouTube, most if not all examples of 'shaman states' use the power and intensity of the drum.

Concerning Michael Jackson, in a 1993 interview with Oprah Winfrey, he explained the sexual gestures in his concerts. 'It happens subliminally, it's the music that compels me to do it. You think about it, it just happens. . . . I'm a slave to the rhythm.'5

Rhythm has power. Read this following quote:

Since fast rhythm releases into the bloodstream chemicals which excite the organism, such music can literally be said to give a 'kick.' When a young person is used to listening to fast rock music for a number of hours per day, such kicks literally become a form of addiction, and a sense of emptiness is experienced if for some reason music cannot be listened to for a prolonged period of time. (David Tame, *The Secret Power of Music*, p. 139)

There seems to be research that supports the connection of the *strong* beat being rooted in paganism.

The drum is the oldest-known instrument in the world dating back to 4000 BCE in Egypt in the northeast corner of Africa. It is present throughout every region of Africa, playing different roles among the various peoples.

Drums made with alligator skins have been found in Neolithic cultures located in China, dating to a period of 5500–2350 BC. In literary records, drums manifested shamanistic characteristics and were often used in ritual ceremonies.[6]

Drums are divided into three classes according to construction: (1) Instruments having a skin stretched over one end of the resonant cavity, the other end open, such as the tambourine (*q.v.*) and the *darabukkeh* or Egyptian drum, shaped like a mushroom; (2) instruments consisting of a cup-shaped receptacle of metal, wood, or earthenware entirely closed over by a skin e.g. kettledrum; and (3) a receptacle in the shape of a cylinder closed at both ends by skins e.g. bass drum or side drum.[7]

Having said all that, let's look at the concept of the drum briefly as the word in a biblical context. Firstly, the word *drum* does not appear in bible language.

In Nahum 2:7, where the word *tabering* occurs, it means beating on the breast as drummers beat on the tabret. The Israelites learnt to use the timbrel during their sojourn in Egypt, and Kathleen Schlesinger, in the eleventh edition *Encyclopædia Britannica* of 1911 volume, stated, 'It has been suggested that as the Egyptians used it to scare away their evil spirit Typhon.' The word *tof* is derived from the latter. [8]

An interlinear concordance helps with the meaning of the word toph.

The word as stated is *toph* (Strong's Concordance – H8596)

תֹּף **tôph**, tofe; from H8608 contracted; a tambourine:—tabret, timbrel.[9]

תֹף m. plur. תֻּפִּים (from the root תָּפַף)—(1) *a drum, timbrel* (Arab. دُفّ, whence the Spanish *adduffa*), beaten in the East by women when dancing; it is made with a wooden circle, covered with membrane and furnished with brass bells, Exod. 15:20; Jud. 11:34; Jer. 31:4 (compare Ps. 68:26). Compare Niebuhr's Travels, vol. i. p. 181.

(2) Eze. 28:13, the bezel or hollow in which a gem is set; compare נֶקֶב.

Noun (1) *timbrel*, small hand drum similar to a tambourine, formerly carried by itinerant jugglers.

According to the free dictionary, a drum is a musical percussion instrument usually consists of a hollow cylinder with a membrane stretched across each end.[10]

Some in their research have tried to equate the timbrel to a drum seen in places like Egypt and Mesopotamia, but this cannot be assumed to be the same as the one used in Israel's music. The Timbrel was a handheld portable instrument, similar to what we have today, or like the Irish Bodhran drum.

Here are some other examples.

'Begin the music, strike the timbrel' (Ps. 81:2).

'Let them praise his name with dancing and make music to him with timbrel and harp' (Ps. 149:3).

'Then Miriam the prophetess, Aaron's sister took a timbrel in her hand, and all the women followed her, with timbrels and dancing' (Exod. 15:20).

'In front are the singers, after them the musicians; with them are the maidens playing timbrels' (Ps. 68:25).

'Praise him with the sounding of the trumpet, praise Him with the harp and lyre, praise Him with the timbrel, and dancing, praise Him with the strings and flute, praise Him with the clash of cymbals, praise Him with resounding cymbals. Let everything that has breath praise the LORD' (Ps. 150:3–6).

It is worth noting that of the many instruments listed for use in the sanctuary, timbrels were not included among those cited (1 Chron. 16:42, 23:5, 25:6,7; 2 Chron. 5:12,13, 29:25,26).

By nature, the drum is not a particularly melodic instrument apart from the steel drums of the Caribbean. Drums tend to excite the emotions and appeal to the carnal nature; therefore, the Bible does not seem to record them as being used in the sanctuary.[11]

Jeremiah 7:31–32 speaks of a place called Tophet.

You may recall in 1 Kings 11:1–8, Solomon turned to pagan idolatry in his later years. His 700 wives and 300 concubines 'turned away his heart after other gods'. Solomon built his pagan wives a garden, originally called The Garden of the King, at the place where the Kedron Brook and the Brook of Hinnom met. It became known as the Garden of Tophet, which means the Garden of the Drum. It was there that Solomon's wives sacrificed to their goddess Asthoreth and the demon god Moloch. There, Israel burnt their children alive in sacrifice to his idol.

Dr Don Nelson did first-hand research in Israel and discovered it was called the Garden of the Drum (Tophet) because the people were brought to a drug-like trance through the driving beat of the drum and then they sacrificed their children.[12]

The pulpit commentary outlines that Jarchi, quoted by Wordsworth, describes the idol Molech as 'made of brass, having the face of an ox, with arms stretched out, in which the child was placed and burnt with fire, while the priests were beating drums, in order to drown the noise of its shrieks, lest the fathers might be moved with pity thereby'. The place where the children were offered, in the later period of the Jewish history, was the Valley of Hinnom (Jer. 7:31, Jer. 32:35, 2 Kings 23:10).[13]

So what is this Tophet?

To understand the significance, it is important to understand the historical context.

One area within the Hinnom Valley was called Topheth (also spelled Tophet or Topeth) where the children were slaughtered (2 Kings 23:10). The name Topheth is derived from either, or both, the Hebrew word *toph*, meaning *a drum*, because the cries of children being sacrificed by the priests of Moloch were masked by the sound of the beating on drums, or from *taph* or *toph*, meaning to *burn*. If anyone questions God's wrath upon paganism, apart from turning their backs on the true God, one need only look at these barbaric acts that were committed in that valley as one example.[14]

Even King Ahaz of Judah, the 12th king from King Solomon, sacrificed his own sons to Molech (2 Kings 16:1–3).

The *Easton's Bible Dictionary* says Tophet is from the Hebrew *toph* meaning *a drum*, because the cries of children were drowned out by the noise of the drum. The *Fausset's Bible Dictionary* says this word comes from *toph*, the drums beaten to drown the shrieks of the children. According to the *Unger's Bible Dictionary*, this word was known as the place or garden of the drum.

Plutarch wrote in *De Superstitiones* 171:

But with full knowledge and understanding they themselves offered up their own children, and those who had no children would buy little ones from poor people and cut their throats as if they were so many lambs or young birds; meanwhile the mother stood by without a tear or moan; but should she utter a single moan or let fall a single tear, she had to forfeit the money, and her child was sacrificed nevertheless; and the whole area before the statue was filled with a loud noise of flutes and drums took the cries of wailing should not reach the ears of the people.

Incredibly, Hillsong London as part of their Easterfest in 2016 used a voodoo invocation including dramatic dance, which one can only conclude that Satan's hordes sit around the board table in their creative department.[15]

Although this chapter is difficult reading this if nothing else should demand us all to take stock of the inordinate use of drums in Christian music.

I was 11 when I started drumming. Yes, I'm a drummer. My training and background was in highland pipe bands. However, at one stage as a teenager, I thought that being in a rock band out on the road was an exciting career.

Fast-forward and I still drum but not in a rock band. In fact, no band as church is a place for worship, where individual musicians play in harmony to hopefully bring glory to God. I deliberately do not play loud. My role is to provide timing, and I am never there to be overbearing. I am also one of the worship leaders at church.

So drums should not dominate or be a gaudy display. 'Love does not vaunt or promote itself' (1 Cor. 13:4).

This is the point of this chapter. One will have to make up one's own mind on the topic.

For most modern Christians however, this is a bitter pill too difficult to swallow.

16
ANOTHER JESUS,
ANOTHER 'GODSPELL'

Take thou away from me the noise of thy songs; for I will not hear the melody of thy viols. But let judgment run down as waters, and righteousness as a mighty stream.

—Amos 5:23,24

Remember Rick Warren's rhetoric, 'There is no such thing as "Christian" music; there are only Christian lyrics'?

Now we have neither!

In his article 'Match the Music to the People', Rick Warren goes on to say, 'It's the words that make a song spiritual. If I were to play a tune for you without any words, you wouldn't know if it was a Christian song or not.'[1]

Has he never watched a Metallica concert? Doesn't the tune of amazing grace not provide some clue?

Around four years ago, I had an experience that would forever make Warren's naive statement completely false. I walked into an alternative music store, and some music from a death metal band was playing over the speakers. The beat was loud, and the music overpowering. It seemed

97

I was being engulfed by the music. And yet somehow I was. It was throbbing and pounding through my body as its energy targeted me. The impact was so overwhelming it seemed like I was no longer in the shop but down in some kind of abyss, in a dark cavern, where the walls were closing in around me. I was looking around for something to hold on to. I experienced this frightening episode for about 10 seconds until I came to my senses and realised it was time to leave the shop.

There is a solemn warning here that the church has not heeded. Atmospheres are going to come, and one of the major vehicles through which it will come to this new generation of young rockers—through the electric church. The church of God playing the music of the world in the name of God! Deceived by seducing spirits, we now are no longer in control of the way the music is going.

When they introduced this new type of music, it was never just to have a new style of music. It was never just to make things more appealing. It was to lead us away from everything sacred and everything that had a scriptural basis.

I hope you will put up with a little of my foolishness; but you are already doing that. I am jealous for you with a godly jealousy. I promised you to one husband, to Christ, so that I might present you as a pure virgin to him. But I am afraid that just as Eve was deceived by the serpent's cunning, your minds may somehow be led astray from your sincere and pure devotion to Christ. For if someone comes to you and preaches a Jesus other than the Jesus we preached, or if you receive a different spirit from the one you received, or a different gospel from the one you accepted, you put up with it easily enough. (2 Cor. 11:1–4 NIV)

Whatever the inspiration for the music and with its subsequent industry that has produced album after album, year after year, we know that something has changed in the attitude, style, lyrics, and overall message of the music.

Receiving 'another' Jesus also entails the receiving of a 'different spirit' (v. 4b). And if the 'Jesus' they believe and the 'Spirit' they receive are not the ones Paul preached, then clearly, the 'gospel' they have embraced is false and damning! There isn't another Jesus. There's only one.

When they introduced this new music, it was always to lead us away from everything sacred and scriptural.

These heavy metal bands have become the new benchmark of inspiration for the modern church. This rampant deterioration brings a deep sense of foreboding when reflecting on the sound and the lyrics now coming out of the Hillsong and the Planetshakers music machine.[2]

And this is the judgement. Hillsong and Planetshakers are now all over world! This cancer has spread from the very shores of Australia!

A different spirit is now taking over!

The spirit of this age is taking over popular bands, and this is becoming more and more obvious with successful Christian bands like Skillet who have released recent albums with the titles of *Awake* and *Rise*. The cover of *Awake* features a person wrapped in white rags exposing only one eye. We will look at these two words later in chapters like 'Oceans: Bridge Over Troubled Waters'.

[12]And what I do I will continue to do, in order to undermine the claim of those who would like to claim that in their boasted mission they work on the same terms as we do.[13] For such men are false apostles, deceitful workmen, disguising themselves as apostles of Christ.[14] And no wonder, for even Satan disguises himself as an angel of light.[15] So it is no surprise

if his servants, also, disguise themselves as servants of righteousness. Their end will correspond to their deeds. (2 Cor. 11:12–15 ESV)

Now the Spirit speaketh expressly, that in the latter times some shall depart from the faith, giving heed to seducing spirits, and doctrines of devils. (1 Tim. 4:1 KJV)

Why are we pushing the envelope? Or perhaps a better question is, who is pushing the envelope?

17
CELEBRITY DRIVEN CHURCH

Therefore as the fire devours the stubble, and the flame consumes the chaff, so their root shall be as rottenness, and their blossom shall go up as dust: because they have cast away the law of the Lord of hosts, and despised the word of the Holy One of Israel.

—Isa. 5:24

Hillsong Music is Christian music produced by Hillsong Church in Sydney, Australia.

Their albums are released and distributed by Hillsong Music Australia, the resource arm of Hillsong Church. Hillsong is one of the world's fastest-growing ministries, with a now 30,000-plus-strong congregation in Australia, as well as one of the largest evangelical churches in various cities throughout the globe, such as London, Cape Town, and Kiev. Hillsong also has churches in Stockholm and Paris and recently established new churches in New York City and Los Angeles.[1]

For the past 20 years, Hillsong worship music has been a global phenomenon. The songs from Hillsong church in Sydney, Australia—

with their quirky punk rhythms and euro pop harmonies—are sung around the world. You can even find Hillsong CDs in small-town Lutheran bookstores, as I did recently.

Hillsong's popularity in Christian praise and worship music stems from the inauguration of their conferences in the late 1980s and the first publication of choruses written by Hills CLC members, especially Darlene Zschech. Their first live worship CD *The Power of Your Love* was released in 1992. Since then, live praise and worship albums have been produced each year. Other music series include the Worship series, United, Youth Alive, Hillsong Kids, and Instrumental series as two Christmas albums and several compilation albums.[2]

Since its first release in 1988, Hillsong has recorded more than 60 albums, including live worship and kids and youth CDs. They have been distributed in 80 countries and collected more than 30 gold and platinum awards in Australia and the United States.[3] Hillsong's Sydney location *reported* $64 million in revenue in 2010, but its report does not reveal income from its worldwide music sales.[4]

And all this is achieved by its army of volunteers and performers who are not paid, and so Hillsong is able to make even more money from the album sales because of its tax-free status.

And yet according to Tanya Levin, ex-Hillsong member and author of the book *People in Glass Houses*, Hillsong (as Hills Christian Life Centre back then) 'had advertised for a long time that rock 'n' roll music was evil, that it was of Satan.'[5]

Joel Houston (oldest son of Brian and Bobbie Houston, senior pastors of Hillsong) said in one interview, 'As long as we're always committed to our call to "serve the church", and keep that the basis for why we do, what we do. We could tour 365 days a year, but we don't, because that's

not our call. Record labels will tell us to do it 'cause it will help sell more albums, but at the end of the day that's not what we do.'

So being at the top of the charts isn't your thing?

Joel Houston: 'The desire is to reach as many people as we can, so that's probably demonstrated when more people buy the albums. But that's not the business of what we're doing. What we're doing is reaching as many people as we can with the message that we have.'[6]

The question has to be asked, what is the message?

On the back cover of the CD *Mighty to Save*, Hillsong quotes 2 Chronicles 7:14: 'If my people who are called by my name will humble themselves and pray, and seek my face . . . then I will hear from heaven and heal their land.' They left out the '*and turn from their wicked ways*'.[7]

They continue to massage the gospel. They have just pulled away the lynchpin. Live as you please. There's no need to change your lifestyle and no need to take seriously the demands of Christ and the challenge of the gospel. This then is the message, the mindset, and culture of Hillsong.

Speaking of being on tour, in 2006 Darlene Zschech lead the praise and worship at Joel Osteen's Lakewood Church in Houston, Texas.[8]

Hillsong United band is a praise and worship band that originated as a part of Hillsong. The band tours the world, performing at the various Hillsong church locations as well as general concert venues. The music style now is known as hard worship or rock worship.[9]

Dr Mark Evans (Macquarie University) states in his PhD thesis, 'A youth band was formed from the Hillsong music team, which took what was happening in the church musically and played it louder and rockier, appealing directly to a youth demographic.'[10]

The Christian music industry is now celebrity driven. The song is irrelevant. The focus is on the person, and the songs have become disposable. Most of our ills can be directed at this circus of Christian entertainment, which is giving a generation a palatable Christianity, a people who know nothing of seeking after God. We are now seeing a crisis among today's Christian youth.

Andrew Strom provides an accurate analysis. Today this error is flooding into the church under the guise of 'relevance'. In the name of relevance or purpose, we are rushing around, desperately trying to make our music cool, our leadership cool, our gospel cool, and our youth events cool—all in an effort to attract the world on its terms. Instead of 'holier than thou', we are cooler than thou. Our whole effort is aimed at proving to the world that Christianity is just as much cool, just as much fun, and just as much of a party as the world has to offer. We feel we have to become just like the world in order to impress the world. Thus, we now need to be seen in fashionable (or, better still, hip or alternative) clothes. And our youth events become an excuse for a party. And our presentations become entertaining multimedia extravaganzas.[11]

This is all in an effort to be equal or out-cool the world, which is why you now see 'moshing' heads, slam dancing, and stage diving at youth concerts, matching the world's mindless hedonistic ways. We have become lovers of pleasures more than lovers of God. Being cool yet full of pride, worldliness, and rebellion—all in the name of relevance. Just like the world in every sense. Unfortunately, many of these 'cool' Christians do not realise that in order to impress the world, they have to compromise some of the most vital elements of New Testament Christianity.

There is a real danger of the emergence of the 'concert Christian', the semi-converted, shallow, committed teenager whose Christianity means little more than that he enjoys conferences and festival going.

And the tragic fact is that such concert Christians are now found in their multiplied thousands around the globe. It is not just the large festivals and concerts that have succumbed to this spirit of entertainment.

We now find this 'entertain-them-at-all-costs' approach to youth ministry everywhere, from local church youth right up to large regional gatherings. This spirit has pervaded everything, particularly those areas in the church that are connected with young people. In fact, it has become increasingly rare to find gatherings of Christian youth now in which these attitudes do not prevail.

This begs the question, can Carl Lentz be an 'apostle of cool' and an apostle of Christ? New York's trendy Gen-Y crowd are drawn every Sunday by this new pastor of chic. Can Christianity be this cool and still be Christian?

Show up for a Sunday service at Hillsong NYC and the first thing you notice about the audience is it's seems they're all united in wearing the same thing, like a badge or a uniform. Conformity seems to be the way Hillsong is reforming Christianity.

In the world of sales, if a product is not selling, you revamp it, rename it, give it different packaging, and promote it to a different audience. That's what they have done. They have made Jesus a product. You see, a product can change, but the TRUTH cannot.

Just because you follow Carl or Joel doesn't mean you follow Jesus

Why is Hillsong offering a repackaged celebrity? In our culture driven by and obsessed with celebrities, ones like Jay-Z and Justin Timberlake admit that it is not all it appears to be on the surface.

King Solomon came to realise the answer to finding purpose, and it wasn't in endless pleasures. 'Let us hear the conclusion of the whole matter: Fear God, and keep his commandments: for this is the whole duty of man' (Eccl. 12:13 KJV).

18
YOU CANNOT SERVE
GOD AND EMI

*No man can serve two masters: for either he will hate the
one, and love the other; or else he will hold to the one,
and despise the other. Ye cannot serve God and mammon.*

—Matt 6:24

Hillsong's Music Industry (HMI) has joined forces with EMI. In April
2010 EMI CMG Label Group and its Sparrow Records label started
marketing Hillsong Music, as well as their other music and video
products. The plan is to expand its reach into North and South America[1]

Capitol Christian Music Group (Capitol CMG) (formerly known as
EMI Christian Music Group) is the leader in the Christian Gospel
Music Industry.[2]

The music group was founded by Billy Ray Hearn in February 1976 as
Sparrow Records. Formerly known as EMI Christian Music Group,
Capitol CMG is a division of Capitol Music Group, a Universal Music
Group company. Over the years, the venture has grown into a multi-
faceted business incorporating several labels. The company's roster
features top names in the Christian and gospel communities, among
them Jeremy Camp, Michael W Smith, Hillsong United, Smokie

Norful, Tye Tribbett, Britt Nicole, David Crowder Band, Newsboys, and Matt Redman.

According to former president/CEO Bill Hearn, 'we want to impact popular culture and resource the church through music and music-related content and services consistent with a Biblical worldview, and finally, lead with excellence and be profitable'.

Based on this vision, Hearn and Hillsong are clearly *united*.

It raises the all-important question as to whether these Christian labels are now essentially ministry-driven or profit-driven entities. And it also gives a pointer to just how much MONEY is involved in the Christian music industry today.

Today the largest Christian publishers are owned by secular corporations or have shares held by Wall Street investors. As ministries turn into big businesses, theological integrity can easily give way to marketing considerations.

The Christian marketplace thus follows the lead of the world's pop culture. A common saying in the industry is 'Whenever a trend emerges in the secular arena, wait six months and a Christianised version will appear in the religious bookstores.'

The early songs of Hillsong such as 'Power of Your Love' (1992) covered some basic Christian themes. An acknowledgement of God, the need to change, our weaknesses, God's grace, our need for Him, the power of God's love to forgive and overcome in our lives.

In this past decade, we have seen a steady well-orchestrated decline into the worship of entertainment.

Hillsong United's Break Free (Abridged) 2007

Would you believe me, would you listen if I told you that

There is a love that makes a way and never holds you back?

So won't you break free, won't you break free Get up and dance in his love (x2)

Who would have thought that God would give His one and only Son.

Taking a stand up on the cross to show his perfect love?

Now we have a Christ whose love doesn't hold us back and a love that is taking a stand on the cross. When you look at the importance of songs in conveying a message, this song falls far short of the traditional Christian canon. In fact, it is downright repugnant. I could say more but will refrain!

Christ paid our price on the cross. He took our place. He took our penalty for sin and received the very wrath of God poured out on him. He died a physical death. As the Eternal God, He who had no beginning, ever present with the Father, he was cut off for the first time from God. He who knew no sin was made sin for us. He endured agony emotionally, physically, and spiritually. All for us!

'Christ demonstrated his love, that while we were yet sinners, Christ died for us' (Rom. 5:1). In the words of the popular modern Christian worship song - *In Christ Alone* by Keith and Kristyn Getty we are given clarity;

Till on that cross as Jesus died,
The wrath of God was satisfied
For every sin on Him was laid; Here in the death of Christ I live.

Not quite the same as *making a stand*, to show His love. These types of glib lyrics are unacceptable. But the loose modern Christian accepts all this under the guise of interpretation, and creative license.

19
THE CROSS AND THE PHOENIX

If any man will come after me, let him deny himself, and take up his cross daily, and follow me.

—Lk. 9:23

Hillsong United released a new studio album called *Aftermath* released back on 15 February 2011.[1]

When I read this album title, I questioned the name with a great deal of unease. These days we like to talk about the cross, even talk up the cross, but not take up the cross.

Definition of *Aftermath*

The meaning of the word *aftermath* is linked to the consequences of an event (especially a catastrophic event) e.g. the aftermath of war. In the wake of the accident, no one knew how many had been injured. A consequence, especially of a disaster or misfortune: famine as an aftermath of drought. Aftermath is defined as a period of time following a disastrous event.

Aftermath, by the way, doesn't feature as a word in the Bible anywhere.

Back in 2001, Youth Alive, who reached out to young Australians with a positive message, produced an album called *Elevate*. Again, *Elevate* is not a word found in the Bible either. It is a term linked to evolution and the ascendancy of man. It is found in Masonic literature and the business world.

Why does Steven Furtick use it as the name of his church? He even had a worship night bearing the same name.

But continuing on, let me make it loud and clear: the cross of Christ and His choosing to go there has nothing to do with Greek or Roman tragedy, calamity, or some sort of cosmic fallout. Christ, on the cross, declared it is finished! He was not the messiah, as Mary Magdalene, and the disciples thought he was. To them, his death was a tragedy. All their hopes and dreams lay silent with the Lord in the tomb. But Jesus, the only Son of God, rose up that Sunday morn, conquering the grave, just as he said!

'For you will not leave my soul in sheol, nor will you allow your holy one to see corruption' (Ps. 16:10).

The Lord Jesus did not experience death and decay as we mortals.

'And having spoiled principalities and powers, he made a show of them openly, triumphing over them in it' (Col. 2:15).

Christ rose from the dead and is now seated at the right hand of God. He has defeated death, sin, and the devil. Let me repeat this so I'm clear: there is no aftermath with God, and there are no surprises. He makes all things new. Hallelujah!

The unusual name of the album and single are even more pronounced by its association with other songs and a short film of the same title.

In 1994, *Aftermath*, a short film, was produced where a man working in a morgue mutilates and defiles one of the corpses. Then he takes the heart home to his dog.

Other songs entitled 'Aftermath' are the following:[2]

- 'Aftermath' by REM

- 'Aftermath' by Adam Lambert from *For Your Entertainment* (2009)

- 'Aftermath' by Edge of Sanity from *Crimson II*

- 'Aftermath' by Phish from *Phish*

- 'Aftermath' by The Rolling Stones (an unreleased song)

- 'Aftermath' by Sonic Syndicate from *Only Inhuman*

- 'The Aftermath' by Bob Seger and the Silver Bullet Band from *Like a Rock*

- 'The Aftermath' by Iron Maiden from *The X Factor*

- 'The Aftermath' by Kashmir from *Zitilites*

- 'The Aftermath' by Origin from *Antithesis* (2008)

- 'The Aftermath (G3)' by Escape the Fate from *Escape the Fate* (November 2010)

Adam Lambert (listed above), this modern Elvis look-alike, had photos showing him romantically kissing another man while he was competing on the eighth season of *American Idol*. Lambert confirmed that the photos were of him, stating he had nothing to hide and had always been open about his life. Mainstream media speculation centred on Lambert's sexuality; presuming he was gay, he would be the first gay American Idol.[3]

He appeared on *Australian Idol* as a guest singer in the same year.

Lambert released his album *For Your Entertainment* in November 2009, but 'The Aftermath' remix single was released in March 2011. The timing, with Hillsong United's release date of February 2011 for their album, raises some speculation that it was more than a coincidence.

If you research the above list, most of the groups are rock, hard rock, metal, or heavy metal.

Origin is a technical death metal band!

Hillsong's album *Aftermath* has the theme of destruction and nuclear annihilation associated with it, which we will see later. It is a major theme of heavy metal bands.

How can a seemingly innocent title of a song stir up some much questionable connections and controversy? There must more to the name than meets the eye.

Aftermath (February 2011) (Abridged Lyrics)[4] You were broken for all the world to see

Lifted out of the ashes

I am found in the aftermath

The above lyrics are taken from the single 'Aftermath' by Hillsong United.

Firstly, I want to say these lyrics seem as though they were intended to be metaphorical. However, there must be concern over lyrics that refer to Christ's death as an aftermath. Christ's death can no way be considered a disaster or human tragedy.

Christ's death was a propitiation (payment) for our sins to deal with

God's righteous justice against our sin and rebellion. His death was part of the overall plan of salvation. God was in Christ reconciling us back to Himself, taking away the barrier of our sin, through the death of His son. Christ the victor gives us life through His life. Do we come forth anew, raised out from Christ's death or from Christ's ashes? If that was what was meant, then the analogy smacks of a modern-day take on reincarnation. And if this is not what they mean, then what? Why is Hillsong using the symbology of ashes in the first place?

The scripture makes it clear: 'We are buried in Christ, and we are raised again with him' (cf. Rom. 6:4–11). We are raised with Christ.

Therefore we are buried with him by baptism into death: that like as Christ was raised up from the dead by the glory of the Father, even so we also should walk in newness of life.'

To be 'lifted out of the ashes' is a weighted reference to the phoenix. The phoenix bird symbolises rebirth, especially of the sun, and has variants in European, Central American, Egyptian, and Asian cultures.[5]

Even Chris Tomlin uses it in one of his songs called 'Our God'.[6] Search any song title on the phoenix, and there is this explicit reference to the phoenix rising from ashes or out of the flames. How can Christians not know this?

In the 19th century, Danish author Hans Christian Andersen wrote a story about the phoenix. Edith Nesbit features a phoenix in one of her children's stories, *The Phoenix and the Carpet*, as does J. K. Rowling in the infamous Harry Potter series. In one volume of Harry Potter, the phoenix does its usual resurrecting routine. J. K. Rowling wrote *Harry Potter and the Order of the Phoenix* in 2003.

According to Egyptian sources, a sacred bird was occasionally seen at the temple in Heliopolis, the city of the sun god. On some of the oldest and best pictures, the bird resembles a heron. The bird symbolised the rising sun, i.e. the day and eternal rebirth. According to an Egyptian myth, Osiris transformed into a phoenix in Heliopolis. The bird was from time to time depicted sitting in a tree next to Osiris's coffin, thus symbolising Osiris's death, and resurrection. The myth spread and has lasted until today. Catholic monks in the Middle Ages employed the phoenix as a symbol of Christ because of its voluntary death and rebirth.[7]

A new phoenix always rises from the ashes.[8]

Manly P Hall, in his book entitled *The Secret Destiny of America* (1958, p. 176,177)wrote:

'All symbols have their origin in something tangible, and the phoenix is one sign of the secret orders of the ancient world, and of the initiate of those orders, for it was common to refer to one who had been accepted into temples as a man twice-born, or reborn. Wisdom confers a new life, and those who become wise are born again.' Hall was referring to the illumination through the phoenix.

A former witch had this to say regarding the occult belief in the phoenix bird: 'The Phoenix . . . is believed to be a divine bird going back to Egypt. . . . This Phoenix destroys itself in flames and then rises from the ashes. Most occultists believe that **the Phoenix is a symbol of Lucifer** who was cast down in flames and who they think will one day rise triumphant. This, of course, also relates to the rising Hiram Abiff, the Masonic "Christ"'(C. Burns, *Masonic and Occult Symbols Illustrated*, p. 123).

Thus, what we have here is a bird, the occult phoenix bird that has its roots in ancient mythology. This mythical bird symbolises the new age concept of being born again.[9]

It is definitely NOT Christian. Rather, it is linked to the rising of a New

World Order as illustrated in detail on the back of the United States One-dollar bill. The eagle replaced the phoenix in 1841 as the national bird. But the phoenix has been a brotherhood symbol since ancient Egypt. The phoenix was adopted by the founding fathers (Freemasons) for use on the reverse of the first official seal of the United States after a design proposed by Charles Thompson, secretary of the Continental Congress. The Great Seal played a prominent role in the 14 January 1784, ratification of the Treaty of Paris.

In May 1782, William Barton, who had a reputation for his knowledge of heraldry, was consulted by the Third Great Seal Committee to contribute to the design of a national coat-of-arms for the United States.

He introduced an eagle with wings 'displayed', an element that Secretary of the Continental Congress Charles Thomson greatly emphasised in the final proposal. The new design for the reverse of the seal incorporated the Eye of Providence atop a pyramid of thirteen steps. This combined the influence of Pierre Eugene du Simitiere, who had included the Eye of Providence in his designs for the First Great Seal Committee, with that of Francis Hopkinson, who had consulted for the Second Great Seal Committee and who had included a similar pyramid in his 1778 design for the Continental currency. On 20 June, the design, as amended and expanded by Thomson, was adopted by the Continental Congress.

In Barton's design, at the top is an eagle and on the pillar in the shield is a 'phoenix in flames'. The mottos were 'In Vindiciam Libertatis [In defence of liberty]' and 'Virtus sola invicta [Only virtue unconquered]'.

The great seal of 1782, if compared with the present design on the dollar, is clearly different. It is immediately evident that the bird on the original seal is not an eagle but a phoenix, the ancient symbol of human aspiration towards universal good. The beak is a different shape, the neck is much longer, and the small tuft of hair at the back of the head leaves no doubt as to the artist's intention.[10]

For the reverse side of the seal, Barton used a pyramid of thirteen steps, with the radiant Eye of Providence overhead, and used the mottos 'Deo Favente [With God's favour or, more literally, God favouring]' and 'Perennis [everlasting]. The pyramid had come from another Continental currency note designed in 1778 by Hopkinson, this time the $50 note, which had a nearly identical pyramid and the motto 'Perennis'.

For the reverse, Thomson essentially kept Barton's design but re-added the triangle around the Eye of Providence and changed the mottos to 'Annuit Cœptis' and 'Novus Ordo' Seclorum' (wingtips up) instead of rising. Barton also wrote a more properly heraldic blazon.

On the 1782 resolution of the dollar bill, the seal blazons the image on the reverse side as an 'unfinished pyramid. In the zenith was an eye in a triangle, surrounded by a glory, proper'. The pyramid is conventionally shown as consisting of thirteen layers to refer to the thirteen original states. The adopting resolution provides that it is inscribed on its base with the date MDCCLXXVI (1776) in Roman numerals. Where the top of the pyramid should be, it is the Eye of Providence that watches over it. Note the number thirteen (13) throughout this design.

On the subject of heraldry, Barton wrote a 1788 letter to General George Washington:

I am likewise persuaded, Sir, that Blazonry not only merits the notice of an inquisitive mind, viewed merely as an affectative science; but that Coat-Armour, the Object of it, may be rendered conducive to both public and private uses, of considerable importance, in this infant nation, now rising into greatness.

Two mottos appear. 'Annuit Coeptis' signifies that Providence has 'approved of [our] undertakings'. 'Novus ordo seclorum', freely taken from Virgil, is Latin for 'a new order of the ages'.[11]

The coming new order will one day rise up out of the ashes, out of the chaos (aftermath) of the old regime.

The motto of 33rd degree Scottish rite Masonry is 'Ordo Ab Chao', or 'Order from Chaos'. In fact, the Masonic Christ is said to arise out of the chaos of this present age!

But the story is only half told. How did these two great seals originate?

Thomas Jefferson, a Mason; Benjamin Franklin, a Rosicrucian; and John Adams, also a Mason, were commissioned on 4 July 1776 to design the seals.

However, as strange and bizarre as it seems, these patriots were *given* the design. On 17 June 1782, while at his home reviewing the drawings, Thomas Jefferson was suddenly approached by a strange figure cloaked in black. The man allegedly presented Jefferson with a red velvet bag, which contained two plaques. Turning around, the 'man' walked into Jefferson's garden and mysteriously vanished.

The two plaques were the two great seals of the United States. The detail in these seals are brilliantly put together and can be nothing but be inspired by Satan. Whatever you believe, one outstanding fact remains unchanged: these seals were not to inaugurate the declaration of freedom but were designed as a tribute to a New World Order.[12]

During the 1932 presidential campaign, Franklin D. Roosevelt, a 33rd-degree Mason, came to power. His political platform was based on what he termed the New Deal.

As Roosevelt's New Deal was put into motion in 1935, every new dollar bill coming off the presses carried with it these two new seals that had never been seen before: the two seals of the Illuminati. They could now openly declare that their conspiracy had finally borne fruit, their 'Novus Ordo Seclorum', or 'new deal of the ages', had come to the fore. Christian J. Pinto and Cutting Edge Ministries have a great DVD called *Eye of the Phoenix* that covers this topic in depth.

The phoenix symbol is important in another way as an emblem among nearly all civilized nations of royalty, power, superiority, and immortality. The phoenix of China is identical in meaning with the phoenix of Egypt, and the Phoenix of the Greeks is the same as the thunderbird of the American Indians.

But if this design on the obverse side of the seal is stamped with the signature of the order of the quest, the design on the reverse is even more definitely related to the old mysteries.

Here is represented the Great Pyramid of Giza, composed of thirteen rows of masonry, showing seventy-two stones. The pyramid is without a capstone, and above its upper platform floats a triangle containing the all-seeing eye surrounded by rays of light.

The combination of the phoenix, the pyramid, and the all-seeing eye is more than chance or coincidence. There is only one possible origin for these symbols, and that is the secret societies, which came to this country 150 years before the Revolutionary War. There can be no question that the great seal was directly inspired by these secret orders and that it set forth the purpose for the United States, and that purpose was seen and known to the founding fathers.[13]

The lotus flower, the egg, the swastika, and the yin yang are all symbols for birth and rebirth.[14]

These symbols of rebirth and the phoenix alluded to in Hillsong United's 'Aftermath' is totally misguided, linking Christian thought with new age mythology and Masonic symbolism. This is a mixing of metaphors.

And just to make sure I wasn't reading anything into this song that wasn't there, I read on and found these additional lyrics of 'Aftermath': *Lifted out of the wreckage I find hope in the aftermath.*

If I really understand the reference to aftermath, it is not light but always darkness, confusion and despair. Indeed, the picture appears as loss, disaster, wreckage, ashes, fire, crumbling, ruins and downfall. How can this be the symbol for Christ and His resurrection?

To be blunt, it sounds more like tragedies such as 9/11. It is this strange and persistent merging of two different ideas or philosophies into a homogenised heterodoxy that is the concern. Although these things contain an element of truth, you cannot press them too far.

Has Hillsong been given over to a dark spirit?

Maybe a better question is, how long has Hillsong been under this beguiling spirit?

The departing from the faith as was foretold is happening right before our eyes, and yet most don't see it!

To further clarify the inspiration of this style of music, iTunes wrote this brief review back in February on the day of the release of the album:

Historically, if there's one complaint about modern Christian worship music, it's that it can lack variety and rarely ventures outside its safe zone. In that context, listening to Aftermath is truly an experience: an event as real and engaging as the worship team's well- documented stage show that has been seen by the masses on six continents. . . . The team shouts refrains on 'Nova' and 'Go' amid percussive rhythms that sound like a cross between Chris Tomlin, Coldplay, and even Kings of Leon. The guitar work on 'Take Heart', 'Father' and 'Rhythms of Grace' is delicate and captivating, evolving into a Sarah McLachlan-like trance on 'Like an Avalanche' and 'Bones'. Aftermath shows that Hillsong continues to set the bar high, and blur the lines between studio albums, and live worship.[15]

How can worship meant for God be compared to Coldplay, Kings of Leon, and Sarah McLachlan and setting the bar for biblical worship?

Not only do they blur the lines between studio albums and live worship, the lines between the holy and the profane are redefined. And the lines between true worship and false are blurred also. This compromise to entertain with the world's tunes leaves us blunted and unable to challenge the present culture.

The current brand of Christianity wears a fair exterior, which makes a fair show in the flesh, speaks well of Christ, and yet betrays him with a kiss.

Spurgeon declared in his sermon in 1885 to his congregation called 'Coming judgment of the secrets of the sons of men':

God [has] appointed a day in which He will judge the world, and we sigh and cry until it shall end the reign of wickedness, and give rest to the oppressed.

Brethren, we must preach the coming of the Lord. . . . It is absolutely necessary to the preaching of the gospel of Christ that men be warned as to what will happen if they continue in their sins. . . . You hope to heal the sick without their knowing it. You therefore flatter them; and what happens? They laugh at you; they dance upon their own graves. At last they die! Your delicacy is cruelty; your flatteries are poisons; you are a murderer. Shall we keep men in a fool's paradise? Shall we lull them into soft slumbers from which they will awake in Hell? Are we to become helpers of their damnation by our smooth speeches? In the name of God we will not.[16]

It is ironic that at the writing of this chapter, Hillsong United had their most successful concerts in the United States ever and have received nomination for ten Dove Awards.

They have sell out concerts but in so doing have sold out Jesus and the message of the gospel.

20
HILLSONG'S TATTOO CULTURE

Do not cut your bodies for the dead or put tattoo marks on yourselves. I am the LORD.

—Lev. 19:28 NIV

Australia's Christian sensation Guy Sebastian has gained success in the secular charts, fans, as well as respect from the world. It's called influence. God calls it apostasy and backsliding.

Guy's hit about a girl in club is a reflection of the modern Christian outlook on the world's nightlife. It's okay to be there in a club.

For World Youth Day, July 2008, 'Receive the Power'[1], a song written by Sebastian and Gary Pinto, was chosen as the official anthem for the Roman Catholic Church's XXIII World Youth Day (WYD08) held in Sydney, Australia, in 2008.[2]

Guy, on his rise to success, got himself a tattoo. The Bible condemns the branding or marking of our body. 'Ye shall not make any cuttings in your flesh for the dead, nor print any marks upon you: I am the LORD' (Lev. 19:28).

Tattoos used to be worn by the sordid criminal, the drunkard, and the seaman.

'Do you not know that your body is a temple of the Holy Spirit, who is in you, whom you have received from God? You are not your own; you were bought at a price. Therefore honor God with your body' (1 Cor. 6:19–20).

Guy Sebastian got a tattoo in 2009. So what was it? You guessed it, a phoenix!

Guy has other tattoos including one to commemorate Martin Luther King, with Guy's latest 2014 tattoo, which is a quote from John Lennon to remind him about life. It's the famous quote 'Life happens while you're making plans.'[3]

So he gives himself a tattoo of a quote from a man who was an atheist and had an absolute disdain for the Lord and said imagine there is no heaven or hell etc. and also said the Beatles were more popular than Jesus to remind him about life and the balance of it. This shows where Guy Sebastian's head is these days. Was he ever saved, or did he just play church as a youngster because of his mum and dad taking him there every Sunday?

Paradise AOG in Adelaide, Australia, sought to cash in on his popularity. They hoped it would bring people to their church, but it never did.

You can spot irrefutable evidence a society has embraced Satanic values in many ways, but the visible evidence of multiple body piercings and tattoos are the strongest of all. Few people understand the use Satan makes of piercing and tattoos to *control* the person!

Chris Brown (American R&B singer), and Todd Bentley (preacher/

evangelist, Lakeland Revival, Florida) are two obvious examples why you don't get a tattoo!

Joel Houston of Hillsong has a tattoo on his upper right arm. Houston's tattoo (a Japanese artwork of a wave on his inner bicep) caused a stir among bloggers who debated whether tattoos are prohibited.

With some additional research on various websites, there appeared a list of spiritual meanings for all Japanese tattoos to do with the waves, which have a variety of meanings.

However, it seems as though it is a Japanese wave design with a sun combo motif. It would seem Joel's is in reference to the waves and sea and the sun, the world of surfing, and being carefree.

He has another tattoo on the other arm, but this to date is indistinguishable. His wife, in Joel's Facebook, has a tattoo on her torso with was some writing.

By going to Facebook and Twitter, you can see that these people are very worldly Christians in many ways.

Oh, and his bro. Benjamin (Ben Houston) has a tattoo on his arm as well. The amusing thing is Brian Houston doesn't seem to like them.

If you put the brethren in remembrance of these things, you shall be a good minister of Jesus Christ, nourished up in the words of faith and of good doctrine, whereunto you have attained. But refuse profane and old wives' fables, and exercise yourself rather unto godliness. For bodily exercise profits little: but godliness is profitable unto all things, having promise of the life that now is, and of that which is to come. This is a faithful saying and worthy of all acceptation. (1 Tim. 4:6–9)

Paul admonished Timothy about faith and good doctrine, but never once did he mention the need for a well-placed tattoo.

Then there's the pastor of Hillsong NYC Carl Lentz who has an armful. Both of Lentz's inner biceps are covered down to his forearm. Famous witch and author Laurie Cabot writes of the tattoo: 'The origins of tattooing came from ancient magical practices' (Laurie Cabot *Power of the Witch*, cited in *Masonic and Occult Symbols Illustrated* by Dr Cathy Burns, p. 301). [4]

Even today, in many countries (including the United States), the tattoo is believed to be a bridge into the supernatural world.

21
HIGHWAY TO HELL

There is a way which seemeth right unto a man, but the end thereof are the ways of death.

—Prov. 14:12

Perry Noble, one of the new breeds of pastors who will try anything once, ran with the idea of playing AC/DC's Highway to Hell back in 2009 at their Easter service at NewSpring church in Anderson, South Carolina. He said recently he had no regrets about the decision but would like to use it again in a mash-up with the Aussie band's other anthem 'Hell's Bells'.[1]

Clearly, a new generation of Nadabs and Abihus have entered the ministry!

Noble went on to state, 'We are committed to doing whatever it takes to bring people far from God into a relationship with Jesus.' Whatever it takes? This is complete nonsense, if not complete insanity. The logical conclusion is everything and anything is permissible to bring a man to a decision for Christ. How about we try a swingers' weekend or a séance Sunday? Whatever it takes? Monstrous!

The lines are now subtle yet clearly drawn between those promoting the grace of God as a license to sin and those who still hold to the tenet of biblical separation.

After the obvious backlash, one woman at the church defended Noble by saying, 'NewSpring does whatever we can to reach the lost and meet them where they are, exactly like Christ did!' She goes on to suggest that some might walk away, but NewSpring is running the good race, sprinting towards Jesus.[2]

A hymn to Satan and *sprinting towards* Jesus? This isn't just about a satanic Sunday morning service. This is about the mentality, the ministry philosophy, the pastoral propriety, the purity of the church, and the difference between true worship and 'strange fire', the holy and the unholy, Christ and Belial. God says, 'Don't worship me this way.' The end does not justify the means. There are certain fundamental principles that are right, good, and essential; and you cannot justify violating them because you have some 'right' or 'good' goal, or agenda in mind. In 2014 Noble revealed that he had been taking anti-depressants since 2012 after years of struggling with anxiety and suicidal thoughts.[3] In July 2016 after counsel with members of the senior pastoral team, Noble was stood down to deal with his alcoholism and his marriage.[4]

And yet if you say anything against these groups you are a judger, a condemner, and a hater. You are labelled a Christian hypocrite and a proud Pharisee.

One of the most tragic aspects of this ongoing departing is the reality that the whole world lies in the hands of the evil one. We are born part of this world system, dead in trespasses and sin, blind, cut off from God, hostile and wayward in our response to Him. Without God's intervention, we are eternally lost, set on a course for hell and destruction. Without God, we are without hope in the world. Yet the majority of the church wants to use the methods of the world to bring about the new birth.

Various men still resist the truth; and like them men of corrupt minds— men who have their own ideas, understanding, bias, and prejudice against the truth and think the gospel can be peddled like a five-dime watch.

Now as Jannes and Jambres withstood Moses, so do these also resist the truth: men of corrupt minds, reprobate concerning the faith. But they shall proceed no further: for their folly shall be manifest unto all men, as theirs also was (2 Tim. 3:8–9).

These men challenge the true church by saying we are okay as we are. We don't need your God, and yet we think to win them with the new cart of self-esteem and music methods. They are far from being true Christians. Thus, many Christian leaders today have an appearance of all things God, yet they have a counterfeit life and a counterfeit ministry.

Thus, the world's music and its culture has always opposed the church from truly liberating God's people, but worst of all has been the resistance of God's truth and holiness from within the church herself throughout recorded history, which is the greatest crime.

Paul tells us that we are to reprove, *not* approve, of the works of darkness (cf. Eph. 5:8).

Who do we fool? We massage the message and manipulate the multitudes using natural means like rock music to bring about spiritual outcomes. There can be no new birth, no new creation, no sanctification apart from the life and activity of the Holy Spirit. This use of worldly concepts only brings about false conversions, dare I say, 'stillbirths'.

Growth in the modern church over the last three decades has been nothing more than the work of man on the back of a Philistine cart. With the church in decline, someone decided to keep the ark from falling by the introduction of marketing and a man-centred gospel, but we have touched the holy.

Though we have seen this way sweep the world, there has been no change, no repentance, no fleeing from the wrath to come, ' just come to Jesus' and pray a simple prayer. The Holy Spirit's influence is more or less ceased. Instead, we use the world's music, theatre, and other forms of entertainment to draw men, which is nothing more than appealing to the carnal.

The homosexual community tapped into this idea years ago, with their annual Mardi Gras. Give the people what they want—fun and entertainment—and we will make them believe our lifestyle is acceptable. The church is using the same worldly methods without blushing.

Today true salvation is rarely understood. We have gone down the slippery slope of offering the masses a repackaged modern-day version of Catholicism. Atonement is now defined as forgiving yourself.

Emerging is a Romish reformation of form and flattery. God's wonderful plan for our lives, according to scripture, is death to self, denying of the flesh, the path of suffering, the cross, with its shame. Instead, we feed the prodigals the husk of health, wealth, and prosperity, cheap grace, your best life now while still leaving them wallowing in their pigpen. We have preached the message of a 'golden ticket', a Christ-purchased salvation, so we can live as we please, our best life here, and our best life there.

We don't change the message. The message is supposed to change us!

We are fulfilling Christ's words again in our generation, going across seas to make proselytes twice the sons of hell we are. Robert Schuller and his band of reformers have blazed a trail that is bringing in a new dawn of apostasy. Grieved men who put no trust in the flesh cannot stand by and watch this storm of deception roll in.

22
HILLSONG'S HELLRAISERS

If we say that we have fellowship with him, and walk in darkness, we lie, and do not the truth.

—1 Jn. 1:6

Throughout its first three centuries, the church went through severe persecution. Then in the beginning of the third century, from out of nowhere, the Roman emperor himself became a Christian. Within one lifetime, the empire went from gross savagery in persecuting Christians to embracing Christianity.[1]

Emperor Constantine became the pontiff of the great Roman empire from AD 306 to 337. Constantine (27 February c. 272–22 May 337) was also known as Constantine I or Saint Constantine.[2]

Wikipedia outlines that Constantine became the first Roman emperor to claim conversion to Christianity. As the new emperor, Constantine enacted many administrative, financial, social, and military reforms. The government was restructured. The solidus, a new gold coin, was minted to combat inflation. Constantine pursued various successful campaigns against the tribes along the Roman frontiers—the Franks, the Alamanni, the Goths, and the Sarmatians—even resettling territories abandoned by his predecessors during the turmoil of the previous century.

Constantine played an influential role in the proclamation of the Edict of Milan, which decreed tolerance for Christianity in the empire. He called the First Council of Nicaea in AD 325, at which the Nicene Creed was professed by Christians.[3]

He may have even suggested some of the wording for the creed. Yet with all this, he did not formally renounce heathenism and did not receive his baptism until AD 337, near his death.

During this time, Constantine became embroiled in theological controversy, and he called the Council of Nicaea together to settle questions about the deity of Christ. The age of Constantine marked a distinct epoch in the history of the Roman empire.[4]

Acclaimed as emperor by the army after his father's death in 306, Constantine emerged victorious in a series of civil wars against the emperors Maxentius and Licinius to become sole ruler of both West and East by AD 324.[5]

According to the stories told by him, he had a dream in which he saw the sign of the cross (actually a chi-rho)* in the sky, with the words 'In hoc signo vinces [By this sign, conquer].'[6] The next day he added this sign to the standards of his army and won the battle. He entered Rome and became unchallenged as Western emperor.

From this time forward, he began to favour Christianity but did not completely convert all at once. Constantine became a believing Christian who vigorously promoted Christianity without trying to force it down loyal pagan throats. His legislation favoured Christianity more and more. At some time, his mother, Helena, had become a Christian; and along with her son, she began to spend large sums of money building new churches and visiting the Holy Land.

So the emperor and his empire became 'Christian'.

Much of his new faith was reflected in his imperial policy. He outlawed infanticide, gave greater equality for women, stopped the abuse of slaves and peasants and crucifixion, and made Sunday a day of rest.

Philip Schaff—who wrote his eight-volume *The History of the Christian Church* first published in 1882, now in public domain—provides a summary of the emperor's impact:

Constantine, the first Christian Caesar, the founder of Constantinople and the Byzantine empire, and one of the most gifted, energetic, and successful of the Roman emperors, was the first representative of the idea of a Christian theocracy, a system of policy which assumes all subjects are Christians, and connects civil and religious rights, and regards church and state as the two arms of one and the same divine government on earth. This idea was more fully developed by his subsequent successors.

It wasn't just from self-interest, but for the good of the empire, which now shaken to its foundations, and threatened by barbarians on every side, could only by some new bond of unity be consolidated, and upheld until at least the seeds of Christianity, and civilization should be planted among the barbarians themselves. His personal policy thus coincided with the interests of the state. Christianity appeared to him, as it proved in fact, the only efficient power for a political reformation of the empire.

His whole family was swayed by religious sentiment, which manifested itself in very different forms, in the devout pilgrimages of Helena, the fanatical Arianism of Constantia, and Constantius, and the fanatical paganism of Julian.

Constantine adopted Christianity first as a superstition, and put it by the side of his heathen superstition, till finally in his conviction the Christian vanquished the pagan, though without itself developing into a pure and enlightened faith.[7]

How much Christianity Constantine adopted at this point is difficult to discern. His Roman coins minted up to eight years after the battle still bore images of Roman gods. His coins bore on the one side the letters of the name of Christ, on the other the figure of the sun god and the inscription 'Sol invictus'.

In the old language, he had a 'bob each way'.

Nonetheless, it must be acknowledged Constantine's decision to 'embrace' Christianity was a turning point for the Christian church. After his victory, Constantine supported the Church financially, built various basilicas, granted privileges (e.g. exemption from certain taxes) to clergy, promoted Christians to some high-ranking offices, and returned property confiscated during the Great Persecution of Diocletian. Yet it seems the Christian emperor combined Christianity with sun worship.

Between AD 324 and 330, Constantine built, virtually from scratch, a new imperial capital that came to be named in honour of him: Constantinople. The emperor began to enforce doctrine, root out heresy, and uphold ecclesiastical unity.

Constantine created a new system of sorts, of religious liberty, in which pagans continued to worship their deities but without state support. At the same time, the emperor often cited God vaguely enough to incorporate Christians and pagans, creating a vague new form of civil religion, even while he himself lavished personal patronage on the church and granted bishops some juridical authority.[8]

Constantine's son's successor, known as Julian the Apostate, was a philosopher who, upon becoming emperor, later renounced Christianity and embraced a neo-Platonic and mystical form of paganism, shocking the Christian establishment.[9]

Idolatry took root, and much of it was defended even by some so-called church fathers.

John F. Walvoord suggests, as a result, the church soon lost its hope of the early return of Christ, and biblical simplicity was replaced by a complicated church structure that substituted human creeds and the worship of Mary for true biblical doctrine. The church worshipped idols and formed a union with the heathen world. The solemn warning of Christ given to the church at Ephesus was forgotten.[10]

In AD 313, Constantine issued an edict, ordering that all persecution of Christians should cease and that heathen temples should be converted into Christian churches. For his own selfish ends, he favoured Christianity, which, by this time, had millions of adherents. When Constantine came to the throne, with the eye of a politician, he saw that it was to his advantage to favour rather than fight these multitudes. But alas, from that time on, the poor deluded leaders of the church ceased to look for the coming of the Lord. They concluded that Constantine's kingdom must be the 'kingdom of God' that was to be established upon earth, and the union of church and state became an accomplished fact.[11]

Schaff's assessment of Constantine's reign reminds us of the typical ruthless rule of any despot of his day:

The very brightest period of his reign is stained with gross crimes, which even the spirit of the age and the policy of an absolute monarch cannot excuse. The very year in which he summoned the great council of Nicaea, he ordered the execution of his conquered rival and brother-in-law, Licinius, in breach of a solemn promise of mercy (324). Not satisfied with this, he soon afterwards, from political suspicion, brought the death of the young Licinius, his nephew, a boy of barely eleven years. But the worst of all was the murder of his eldest son, Crispus, in 326 AD, who had incurred suspicion of political conspiracy, and of adulterous and incestuous purposes towards his step-mother Fausta, but is generally regarded as innocent.[12]

By all accounts, Christianity failed to produce in Constantine the necessary moral transformation. He was probably never truly converted. He was still a heathen who basked in this newfound power, an instrument in the hands of the devil to bring about an unholy alliance with the world. His professed conversion was a great tragedy.

Schaff cites a story that indicates Constantine's constant pragmatism:

One year [AD 324] twelve thousand men, with women and children in proportion, were baptized in Rome, and that the emperor had promised to each convert a white garment and twenty pieces of gold, is at least in accordance with the spirit of that reign, though the fact itself, in all probability, is greatly exaggerated.[13]

The point is this type of all-embracing Christianity, one size fits all, began to take root; and the religion of the day, Christianity, was given the red carpet treatment, which undermined the single-mindedness and purity of the church's role to be salt and light, instead bringing in the corrupting leaven of compromise. The persecution the church had previously endured was replaced by a period of favour. Under this environment, it soon became popular to be a Christian, and the conscience of the people became dulled.

John Wesley writes of this period:

It does not appear that these extraordinary gifts of the Holy Ghost were common in the Church for more than two or three centuries. We seldom hear of them after that fatal period when the *Emperor Constantine* called himself a Christian. . . . From this time they almost totally ceased. . . . The Christians had no more of the Spirit of Christ than the other heathens. . . . This was the real cause why the extraordinary gifts of the Holy Ghost were no longer to be found in the Christian Church; because **the Christians were turned Heathens again, and had only a dead form left.**[14]

Turned heathen again? Today we **leave them as heathens** and invite them to our churches. In this same blinding zeal, the modern way is to blur these lines of distinction, both morally and theologically. It seems nothing changes. History more or less repeats itself.

In February 2014, Justin Bieber's private jet was reportedly detained in Toronto, Canada, on suspicion of marijuana being on board.

After Justin Bieber's plane was held up for smelling like a pot parlor, the 19-year-old singer was detained for five hours of questioning![15] Bieber continues to be the bad boy of the moment, but in the background, he has been searching for some spiritual help from Australian megachurch Hillsong for a while now.

Multiple sources confirmed to the *New York Post* that Bieber was looking for a Manhattan property with a private pool to conduct some sort of baptism-like ceremony with the Hillsong Church NYC.

One source said, 'Justin and his team spent time on Saturday searching for a place with a pool where they could conduct a baptism for him, a cleansing ritual, with the Hillsong Church. But they couldn't find a place in time.'

Another added, 'Justin is serious about his Christian faith, and after recent events, he needed to take a pause.'[16]

Bieber, who is believed to have been baptised as a child, is a fan of the megachurch after attending a service at their New York City location last September. He tweeted about its hip leader, Pastor Carl Lentz: 'Amazing sermon at church this morning. Love you man. I broke down today.'[17]

Much of Hillsong New York Church's popularity can be attributed to the pastor of the church, Carl Lentz. Lentz is described as an unconventional and hipster pastor. The New York branch of the Australian Pentecostal church is located at its Irving Plaza location near Manhattan's Union Square. Hillsong NYC is attracting more than 6,000 young, attractive urbanites every Sunday with a simple approach to religion: A pastor with pop-idol looks covered in tattoos gets onstage to a rock introduction to preach an anti-Kennedy gospel: Ask not what you can do for God — ask what God can do for you.[18] Lentz's fast-growing flock of groupies includes Justin Bieber, NBA superstars, and young Hollywood celebs. But whom, exactly, is this new apostle of cool seeking to glorify?"

Besides Justin Bieber, these are some other celebrities who visit or are regular attendants of the church, according to US lifestyle and fashion magazine *Details*:

- Anna Sophia Robb, Colorado-raised *Carrie Diaries* star

- Kevin Durant, NBA superstar

- Scooter Braun, Justin Bieber's manager

- Damon Dash, Roc-A-Fella Records cofounder

- Jeremy Lin, basketball player for the Houston Rockets

- Vanessa Hudgens, *Spring Breakers* co-star

- Austin Butler, actor, Vanessa Hudgens's boyfriend

- Tyson Chandler, Basketball center who currently plays for the New York Knicks[19]

According to *GQ* Pastor Carl caters to celebrities. 'Celebrities deserve a relationship with God. Celebrities deserve a place to pray.' So do all of God's children, he adds. And so they save seats in a special section for celebrities, but also for people in wheelchairs and single mothers who might be running late.[20]

And the list keeps getting bigger. Another young entertainer has also graced the halls of Hillsong, known in the rap world as Ja Rule.

He was awestruck at Hillsong's New York service, explaining how it was dark and black inside, with a disco ball in the ceiling. He felt it was different from other churches he had been to, with everyone around him being just like him. What he witnessed convinced him that the leaders were sincere when they tell people to come as they are. He talks of Pastor Carl Lentz who had tattoos, with Jordans on, jeans, and a T-shirt. Lentz came out, and he started preaching, and it felt like he was talking straight to Rule.

'I got saved at that church, me and my wife,' he revealed, adding that he encouraged his wife to take the step with him. 'We went up on stage, we got saved and it just gave me a good feeling.'[21]

Ja Rule, rapper and *I'm in Love with a Church Girl* star, was previously a Jehovah's Witness, but this left him disenchanted with religion and why he and his wife decided to get saved at Hillsong NYC Church.

Although there other great churches out there, Ja Rule explained, it didn't feel much like they were talking to him. He was surprised to see the Irving Plaza concert ballroom transformed into a worship setting.

The New York rapper admitted that although he made a decision to get saved, he wasn't ready to go all the way and was still going to make his music in a way that feels good to him. He added, 'I'm taking baby steps, and I want to get closer to God. I feel it's something that you should do in life.'[22]

So I have some obvious questions:

- Is Ja Rule really saved?

- He made a decision and dragged his wife onstage?

- It gave him a good feeling?

- Just as he made a decision earlier in his life as a Jehovah's Witness, now he makes a decision for Jesus?

- But he's *not* ready to go all the way!

- His pastor Carl Lentz told him to take baby steps, do it your way?

- Ja is still going to make his music in a way that feels good to him?

- He still wants his professional career without jeopardizing his Christian faith?

- Or does he mean he wants religion without affecting his singing career?

- Ja Rule realises he wants to get closer to God and feels it's something that he should do in life, but this could apply to many things.

So the real question is, who is ruling who?

A proper decision must come from the inner work of the Holy Spirit.

Only this will bring a complete life change. Committing your life to God is not the same as a membership to a church or a subscription to a magazine. He's asking for your Lordship! You don't give up complete control of your life because you get caught up in the music and emotion of a service. Living for God is a sacrifice you make every single day.

Most want to be aligned to Christ but few want allegiance to Christ

Listen to the words of Waldensian pastor Jean Louis Paschale, who died 9 September 1560. 'I know I must go the narrow way of the cross, and seal my testimony with my blood. I do not dread death, and still less the loss of my earthly goods; for I am certain of eternal life and a celestial inheritance, and my heart is united to my Lord and Saviour' (Thomas M'Crie, *Reformation in Italy*, 1842, p. 173).

So much for there being any gospel in our modern evangelism!

And what of the Hillsong's coveted convert Justin Bieber, who, although has made Hillsong home, is still acting up with all sorts of antics starting in 2014 with a DUI? Bieber who was at the wheel of a rented yellow Lamborghini and was arrested and charged with driving under the influence, driving with an expired licence, and resisting arrest 'without violence', yet at the same time going to Bible studies with his ex-girlfriend Selena Gomez at Judah Smith's Church in Los Angeles?[23]

In a recent Calvin Klein photo shoot for *Interview* magazine, Justin is seen wearing a black-studded S&M mask and red shiny PVC gloves. Bieber looks like some toy-boy for the Illuminati. And all this just after his week-long jaunt to Hillsong's Sydney conference in early July 15?[24] Over the week of the conference, Justin just 'happened' to roll out his Sunday best, wearing the best conference memorabilia money can buy: a Marilyn Manson Antichrist T-shirt.[25]

What is born of the spirit is spirit, and what is born of the flesh is flesh.

You must be born again. For flesh and blood cannot inherit the kingdom of God (Jn. 3:6, Jn. 3:3, 1 Cor. 15:50).

And the list goes on and on. Justin continues showing off his body on covers of magazines and strutting his stuff on stage in another Marilyn Manson creation, 'bigger than Satan', during his Purpose World Tour. Ironically, this new clothing line is called Fear of God.[26]

This religious practice by pastors just to get and keep converts, having them attend church week after week without apparent correction or guidance, is absolutely deplorable, and we wonder why things are not turning around.

These words of Hillsong's newest hellraiser—'We went up onstage, we got saved, and it just gave me a good feeling'—are some of the worst things I've heard.

'I got saved and got me a good feeling'—this is the worst kind of blindness because all he has done is make a decision for Jesus based on a feeling that was good at the time. But now what? Does he know the difference between the JW version of Jesus and Hillsong's version of Jesus, let alone the Jesus of the Bible?

Does the truth matter anymore? Does it even factor in his decision? Where is repentance, righteousness, faith? We are telling them to come as they are and receive Jesus: 'Jesus accepts you, and you can work through your faith over time.'

This is easy believism!

This view was promoted by Robert Sandeman (1718–1781). The Sandemanian doctrine was the nature of saving faith reduced to mere intellectual assent to a fact or proposition. This is illustrated rather clearly in the following quote: 'In a series of letters to James Hervey, the author of *Theron and Aspasia*, he [Sandeman] maintained that justifying faith is a simple assent to the divine testimony concerning Jesus Christ, differing in no way in its character from belief in any ordinary testimony.'[27]

We have fallen for the error of Constantine—of creating half a convert and half a pagan—all for the sake of numbers.

However, this is the bible's formula and order: 'Repentance toward God, and faith toward our Lord Jesus Christ' (Acts 20:21).

Notice repentance first. Repentance is essential to salvation. Without repentance, there is no salvation. Repentance is a lifestyle, not a one- off. The more I turn, the closer to God I get, and the more I become like Him.

'Whoever offers praise glorifies Me; And to him who orders his conduct aright I will show the salvation of God' (Ps. 50:23 NKJV).

The church has torn up the new covenant exacted in Christ's blood and rewritten the contract. It has removed the 'die to self ' clause and replaced it with 'live for self' instead.

To help a little further, consider briefly the story of the rich ruler in Luke 18:18–30:

Verse 26: And they that heard it said, who then can be saved? 27. And he [Jesus] said, the things which are impossible with men are possible with God. 28. Then Peter said, Lo, we have left all, and followed thee.

Most modern churches would stop at verse 27 – saying see it is impossible with man but with God it's possible. Which is true, but again it is only half or part of the story. Here Peter says, 'Lo, we have left all, and followed thee.' Salvation therefore requires deliberate action on our part, in the light of the truth. It's not just all one way traffic. (cf. Phil. 2:12,13)

Dr Martyn Lloyd-Jones shows the error of those who have this faith without works mentality:

There are people who say 'I have believed on the Lord Jesus Christ, therefore I am alright'.

I don't need your doctrines, your deep teaching, I have believed on Christ. I am saved. I went forward and made a decision.' And they go on living more or less as they did before. This is separation of doctrine and life.[28]

Indeed, such wide-road teaching it is reaping a whirlwind in our time.

We have whole church movements undermining the truth of God's word and riding on the coattails of God's mercy and goodness.

The grace of God is a FULL grace, not a FRACTURED grace.

It's not so that we can remain in our sin. Sin is not to be normalised, yet this seems to be modus operandi for many a church.

'**For the grace of God** that bringeth salvation hath appeared to all men; **Teaching us that, denying ungodliness and worldly lusts**, we should live soberly, righteously, and godly, in this present world; Looking for that blessed hope, and the glorious appearing of the great God and our Saviour Jesus Christ' (emphasis mine) (Titus 2:11–14).

This is another 'gospel' full of 'feel good' experiences and ones like Ja Jule are being 'churched' and not saved. They never get saved (born again.) All you end up with is well-dressed, well-mannered people, still living worldly lives under a cloak of Pharisaical religiosity, but no one is actually saved. They want the outward appearance but not the price. This false gospel works a false conversion. You welcome them in, and you dress them up and program them for participation in 'church'.

Hip Christians are nothing more that hip-o-crites!

A whole generation of believers are being deceived to this fact. They remain ignorant of the fact that God's judgement is always according to truth; God is not mocked! Where is our struggle against sin? Where is our fight of faith? If we say we confess Christ and still live happily in our sin we deceives ourselves and the truth is not in us. Such a position is inconsistent and fails the true biblical standard. (1 Jn. 1:8, 1 Jn.2:4).

We have a theology that makes crass cool, casual faith something to aspire to, and Christ is now our mentor and not Messiah.

I can only quote here the famous words of A W Tozer:

So we have the strange anomaly of orthodoxy in creed and heterodoxy in practice.

Any objection to the carryings on of our present golden- calf Christianity is met with the triumphant reply, 'But we are winning them!' And winning them to what?

To true discipleship? To cross-carrying? To self-denial? To separation from the world? To crucifixion of the flesh? To holy living? Of course the answer to all these questions is no. (*Man: The Dwelling Place of God*: Chapter

30. Religious Boredom, page 138)

This religion of the New Evangelicals boasts of converts and decision cards; they are done with making disciples. Because of this downgrade, Christianity has become nothing more than cheap forgiveness, and sentimental love. The great tragedy is, we have believed in a subversive theology, akin to the Trojan horse of Troy. And like the horse, which was welcomed inside the city walls, its belly hid the Greek warriors who emerged in the dead of night, the gates were opened, and Troy was overthrown.

We are birthing the wind!

Footnotes

Constantius I Latin: Marcus Flavius Valerius Constantius Herculius Augustus; 31 March c. 250 – 25 July 306), commonly known as Constantius Chlorus, (in greek Κωνσταντίνος Χλωρός), was Roman Emperor from 293 to 306. https:// en.wikipedia.org/wiki/Constantius Chlorus

Maximian (Latin: Marcus Aurelius Valerius Maximianus Herculius Augustus; c. 250–c. July 310) was Roman Emperor from 286 to 305. He was Caesar from 285 to 286, then Augustus from 286 to 305. https://en.wikipedia.org/wiki/Maximian

Licinius I (Latin: Gaius Valerius Licinianus Licinius Augustus; c. 263 – 325), was a Roman emperor from 308 to 324. For the majority of his reign he was the colleague and rival of Constantine I, with whom he co-authored the Edict of Milan that granted official toleration to Christians in the Roman Empire. He was finally defeated at the Battle of Chrysopolis, before being executed on the orders of Constantine I. https://en.wikipedia.org/wiki/Licinius

*The Chi Rho (/ ˈkaɪ ˈroʊ/) is one of the earliest forms of christogram, and is used by some Christians. It is formed by superimposing the first two (capital) letters chi and rho (XP) of the Greek word "ΧΡΙΣΤΟΣ" = Christ in such a way to produce the monogram. Although not technically a Christian cross, the Chi-Rho invokes the crucifixion of Jesus, as well as symbolizing his status as the Christ. https:// en.wikipedia.org/wiki/Chi Rho

Arius (Ancient Greek: Ἄρειος, AD 250 or 256–336) was an ascetic Christian presbyter of Libyan origins, and priest in Alexandria, Egypt, of the church of Baucalis. [1] His teachings about the nature of the Godhead, which emphasized the Father's divinity over the Son, [2] and his opposition to Homoousian Trinitarian Christology, made him a primary topic of the First Council of Nicea, convened by Roman Emperor Constantine in AD 325. https://en.wikipedia.org/wiki/Arius

*Ecumenical here means worldwide. teachings about the nature of the Godhead, which emphasized the Father's divinity over the Son,[2] and his opposition to Homoousian Trinitarian Christology, made him a primary topic of the First Council of Nicea, convened by Roman Emperor Constantine in AD 325. https://en.wikipedia.org/wiki/Arius

23

JESUS CHRIST SUPERSTAR

He said unto them, But whom say ye that I am? Peter answering said, The Christ of God.

—Lk. 9:20

Hillsong's mission, which is found on their main website, is 'championing the cause of the local church' while their conference positioning statement is 'The church is God's solution for the earth.

Jesus commissioned us to be builders of the church and the church to be builders of people.'[1]

Disturbingly, Masonic branding says something similar in the phrase 'making good men better'.[2]

Yes, that's right. According to Hillsong's mission statement, an institution is God's answer for the world! You know the verse: 'Go into all the world and build churches' (see Matt. 28:18–20).

No, Jesus's mission statement was 'Go into all the world and preach the gospel,' and He said, 'I will build my church'! The Lord Jesus isn't abdicating His throne anytime soon.

The cross is God's solution for the earth!

Hands up all those who *still* think the local church is God's solution for the earth. In fact, the correct answer is more straightforward. God was in Christ, reconciling the world to Himself (see 2 Cor. 5:19, Rom. 1:16, Col 2:15).

Some accuse me of writing this out of jealousy. Yes, I am jealous but for God's name and the insult that churches and ministries like Hillsong make to the gospel and for blaspheming the name of God. The church is pouring energy into making the message popular, a message that is a forgery. These churches are nothing more than a burger franchise.

The gospel is nothing but a product. God is sold as a product to benefit our lives. To make our lives easier or better. But this is not the gospel. This is a sham. It's a nice way to entertain and to 'introduce' Jesus. But again, this is not the gospel.

We have come to this weird idea that church has to be fashioned after the entertainment offered by the world and that we are competing with the world on the basis of market share.

Jesus said, 'Unless you take up your cross and follow me, you cannot be my disciples.'

I protest because there is a need to. To not to do so is to be like Peter, warming himself by the fire and enjoying my comfortable life and denying my Lord. The signs of the times are all around; apostasy and a great falling away is happening in our day.

They are of the world. Therefore, speak they of the world, and the world hears them (1 Jn. 4:5).

The cross of Jesus Christ is our only way out, the only way of salvation, freeing us from the destruction, woes, and suffering that comes from sin.

That's why Christianity is unique. It is God's work in Christ. Not man's effort or good works are good enough to bring us to God. Over 2,000 years ago, the Lord Jesus took our punishment so that we may not have to suffer the punishment of God. Christ's intention in dying was to save out of the world a people for Himself.

We don't need entertainment, we need the Truth.

Nevertheless, it seems the House of Houston, and its dazzling dynasty are set on building global success regardless. *Destined to Reign* in an earthly realm of their own making! They have deceived themselves into believing they have a divine mandate to accumulate power, wealth, and influence!

The *true* cause of this now $100 million juggernaut is to amass wealth and property, which is nothing more than psychology and satanic philosophy dressed up in 'Christian' phraseology.[3]

Read the lyrics by hard rock band Van Halen who produced songs like 'Runnin' with the Devil'. Compare Hillsong's definition of success with Van Halen's song 'Best of Both Worlds':

> You don't have to die and go to heaven . . . Or hang around to be born again
>
> Just tune in to what this place has got to offer . . . We may never be here again.
>
> I want the best of both worlds . . . I know what it's worth
>
> Give me the best of both worlds . . . I want heaven right

here on earth.[4]

The blight of this type of thinking is heaven is no longer our aspiration—the church has forgotten the blessed hope. Many have fallen to Satan's temptation of desiring the kingdoms of this world (Matt. 4:8,9). We no longer live under the shadow of the cross, but under the bright lights of the world.

Anton LaVey, the high priest of the satanic church, explains the essence of satanism:

Knowing this, realizing *what human potential is* . . . here is one of the essential points of satanism; (to) attain his own godhead in accordance with his own potential. Therefore, each man, each woman, is a god or goddess.[5] (emphasis added)

It seems satanist Anthony LaVey would enjoy the sermon at Hillsong on any given Sunday.

Just to make it plain, go to their main website hillsong.com, and what you will read is this:

Our singular, all-consuming passion is to build God's Church and Kingdom on the earth, and see everyday people released into their purpose and calling. We believe in people—*we believe in their potential* and we believe in their amazing capacity to influence the world with good.' (emphasis added) (Brian and Bobbie)[6]

With good? Good is not the gospel. You see, human potential, making good men better. It appears we are denying Christ on purpose.

The Church of Scientology's ethos is almost word for word.

"Man is a spiritual being endowed with abilities well beyond those which he normally envisions [potential]. He is not only able to solve his problems, accomplish his goals, and gain lasting happiness…."

It goes onto to say; Scientology further holds man to be basically good, and that his spiritual salvation depends upon himself. [7]Interestingly there is good evidence that the founder of Scientology,L. Ron Hubbard said 'The way to make a million dollars is to start a religion.'[8]

In an interview with CBN news reporter Kristi Watts, Joel Osteen said;

'When I grew up, the devil was a reason why I had a headache or the devil was the reason I got mad today. We always blamed the devil. I think today when I say the enemy, I like to make it broader. Sometimes the Enemy can be our own thoughts.'

For Joel Osteen, the enemy Satan is symbolic—exactly what Anton La Vey taught and what the Church of Satan teaches. If the enemy is just symbolic, the implication is that there is no need to be concerned about sin or Satan.

The shocking truth is Hillsong and the other counterfeits like Warren, Prince, and Osteen are promoting health, wealth, prosperity and human potential—the antithesis to true biblical Christianity! The true church is composed of those who have signed up for slavery and death (see Phil. 2:5–10; 2 Cor. 5:14,15; Matt 6:24; 2 Cor. 6:3–10).

Has the serpent subtly crept in and changed the emphasis at Hillsong and elsewhere without anyone knowing? And all these guys are pals with the New Age TV icon Oprah Winfrey.

The pages of the scripture yell out that we cannot have divided allegiance. For me, some of the most terrifying verses in all of scripture are the following verses in the gospel of Matthew:

Not everyone that saith unto me, Lord, Lord, shall enter into the kingdom of heaven; but he that doeth the will of my Father which is in heaven. Many will say to me in that day, Lord, Lord, . . . and then will I profess unto them, I never knew you: depart from me, ye that work iniquity. (Matt. 7:21–23 KJV)

He says, 'Depart from Me. I never knew you', even though they were doing all kinds of works on the Lord's behalf. They are rejected because they 'work iniquity.' Those who enter do the will of the Father who is in heaven.

We call them wonderful works, but He rejects them. All our righteous acts are a stench to God if they are not linked to grace and submission to his will and are instead a sign of rebellion because they are done for selfish ends and selfish gain. A man may be a preacher with an amazing ministry, yet it's done for a name and a pay cheque.

Often, our programmes and social action are what we think are the right things to do rather than knowing that's what we are supposed to do. Most ministry today is initiated out of Martha ministry, 'running to and fro', rather than a Mary-focused ministry. It should come from an overflow of what God has placed on our hearts rather than simply seeing duplicating others and meeting needs. Selfish works become the religion of Cain!

'A man's most glorious actions **will** at last be found to be but glorious sins, if he hath made himself, and not the glory of God, the end of those actions.' —**Thomas** Brooks

Service is all about motives. I can serve God but still hold on to a heart full of pride and adultery. I may be serving God, but I'm really there to make a name for myself. I'm up the front so that everyone will think I'm wonderful. I'll serve God so I can accomplish my own goals and ambitions—to achieve success, to become a Christian rock star—but the

Lord is looking for servants. The Lord said, 'I never knew you' because He never owned you. 'You never wanted my Lordship.'

Charles Spurgeon speaks to us: 'If your heart is set upon iniquity, where your heart is, there your treasure is—and if sin is your treasure, then in the end you are not an heir of Heaven! That which governs your heart is your Lord and your God—what your heart loves, by that you shall be judged'.[9]

The false church is full of rock stars. The true church is full of unprofitable servants.

He is not just talking about Roman Catholics. He is talking to modern-day evangelicals, members, volunteers, leaders and teachers, missionaries and men who manufacture religious enterprise; but the Lord Jesus is nowhere to be seen.

Martyn Lloyd-Jones expressed his concern of this very thing, of a church full of activity. 'The fact that the church is very active does not of necessity prove that what she does is right; it may be all wrong. A church may be living on her own energy, doing things on her own initiative, and deliberately ignoring the head. And refusing to be subservient to Him.' (Christian Unity, Ephesians 4:15,16 Chap. 22, Banner of Truth, p. 274)

Their wonderful works are self-initiated, self-propelled, self-reliant, self-gratifying, self-congratulatory, and self-fulfilling. These modern endeavours of cash, conferences, and costumes will burn up when the books are opened. Their justification before Him—'Did we not do wonderful works?'—is falling back to righteousness by works and not righteousness by faith. The true servant will always testify that what they did was only what was required of them in simple obedience. What he did is only what he should have done in accordance with the Lord's will.

Yet, often the Lord's will is completely ignored. Our religion has become a form of deism. Our theology incorporates a simplistic creed: be nice to others, call on God when you need him, feel good about yourself, and be good enough for heaven in the next life.[10] Christianity is nothing more than the rubbing of the 'Jesus genie' lamp.

For many of these churches, the Lord Jesus is like a grey old geriatric CEO who has no say or control and is never invited to even *one* board meeting!

He is a mere figurehead. He is not expected to object. The corporation is running along quite nicely without him. The Lord has become an absenteeGod, who ignores and winks at any misdemeanor. Our unspoken creed is God is at a safe distance, looking the other way. This prevailing heresy that God is absent leaves us with this mindless activity that He is pleased with whatever we are trying to do.

It reminds of the latest Alvin and the Chipmunks movie, *The Road Chip*. In the opening scene, the crowd is having a great time in the front yard, celebrating Dave's birthday; and yet, Dave isn't even there, still driving along the street, making his way home, oblivious to a party in his honour. These are our churches today—pool parties and dance clubs all in the name of Christ!

Charles Finney describes how we are still rebels without yielding to God's will. A Christian can still be living a life of self-interest. We must cease putting our own interests first. 'The man who does not do this is still a rebel against God.'[11]

The question is, have we made him Lord, or have we just added him to our existing lives?

We cannot serve God and money! God and ourselves! Yet we have books and manuals on like 'Teach your church to give' and 'You need more money'.

Most people believe these mega churches are just another Christian 'flavour'. Their goal is to make God famous. But this is an oxymoron! Umm, who's been around the longest? The idea is ridiculous. The only thing they are promoting is themselves, their music, and their brand. The church is to preach the gospel, not fill concert venues.

This popular 'faith' movement budded from Robert Schuller's self-esteem and Freemason Norman Vincent Peale's possibility thinking; this insidious seduction slithered into the church over a jubilee ago.

Meanwhile, Bobbie Houston has already dusted off the welcome mat for Beth 'Mystic' Moore. Beth Moore was one of the guest speakers for the girls-glam-it-up Hillsong Colour Conference for 2014, with a repeat performance in London in 2015.[12]

Moore, from Southern Baptist roots, is happily promoting this contemplative/centering prayer (CCP), which is a form of meditation, an altered state of consciousness.

In *Be Still*, a DVD released in 2006 by 20th Century Fox, Moore uses contemplative speak to praise 'a true lover of God' who 'spoke about practising God's presence'. She is speaking of a Roman Catholic Carmelite mystic Nicholas Herman (1614–1691), a.k.a. Brother Lawrence.[13]

Lectio divina (Latin for *divine reading*) is a traditional Roman Catholic practice of scriptural reading, meditation, and prayer intended to promote communion with God. It does not treat scripture as texts to be studied but as the Living Word.[14]

Traditionally, lectio divina has four steps: read, meditate, pray, and contemplate. First, a passage of scripture is read. Then its meaning is reflected upon. Although lectio divina involves reading, it is about listening to the inner message of the scripture supposedly delivered through the Holy Spirit. These dark roots go back to Origen in the third century, after whom Saint Ambrose taught them to Augustine. Origen believed that the Word (i.e. Logos) was incarnate in scripture and could therefore touch and teach readers and hearers. Origen taught that the reading of scripture could help move beyond elementary thoughts and discover the higher wisdom 'hidden' in the Word of God.

In his 6 November 2005 Angelus address, Pope Benedict XVI emphasised the role of the Holy Spirit in lectio divina.

John Piper and Beth Moore had a contemplative time at Passion 2012.[15] They read Paul's letter to the Ephesians—all about our wonderful Saviour, His power, His dominion, His salvation, His work, His blood— yet they stood there in deathly silence for almost two minutes. This is eerie. Contemplative monasticism subtly brought in by evangelicals if you please.

The question is why are the Roman Catholic mystic practices developed in monasteries by men who rejected the gospel of salvation by grace alone, through faith alone by Christ's work alone being allowed and even promoted in supposed Protestant evangelical churches?

Not to be left out, Rick Warren invited Pete Scazzero to teach Roman Catholic monastic mysticism at the Radicalis Conference at Saddleback Church in February 2010. Scazzero with his wife, Geri, are co-founders of Emotionally Healthy Spirituality, a ministry that integrates emotional health and contemplative spirituality to pastors, leaders, and local spirituality.[16]

If Warren continues with this magical mystical tour, he may find himself 'back in Rome in 40 days'.

Rob Bell and Shane Hipps of Mars Hill Bible Church promote the use of lectio divina.

Ignatius Loyola believed his church held the truth:

That we may be altogether of the same mind and in conformity with the Church herself, if she shall have defined anything to be black which appears to our eyes to be white, we ought in like manner to pronounce it to be black. For we must undoubtingly believe, that the Spirit of our Lord Jesus Christ, and the Spirit of the Orthodox Church His Spouse, by which Spirit we are governed and directed to Salvation, is the same.[17]

It seems the Jesuit's Loyola and Hillsong's Houston have more in common than they realise!

24
CHURCH OF THE POISONED MIND

They have sharpened their tongues like a serpent; adders'
poison is under their lips.

—Ps. 140:3

Regardless of the seemingly impressive numbers these churches are
drawing, we have given in to the culture of celebrity.

We have fallen into the error of Lucifer himself who became proud of his
place and position within God's hierarchy. How many men of God have
allowed power and position in their ministry to corrupt God's purposes?

And this is the whole reason we have the decay and this crowds-by-any-
means mania in the first place. This world is all about money, fame, and
fortune and all its vices in between. How then can the church take that
which is tainted by the world and use it for the kingdom of God, except
we have fallen backwards?

Spurgeon, burdened in his day, wrote of this compromise: 'The new plan
is to assimilate the church to the world, and so include a larger area
within its bounds. By semi-dramatic performances they make the house
of prayer to approximate to the theatre; they turn their services into

161

musical displays. . . . In fact, they exchange the temple for the theatre, and turn the ministers of God into actors, whose business it is to amuse men'

(C H Spurgeon, 'No compromise' sermon, 7 Oct 1888, Metropolitan Tabernacle).

Yet again, with all the brash sacrilege it could muster, Hillsong put on an end-of-year musical production around 2011 *Someone Has Stolen the Star* based on the theme of Christmas![1]

They included characters, such as Mr Incredible, Gingerbread Man, Tooth Fairy, Batman, and Superman along with Santa Claus to present to us that Jesus was God's present from God to us. Have I missed something?

In London, Hillsong outdid themselves by filling Wembley Stadium for Hillsong's 2015 mega Christmas carols pageant with 1920s flapper girls and leggy dancers for the traditional carol 'Silent Night', which ended up being a sordid night.[2]

When are we going to wake up, making the gospel a vehicle of enterprise? Do we no longer read our Bibles? Will Jesus not come again, take up the cords in His hands, and throw over our tables of merchandise and marketing? It's only a matter of time (2 Pet. 2:1–3).

Spurgeon again speaks to our generation when he wrote in his magazine

The Sword and the Trowel, December 1887 edition, saying:

The Lord our God is holy, and he cannot compromise his own glorious name by working with persons whose grovelling tastes lead them to go to Egypt—we had almost said to Sodom—for their recreations. Is this walking with God? . . . It is a heart-sorrow to have to mention such things, but the work of the Lord must be done faithfully, and this evil must be laid bare. There can be no doubt that all sorts of entertainments, as nearly as possible approximating to stage-plays, have been carried on in connection with places of worship, and are, at this present time, in high favour. Can these things promote holiness, or help in communion with God? Can men come away from such things and plead with God for the salvation of sinners and the sanctification of believers? We loathe to touch the unhallowed subject; it seems so far removed from the walk of faith, and the way of heavenly fellowship. Brethren in Christ, in every church let us purge out the things which weaken and pollute.

25
NIGHTS ON THE BROADWAY

Enter ye in at the strait gate: for wide is the gate, and broad is the way, that leads to destruction, and many there be which go in thereat.

—Matt. 7:13

Brian and Bobbie Houston at one time had this vision. 'I see a Church whose heartfelt praise and worship touches heaven and changes earth. With worship that exalts Jesus Christ through powerful songs of faith and hope. I see a Church whose altars are constantly filled with repentant sinners responding to His call to salvation.

Yes, the Church that I see is so dependent on the Holy Spirit that nothing will stop it, nor stand against it. A Church, whose people are unified, praying, and full of Spirit-filled believers.'[1]

For Pastor Dixon, it's all about the 'fantastic', the numbers and momentum. You know, go into all the world and build momentum!

But even with all this vision casting and seeming momentum, can we really say that we have produced anything close to repentant sinners, dependent on the Holy Spirit, praying, Spirit-filled believers as mentioned by Brian and Bobbie Houston? Instead, I believe we have a brood of candlelight Christians, living half in the world and half in Christ. This rank version of common faith is defecting from the excellency of Jacob. These ones who are at ease in Zion are dancing with the devil in the name of Christ, divided in the twilight of commitment and conviction and the delights of nightclubs and disco halls.

We have Christians facing both ways, halted by two opinions, enjoying Christ and enjoying the world.

We've become enemies of God, but that no longer seems to matter, the warning falling on deaf ears. We cry God will not reject his people? (See 1 Sam. 12:14–25).

When I was still part of Hillsong, I would hear the leaders talk about an upcoming encounter weekend. This was where over 140 young people would get together to meet God. You know, to set aside the weekend to seek God and be filled with His Holy Spirit! But not as you would anticipate. A YouTube clip of the encounter weekend (October 2010)[2] if you view it, leaves you dismayed and heartbroken. Once more, the room is pitch black, the coloured lights flash all around, more like a searchlight, blinding. The green strobe laser lights, the crowded room, the youth pumping! The same noise, beat, and licentious sound. **We have made entertainment the new god!**

Like Xbox, Wii, and every other form of self-gratification, we have replaced the true God with a god we are comfortable with. We do not know what has become of this Moses, the man that brought us up out of the land of Egypt, so we have made for ourselves gods we can worship after the gods of Egypt (see Ex. 32:1).

Like the children of Israel, in the wilderness of sin, we have Christianised our idolatry and sanctified our blasphemy. We do not know what has become of this Moses (type of Jesus). We cannot see Him or touch Him, so the cry is make for us gods we can worship, the gods we know, that we are familiar with. So we bow to the gods of this world. We rock with the best of them and get away with as much as is socially acceptable. If it's not mentioned in the Bible, then we should be fine. Everything else goes, and the values that Christ scorned are being used to attract people to the gospel today.

If it's not mentioned in the Bible, then we should be fine.

It's one thing for the world to go headlong into hell, but for the church to follow suit is complete madness. We are close to losing our evangelical birthright!

The raucous thing we call Christianity today stems from the basic trouble—a false and unworthy concept of God! Perverse, wretched notions of God inoculate us to holiness and to the seriousness of the gospel and God's wrath against sin. False concepts of God plague our bookstores and seminaries. A view of God so shabby, that men like Rob Bell are allowed to disseminate a hill of beans without question. We have surrendered a high opinion of God and exchanged it for a mentor god. We have thought that God is altogether like us (Ps. 50:21).

We think of him as no better than a god like Krishna, like some glorified deity. Shame on us!

The disciples, although they knew Christ, knew him no longer in the flesh (see 2 Cor. 5:16, Rev. 1:12–18). After Christ was glorified in His body, he was completely changed. An image of the Lord Jesus in human form is no use to anyone. All this does is to reduce the Godhead to man's concepts, and as a result, we worship the creature instead of the creator.

God calls Israel upright (Jeshurun), but He decries her waywardness.

[15]But Jeshurun waxed fat, and kicked: thou art waxen fat, thou art grown thick, thou art covered with fatness; then he forsook God which made him, and lightly esteemed the Rock of his salvation. [16]They provoked him to jealousy with strange gods, with abominations provoked they him to anger. [17]They sacrificed unto devils, not to God; to gods whom they knew not, to new gods that came newly up, whom your fathers feared not. [18]Of the Rock that begat thee thou art unmindful, and hast forgotten God that formed thee. [19]And when the LORD saw it, he abhorred them, because of the provoking of his sons, and of his daughters. [20] **And he said, I will hide my face from them, I will see what their end shall be: for they are a very froward [perverse] generation, children in whom is no faith.** [21]They have moved me to jealousy with that which is not God; they have provoked me to anger with their vanities: and I will move them to jealousy with those which are not a people; I will provoke them to anger with a foolish nation. [22]For a fire is kindled in mine anger, and shall burn unto the lowest hell, and shall consume the earth with her increase, and set on fire the foundations of the mountains. [28]**For they are a nation void of counsel, neither is there any understanding in them.** [29]O that they were wise, that they understood this, that they would consider their latter end! (Deut. 32:15–22,28,29) (emphasis added).

Worship now is of the new gods, the gods that have come up recently, the modern gods of celebrity, of rock and slick programming, the ones that our fathers neither feared nor gave allegiance to.

Worship in these churches, like Hillsong, has become nothing more than a sanctified nightclub without the booze and ecstasy. In fact, it can no longer be called worship but a strange fire in the nostrils of an angry God.

The sanctuary has become so denigrated that the gods of Moloch and Dagon feel at home. The church has become a synagogue of Satan. God created us to be worshippers of Him, but we have corrupted the music and made the worship into entertainment, about us, and for us. Hillsong, in particular, has churned out song after song, love ditties, lyrics nothing more than what you would hear on secular radio, the product of a Christless Christianity.

The standard has reached a new low that Van Halen and Keith Urban could be called Christian. You are hard-pressed now to find Jesus mentioned in any of the new 'worship' songs. It's *you*. We have a lot of biblical language but not necessarily anything biblical.

Over the last decade or so, this style of lyric has become part of the ever-expanding 'Jesus is my girlfriend/boyfriend' genre. This genre is defined as song or songs that mean to appeal to an audience outside of typical listeners of CCM by replacing Jesus with *you* in hopes of making the Christian content of the song less obvious to non-Christian listeners. This has not pervaded the airwaves but has been the norm for Sunday worship.

Take out the line 'I've got a Saviour and He's living in me', and 'What the World Will Never Take' is one of those songs: You would never really know it's about Jesus, or perhaps this one will be more meaningful?

'Love Song,' written by Mia Fieldes from the album *Faithful* (2004) speaks of being closer to Christ than a kiss.

One of the most obvious signs that there is no worship in the church is that true worship requires the humbling and prostrating of ourselves before a holy God, who dwells in unapproachable light. The Apostle Paul was blinded on the road to Damascus. The Apostle John saw the Lord Jesus and fell at his feet as if dead; this is the one who had previously laid his head on his breast. Can you see why we are so undone?

Hellsong

Isaiah's God is not our God!

Worship today is nothing more than Pentecostal 'X Factor'. The Pentecostals and evangelicals of this current dark hour have become the Church of Jesus Christ of Latter-Day Judas Iscariots, worrying only about the poor and the money bags. True worship has been relegated to a nonessential for the modern Christian. We know nothing of worship except the putting on of a religious rock concert. We now have the worship team run by session musicians and an assorted chorale of 'Dixie Chicks'.[3]

26
ALL ALONG THE WATCHTOWER

And every one that heareth these sayings of mine, and doeth them not, shall be likened unto a foolish man, which built his house upon the sand.

—Matt. 7:26

Within the world of rock 'n' roll, and specifically in heavy metal bands, musicians are idolised. These bands promote immorality, Satanism, suicide, sadomasochism and masochistic behaviour, drug abuse, obscene language, and even direct blasphemy of God and His Holy name.

In live performance, loudness—an 'onslaught of sound,' in sociologist Deena Weinstein's description—is considered vital. In his book *Metalheads*, psychologist Jeffrey Arnett refers to heavy metal concerts as 'the sensory equivalent of war'. The essence of metal drumming is creating a loud constant beat for the band using the 'trifecta of speed, power, and precision'.

Following the lead set by Jimi Hendrix, Cream, and The Who, early heavy metal acts such as Blue Cheer set new benchmarks for volume. As Blue Cheer's Dick Peterson put it, 'All we knew was we wanted more power.' A 1977 review of a Motörhead concert noted how 'excessive volume in particular figured into the band's impact'. Weinstein argues that the loudness is designed to 'sweep the listener into the sound" and to provide a 'shot of youthful vitality'.[1]

Nuclear annihilation and death are predominant themes in heavy metal groups. The more extreme forms of death metal and grind core trend to have aggressive and gory lyrics. Romantic tragedy is also a standard theme of gothic and doom metal, as well as of nu metal, where teenage angst is another central topic.

Led Zeppelin lyrics often reference *Lord of the Rings*, as well as other mythology and folklore. Deriving from the genre's roots in blues music, sex is another important topic.[2]

In the 1980s, Christian metal-glam rockers Stryper pranced around wearing mascara, lip gloss, eyeshadow, earrings, spandex, and women's hairstyles, deliberately mocking 1 Corinthians 6:9–10: 'No effeminate . . . shall inherit the kingdom of God.' Stryper's popularity and perversion of Christian music garnished a CCM-record-breaking two platinum and four gold records!

In spite of Maranatha's more 'conservative' image, in 1984 Calvary Chapel allowed the metal band Stryper to do a concert at one of their local churches in Downey, California, *twice* in six months. And I thought what I have been outlining in this chapter so far was bad enough, but to uncover this kind of garbage is beyond comprehension. Watch the YouTube clip for yourself. At the end of the concert, a guy who looked like he was a stand-in for one of the band members of Kiss, with a big mop of jet-black hair, said, 'God's got heavy metal music for his glory', amen, trying to talk over the screams, and hollers of young wired teenage girls.'[3]

That same year Stryper played as the opening act for thrash metal band Anthrax and heavy metal band Raven in Los Angeles.[4] These bands sound like you're standing at the very entrance to the gates of hell.

Yet Robert Sweet of Styrper makes a startling admission about Christian rock in *RIP* magazine: 'As a matter of fact, the band was one thing that was making us turn and walk the opposite direction from Christianity. . . . If you're doing something you like doing, and God says not to do it, then you're not going to pay attention' (*RIP*, April 1987 p. 49).

Tim Gaines of Stryper revealed to *HM* magazine, 'From the end of 1988 'til February of this year [1997], I was drunk every day' (*HM Magazine*, Mar/Apr 1997 #64, p. 47).

Steve Gaines says, 'We never wanted to get caught up in the whole Christian music scene in the first place' (*Inside Music*, Oct/Nov 1990 p. 16). What?

'We're not religious fanatics who are trying to convert everybody we meet. . . . We honestly believe that Jesus Christ is the Savior, but we're about the most unreligious Christian band you could imagine' (Robert Sweet, *Hit Parader*, Nov 1986, p. 21).[5]

And they still are.

In an article on music website www.highermusic.com, Stryper's 2011 CD outlines how they have reproduced covers that run the gamut from 1970s era of classic rock (Led Zeppelin's 'Immigrant Song', Deep Purple's 'Highway Star', Kiss's 'Shout It Out Loud' etc.) to 1980s era of heavy metal (Black Sabbath's 'Heaven and Hell, Scorpions' 'Blackout', Iron Maiden's 'The Trooper' etc.).

That's right. You read it correctly. A 'Christian band' is releasing an album of covers of Christ hating heavy metal bands. These men are deceivers! They have never turned away but instead have turned back to their vomit.

Stryper are nothing more than sanitised Satanists.

'How that they told you there should be mockers in the last time, who should walk after their own ungodly lusts. These are they who separate themselves, sensual, having not the Spirit' (Jude 1:18–19).

Just like other metals bands, Stryper produced an album called *The Yellow and Black Attack*, showing ballistic missiles on the cover, hurtling towards earth, glorifying destruction, and nuclear annihilation. Incidentally, without pushing the point too much, many of their covers and merchandise use the pyramid as a backdrop to their band name to form a logo. Occult magician Aleister Crowley wrote a book called *777 and Other Qabalistic Writings* that is significant to the Illuminati. Stryper just happens to have a 7 in each corner of their pyramid, which is in simple terms a reference to man becoming aware of godhood.[6] 777 is highly esteemed in witchcraft and satanism! The satanic group Danzig has a song titled '777'. The *Treasury of Witchcraft* says of the number seven: "*This number, in occult rites, possessed mystic implications . . . powerful: triple repetition is characteristic of magic ritual*" (*Treasury of Witchcraft*, p.23).

We must agree with the Word of God that by their fruit you will know them. What fruit is the tree of heavy metal producing? From the frank admissions above, these men were not able to make any solid commitment to Christ. We now begin to see that music is more than a few tunes and some lyrics. Music moves men's souls for good or for bad.

So we have this other branch of the contemporary wild stock: Planetshakers. They are a Christian youth movement that began as an annual conference and grew into an international ministry and large church in Melbourne, Australia. The first conference held in 1997 had 300 delegates, growing to reach 20,000 nationwide by 2004.

The conference was born out of Paradise Community Church South Adelaide, Australia, by Pastor Russell Evans. Planetshakers expanded and in 2004 moved to Melbourne to begin a church ministry.

Their stated mission is to 'empower a generation to win a generation'.[7] They may have produced some songs of intensity and dedication over their short history. They may have even begun in sincerity and zeal for God (regardless of the leadership's motives),but in the last few years, they have quickly pushed through all plausible barriers of legitimate Christian worship and have the rest of the church careering down a cliff of musical genres: hard rock, heavy rock, metal, thrashing guitars, and club mix. They have become a milder, softer version of Stryper, without the makeup.

This group of young people have produced their own personal Jesus.

The methodology of the modern church has raised up a new breed of demigods: young people still caught up in the idolatries of the media and the music world, who have come from obscurity into stardom, on the back of today's Christian worship. Gone are the days of not putting novices in places of leadership and responsibility. A young convert no longer wants to follow Christ—'The cross before me the world behind me'—but instead covets the place of the Christian rock star.

But the real crime here is the PROFANING OF THE HOLY!

Planetshakers, has produced songs like 'Jump Around', 'Get Up', 'Dance Now', and 'Boom'. They have all the hallmarks of groups such as We Are Kings, Friday Night Boys, and the Downtown Fiction—all pop punk, alternative rock, and power pop bands. Their performances are now full-fledged concerts with LED panels, light show, smoke, and guitars, amps, keyboard, and drums. These stage sets cost thousands of dollars.[8]

I can only watch these clips for a few seconds. It feels like someone has punched me. I want to be like an old prophet throwing dust in the air, renting my clothes, and yelling STOP! I am grieved because of the destruction of the daughter of my people! (Lam. 3:48). Yes, it may be great entertainment, but please don't call it worship.

You can call Creflo Dollar a Christian, have car clubs, and coffee carts; but to worship God in this way is an outright desecration against all that is holy!

Planetshakers' Pastor Rob Bradbury says, 'It's important that we connect with youth culture.'[9]

[6]But whoso shall offend one of these little ones which believe in me, it would be better for him that a millstone were hanged about his neck, and that he were drowned in the depth of the sea. [7]Woe unto the world because of offences! For it must needs be that offences come; but woe to that man by whom the offence comes! (Matt. 18:6,7)

A recent blog said, 'ROCK ON!! I love this song! I am a guitarist!, and that's the reason I love the Planetshakers. Most of your songs are rock type, and I love rock music!' So much for reaching this generation!

Before we move away from Planetshakers, it seems they have succumbed to concerts with light displays with plenty of pyramids, seen in songs like 'Let's Go' and 'Momentum'.[10] Yet can I say that when the band decided to do a song that glorifies God like 'All Hail' then what a difference, what a contrast. This book is not all about denouncing all that is wrong, but trying to bring correction where it is needed. Where the Lord Jesus central then all is well, if not then we go astray.

In a 2006 Steve Rowe of Mortification was interviewed with *HM Magazine*. Mortification was one of the first and mostsuccessful Christian extreme metal bands in the world and one of the best-known figures in the scene, which implies that evangelism is of secondary importance.

Moberg (2006) suspects that Christian metal music may suggest dissatisfaction with traditional forms of worship among today's young Christians: 'They may not feel comfortable with just going to church and singing hymns, they need an alternative means to express the same faith.'

Apart from evangelism, Christian metal may also provide a means 'to get away from the image of Christianity as something rigid and boring'.[11]

Mmm . . . Christians, dissatisfied with traditional forms of worship, and needing an alternative means to express the same faith. They just need to get away from the image of Christianity as rigid and boring. Christianity has an image problem? These people haven't even dipped their toe in the water. They are in the chains and fetters of Babylon!

God has given us over to believing a lie. We are under God's judgement!

Music is the driver. When we look to the moulding and shaping of our society, music takes centre stage. Lady Gaga's iTunes sermon was 'I was born this way', meaning I can't help being delinquent, it's who I am, and a promiscuous lifestyle is part of my DNA.

'Music doesn't lie. If there is something to be changed in this world, then it can only happen through music' —Jimi Hendrix.

The church should have no appearance of evil, we should reprove, not approve of darkness! We are to be the light to the world, not replicate their destructive behaviour!

Hellsong

We have become rebellious people, reprobate silver, undisciplined children (see Heb. 12:6–8)

To whom shall I speak, and give warning, that they may hear? **Behold, their ear is uncircumcised, and they cannot hearken: behold, the word of the LORD is unto them a reproach; they have no delight in it. ...** [17] Also I set watchmen over you, saying, Hearken to the sound of the trumpet. **But they said, we will not hearken. ....** [28] They are all grievous revolters, walking with slanders: they are brass and iron; they are all corrupters. [29] The bellows are burned, the lead is consumed of the fire; the founder melts in vain: for the wicked are not plucked away. [30] Reprobate silver shall men call them, because the LORD hath rejected them... (Jer. 6:10,17,28–30). (emphasis added)

'Hear, O heavens, and give ear, O earth: for the LORD hath spoken, I have nourished and brought up children, and [yet] they have rebelled against me.' (Isa. 1:2 KJV)

Indeed, we are on shaky ground!

27
SATAN'S SAINTS ROCK ROCKETOWN

And no marvel; for Satan himself is transformed into an angel of light.

—2 Cor. 11:14

It opened in downtown Nashville as a nightclub for teens, but club Rocketown caved into the spirit of the world and the spirit of Antichrist and hosted a show with Satanic mainstream bands on the bill.

Rocketown was founded in 1994 by Michael W. Smith in Franklin, Tennessee, and, in 2002, found a new home in downtown Nashville. The venue is part nightclub, part coffeehouse, and part activities centre, complete with an indoor skate park. Christian bands play music, teens can dance under the disco ball, and there are even weekly Bible studies in the coffeehouse, rounding out the club's mission: to share 'Christ's love with youth through creative programs and mentoring relationships that are culturally relevant and eternally significant'.[1]

It is sad to say, but Michael W. Smith is leading churches into ecumenical apostasy—that is, into the coming world religion.

You'll NEVER hear Michael Smith, Amy Grant, Mercy Me, and others take a stand for Jesus Christ as being THE ONLY WAY TO HEAVEN!

Jesus said that He is ashamed of those believers who are ashamed of Him in this adulterous and sinful generation.

'Whosoever therefore shall be ashamed of me and of my words in this adulterous and sinful generation; of him also shall the Son of man be ashamed, when he cometh in the glory of his Father with the holy angels' (Mk. 8:38).

He also said, 'For whosoever will save his life shall lose it; but whosoever shall lose his life for my sake and the gospel's, the same shall save it. For what shall it profit a man, if he shall gain the whole world, and lose his own soul?' (Mark 8:35–36).

Losing one's life in service to Christ and the preaching of the gospel is God's perfect will is for every believer's life.

Therefore Michael W Smith cannot be a Christian in the true biblical sense.

All of the following information is from Dr Terry Watkins.

Here's what a secular reporter in the *Birmingham News* wrote after watching a Michael W. Smith concert some years ago: 'If you weren't familiar with Michael W. Smith's standing in the world of contemporary Christian music, you might attend one of his concerts and come out none the wiser' (*Birmingham News*, 12 Feb. 1993 p. 5c).

Amazing! After Michael W Smith's concert, there was not even enough of God for the lost world to even know this so-called Christian star was a Christian! What a sad testimony! How are you going to reach the young people with the gospel of Jesus Christ when they cannot even tell you are a Christian?

According to Michael, 'you're always going to have those very very conservative people. They say you can't do this; you can't do that, . . .you can't drink; you can't smoke; . . . It's a pretty bizarre way of thinking' (*Birmingham News*, 12 Feb 1993, p.1B).

God help us!

Several years ago, Michael W. Smith attempted the Amy Grant–inspired 'secular rock crossover'. It was a total failure. Note, it wasn't Smith coming over to Christian music from being a secular artist. So Smith went back to singing to the gullible Christians! The CCM hot seller went back to rockin' with praise and worship albums. Of course, Michael W Smith has a wor$hip album. Did I hear ka-ching?

Michael W. Smith's Rocketown website is full of references to ministry and Christ. [2]

Smith's Rocketown has been a venue for Satanic and dark metal bands with immoral, obscenity-laced, violent, and Antichrist lyrics. These include bands like Thaddeus, Mindless Self-Indulgence, Nearing Daybreak, Adelaide, Triceratops, From the Grave, Love Begotten, Goatblaster, Bloodwake, Kill, Whitney Dead, Whitechapel, Promised Treat, Lokyata, Heavy Heavy, Mr. Satisfaction, Spockadelic, Get Your Guns, Blinded Night Tragedy, Thought so Murderous, and Set the Sky to Flames.[3]

The lyrics sung by many of these and other Rocketown bands are too filthy to quote ('Why Does Michael W. Smith's Rocketown Promote Satanic Bands?' 26 Jul 2007).[4]

The poster at the facility for Promised Treat featured a woman with a chain plunged into her head, a meat hook coming out of the front of her face and a slashed and bloody throat.

Hellsong

Goatblaster's official logo is a goat of Mendes, the infamous goat's head inside of a Satanic pentagram, and their lyrics are both Satanic and pornographic ('Michael W. Smith: Wolves in Sheep's Clothing').[5]

Rocketown hosted a night of hard-core Satanic metal bands on 27 October 2009 (Halloween) with a line-up that included the Black Dahlia Murder, Toxic Holocaust, Skeletonwitch, and Trap Them.

One of the bands, Toxic Holocaust, says in their bio that they have a 'deadly fixation on the evil in man and a post-apocalyptic world' and their songs are 'unforgettable anthems that could be the soundtrack to civil unrest in a post-apocalyptic world gone mad'. That might explain their song 'Nuke the Cross'.

Did you pick up on what they said: 'a post-apocalyptic world' or a world in the *aftermath* of destruction and devastation!

And then you have the lyrics to the song 'Black Valor' from the group the Black Dahlia Murder: 'Join us, black valor's on our side. We'll crust their fabled Christ'.[6]

It gets worse. The song makes reference to the pentagram circle, and each man is a god unto himself. They go onto talk of giving allegiance to the almighty one, the one with horns. Their standard is the number is six hundred sixty six. And as part of their holy war, Satan's plan was to guide the spear that pierced the martyr's ribs.

In case you didn't get that last bit about the martyr's ribs, this is the Lord Jesus! This is overt sacrilege and the worst kind of blasphemy!

This is a complete contradiction in mission from the stated purpose by Rocketown.

Interestingly, some of the bands were booked for 27 October 2009, just three days before Halloween. To have these young kids come to hear about Christ and then to give them this putrid line- up of bands who show a complete hatred and disdain for the Lord Jesus Christ is beyond comprehension! The Rocketown website doesn't offer any disclaimers about non-Christian bands performing at the club, though it does warn about not drinking, not fighting, not crowd surfing, and dancing at your own risk.

Keith Mohr—founder of Indieheaven.com, a resource for indie musicians that help them grow both creatively and spiritually—comments via email, 'I was shocked and appalled to see Rocketown booking hard core Satanic bands for shows. . . . I thought their mission was to be a positive influence for youth?' Mohr's message to the club?

'Take a stand Rocketown, there are plenty of hard core bands of Christians with songs you can't understand what they are screaming about out there, but at least they are believers in Christ!' (really, nice logic).

This is completely fallen thinking. Professing Christians scream out onstage. It doesn't matter because it's all for Jesus, man!

One of the most shocking 'confessions' was made by Michael W Smith in *Inside Music* magazine (Jan/Feb 1991, p. 23). During the interview, Smith was asked, 'There's also the influence of such groups as Alan Parsons in your music. It's especially noticeable on the first record, the Michael W Smith Project [even named after the Alan Parsons Project].' And Smith's reply, 'DEFINITELY!' Alan Parsons is among the most occultic and bizarre groups in rock! Alan Parsons has done such songs as 'Lucifer', the sacrilegious 'Genesis Ch. 1 v.32' (there is no Genesis 1:32) and albums like *Pyramid* and *Eve*.[7]

Then there is Smith's album *Christmastime*, a 1998 holiday release where the cover is displaying rune symbology. For those not that familiar with this alphabet, think of the Nazi SS insignia, as one example. Michael W Smith is standing out in a forest clearing on a chair in the snow. He was forming the runic *T*, with his arms bent downwards, and the bottom of the chair is clearly forming the runic *M*.[8]

In addition, his earlier album *The Big Picture* (1986) had Smith's name spelled backwards on the back cover. I would point out that spelling or talking *backwards* etc. is very significant in satanic circles. Again, Michael uses the runic alphabet for part of his name.[9]

In the book *Web of Darkness*, former Satanist Sean Sellers says, 'Runes are the oldest form of occult knowledge and magic. . . . Their use sets a person against God' (Sean Sellers, *Web of Darkness*, p. 72).

Michael Smith's *Rocketown* organization also uses the actual runic *T* symbol as its logo on Smith's website.

Over his career, Smith has sold more than 15 million albums, has won forty-five Dove Awards and has had thirty-two number one singles, yet he had not recorded one hymn album as the timing was not quite, right? (Tape Rewind) Finally, he recorded *hymns* in 2014. His two recent hymn albums are distributed through a US Southern restaurant chain and gift store.[10]

Larry King interviewed Smith in 2006:

KING: How did you choose that Christian music? Why not just music?

SMITH: Well, I wish it was just music. I mean I've hated labels since day one. You know I wanted to grow up and be like Paul McCartney and Elton John and play pop music but talk about my faith. So, you know, in the early days I didn't even know what Christian music was, so it got a label.[11]

Lance Goodall

Larry King went on to clarify what he meant:

KING: So is it described as gospel? Is that a fair description of what you sing? What do you say it is?

SMITH: You know what, I just think it's pop music, you know.[12]

Smith's faith and lyrics are vague. Most of his music requires some form of interpretation. It is because of these vague lyrics and loosely interpreted music that he has been invited to go on tour worldwide.

Michael W. Smith has received invitations from numerous heathen nations, his website explains:

Prior to recording Sovereign, Smith toured the world extensively sharing the gospel in such remote locales as Bahrain, Malaysia, Sri Lanka and Abu Dhabi. . . . 'In Bahrain, I had to be invited by the king to get in. They've never had a Christian concert ever, but there are a lot of churches there. Somehow a Hindu, a Catholic, a Muslim, a Protestant and a Jew all formed this committee and wanted me to come to Bahrain and do a concert of peace.'[13]

Smith may be touring the world, but he is not preaching to unbelievers and calling them to repentance. Smith won't rebuke the world, for the world loves him. It's not hard to see where Michael W. Smith's heart really is—with the world and things of the world. For example, Smith's 2009 world tour called A New Hallelujah featured Matt Maher, a Roman Catholic worship leader, who gets personal invitations from the pope to lead Catholic worship.[14]

An atheist described the Christian rock band *Skillet*:

> I've loved Skillet for absolutely ages, and **I have only just found out that they're a Christian band!** These four

> people alone might be enough to convert me to religion,
> I've been a strong atheist for as long as I can remember
> but what I love about these guys (and girls) is that **they're
> singing more about good morals and ethics than pure
> religion**. I might yet be converted. Thumbs up if there
> are others out there like this! (emphasis mine)

Before you skip over this and assume that this guy will eventually get saved, look at the atheist's confession. He's been following the band for ages, but has only just realised they're Christians? They sing about good morals and ethics, but notice *not* pure religion. It's as if he is sayin' don't talk to me about some dude who claims to be God, just give me love, hope, joy, and peace in the world, and I might just give you guys a go. **In other words Christianity on the atheist's terms!**

I don't want to say it, BUT I TOLD YOU SO. We have come full circle. Each man has created a god unto himself!

'These *things* hast thou done, and I kept silence; thou thought that I was altogether *such an one* as thyself: *but* I will reprove thee, and set *them* in order before thine eyes' (Ps. 50:21)

This is where we will all end up: at the bottom of the spiritual cliff. If we do not repent and follow the old paths and walk in them, we will have lost the fight.

A W Tozer is again resounding in his criticism:

Religious entertainment has so corrupted the church of Christ that millions don't know that it's a heresy. They don't know that it is as much heresy as the counting of beads or the splashing of holy water or something else. (A W Tozer, *Success and the Christian*, p. 6)

All this is serving God with strange fire that He never condoned or permitted! We have been going in the way of Cain, bringing unacceptable worship. We bring to God worship from lives that have never been placed under the blood.

We offer the halt and the lame to Him. We have mixed in the modern sound with all its rebellion and lawlessness. To these blind leaders of the blind, Christian metal is the logical conclusion to the reaching of the unsaved. The only conduit subscribed to in the Bible is the simple preaching of the Word of God (see 1 Cor. 1:21, 2 Cor. 2:2–5).

Apparently, today's carnal, biblically illiterate, culture-chasing Christians are so blinded by their pursuit of relevance that they're oblivious to just how foolish they look when they produce cheap knock-offs of successful secular entertainers.

This is an hour we need those who are on the Lord's side to stand for truth, but where are they?

28
AGAINST THE WIND

*These things hast thou done, and I kept silence; thou
thought that I was altogether such an one as thyself: but I
will reprove thee, and set them in order before thine eyes.*

—Ps. 50:21

We have talked about revival to the point we should have turned the
world upside down by now, but let me say it: God cannot and will not
send clouds of revival to a stubborn, hard-hearted, stiff- necked people.
We have made church a party playground for prodigals instead a place of
prayer. There has been no repentance, no sackcloth, no ashes. Instead,
we have produced *our own* revivals that have brought nothing but Bentley
Bedlam, Houston Heterodoxy, and Hinn Hysteria. These impostors,
clouds without rain, and others like them have brought God's judgement
of deception and drought of the Word of God to God's people. In fact,
the extent of this rift is such that it has been a systematic tearing down of
the foundations of our very faith. We have desecrated the temple with
our own bare hands! We have committed two sins before God, forsaking
Him: the fountain of living waters and digging cisterns for ourselves,
broken cisterns that hold no water. We have chosen to dig for our own

water when Christ, the living waters, has been our source all the time!

The medicine of Christianity has been so watered down that there is little to no relief or comfort; although we may seek for restored health, we remain in our mortal sickness and ignore the remedy. Dr Paul S. Jones makes this observation regarding contemporary Christian music, that from easy listening to heavy metal, rock is inappropriate for worship because, 'the music's destructive, and purposely anti-God. Its anti-authoritarian nature remains undiminished even if it is played by well-meaning Christians'.[1] In other words holiness and hedonism, sanctity and sacrilege can't mix.

"The chief danger of the twentieth century will be religion without the Holy Ghost, Christianity without Christ, forgiveness without repentance, salvation without regeneration, and heaven without hell."
~ William Booth, founder of The Salvation Army

We have made music and entertainment our new refreshment. In heightened treachery, we have carried on with our programmes regardless of what the style of worship. The music and lyrics have left God out of the picture.

In his book *Prophetic Ministry*, in chapter 2 on 'The Making of a Prophet', British pastor Theodore Austin-Sparks (1888–1971) describes our day:

Divine thought taken hold of by carnal men. . . . There is a condition like that existing today. Divine things have been taken hold of by men carnally, and brought down to an earth level; the direct government of the Holy Spirit has been exchanged for committees and boards and so on. Men have set up the government in Divine things and are running things for God. The way of the New Testament, that in prayer and fasting, the mind of the Lord is secured is hardly known. Well, those who are spiritual, who know, who see, who understand, cannot accept that.

R. A. Torrey (1856–1928), American evangelist, and pastor echoing these same concerns said, 'We are too busy to pray, and so we are too busy to have power. We have a great deal of activity, but we accomplish little; many services but few conversions; much machinery but few results.'[2]

It was this reality of singing the mantra of 'man centred' worship that woke me up one Sunday morning to the need to reassess my long-term involvement with Hillsong Church. I was standing onstage as a member of the choir, singing about freedom. Everything was about man, and my heart changed the actual words so that I could lift praise to God and adoration to Him instead. I left the church six months later.

We now worship our own personal Jesus!

29
ALL YOU NEED IS LOVE

And Aaron said unto them, Break off the golden earrings, which are in the ears of your wives, your sons, and your daughters, and bring them unto me. And all the people broke off the golden earrings which were in their ears, and brought them to Aaron. And he received them at their hands, and fashioned with a graving tool, after he had made it a molten calf

—Exod. 32:1–4

One of the saddest periods in Israel's history was this departing from God at the outset of their journey towards the Promised Land. Aaron melted down the gold jewellery, but rather than it being brought in reverence as an offering to YHWH, it was fashioned it into a golden calf. Idolatry and immorality came flooding back. Israel gave into the flesh and moulded their faith into something that they were familiar with. Aaron was the high priest, which might be a warning that not all who are in the ministry understand their role as leaders of God's people.

And he said, 'These be thy gods, O Israel, which brought you up out of the land of Egypt' (Exod. 32:4).

Oh, how quickly the Israelites forgot. Just because God delivers them out of their slavish bondage didn't necessarily mean He received their automatic devotion. Israel was taken out of Egypt, but Egypt was not yet out of the hearts of Israel.

'O Foolish Israelites, you turned from the truth so quickly. God is drawing you to Himself to worship the one holy living true God, now here you are with your calf.'

This request came first from the hearts of the people, not Aaron.[1] They wanted gods to go before them, undoubtedly, to the Promised Land. They saw how the LORD led them out of Egypt, and they knew the LORD God had revealed Himself at Mount Sinai. Yet they were willing to trust a god they could make with their hands to finish what the LORD began.

Do we not see their failure? And isn't this the great error of our day to make good on what only God himself can breath and bring about. Left to our own devices, we end up worshipping something abstract: an image, a ministry, a man, a teaching, something inanimate, a representation and counterfeit of the real thing. May I say at this point, that our failure in this generation has been forgetting God; and instead like the Corinthians, we have followed men, and their ministries. Because we have little of the eye of faith, we have relied on the eye of the natural.

You see, man must worship something; and in doing so, we prefer something tangible (even if it's wrong) to someone who is omniscient and transcendent. In our fallen state, we worship a form: something earthly, a figment, a taste of God, but not God himself.

'Break off the golden earrings . . . and bring them to me: God gave Moses instructions for taking a free-will offering to be used in making a

191

holy place for God' (Exod. 25:1–7).

Instead, Aaron received an offering that ended up being used for idolatry instead of for God's service. Oh, how this echoes and resounds as one of the greatest crimes in ministry today, the offerings of the people being used for greed and ill-gotten gain. The number of eternally worthless earthly mansions built with granite and marble, nine bedrooms, lavished with seven bathrooms, and five car garages; houses built here of bricks and mortar; men gouging men for money and for their luxury instead of it going to the poor, the hungry, and the dying.

The millions of dollars that have been completely wasted on televangelists, giving the impression to every naive and avid viewer that a hundredfold blessing will be theirs. It seems people are generous in what they give to their idols.[2] Their gold and silver will witness against them in the last day (see James 5:1–6).

The scripture tells us they had learnt the way of the Egyptians for it is said, They did not forsake the idols of Egypt (Ezek. 20:8), Neither left she her whoredoms brought from Egypt (Ezek. 23:8). Thus, they changed their glory into the similitude of an ox (Ps. 106:20) and proclaimed their own folly, beyond that of other idolaters, the nations who worshipped the host of heaven. This shows the foolishness of idolatry. This statue of a calf did not exist the day before, and now they worship it as the god that brought them out of Egypt?

When Aaron saw it, he built an altar before it.

Now Aaron honoured and sanctified the idol with an animal sacrifice. He made the calf, and then he made an altar to worship it. 'Tomorrow is a feast to the LORD.'

This aspect is most interesting and is important for our consideration. The creation and the worship of the golden calf was *not* a conscious rejection of the LORD. It seemed that Aaron and the rest of Israel thought that they could give honour to the LORD *through* the golden calf.

They would worship the true God through this image, and yet this did not excuse them from gross idolatry any more than excusing the papists whose plea it is that they do not worship the image but God by the image, making themselves idolaters.[3]

Aaron was not crass enough to say, 'Let's forsake the LORD God.' He simply accommodated the fashion of Egypt, making worship for Israel more acceptable. In the mind of Israel, Aaron didn't take away the LORD God. He simply added the golden calf to aid and assist their worship.[4]

The golden calf as an image was to be a visible sign or symbol of Jehovah so that their sin consisted not in a breach of the FIRST (Exod. 20:3), but of the SECOND commandment (Exod. 20:4–6).

This is the modern modus operandi.

Leaders who don't do away from God completely but manipulate, reshape, or redefine God into the god they imagine him or need Him to be.

God is liberal, they say, and will not mind a different style of worship. As long as we gather unto Him, that's all that matters. What we are doing is for the Lord. This is all that God requires, that we lift up his name. See, we worship God. God is loving and compassionate towards us. Should we choose to use rock music or lyrics that teach nothing of biblical doctrine, it's still okay. If we say hell is an outdated concept and even atheists will find a home in a better place, doesn't that seem reasonable? Besides, Christ died for all men. And should the world find by scientific discovery that homosexuality is genetic, who are we to denounce and debate on these issues? Our God is love!

It seems the modern view is that what was really happening on the cross was that God was showing he is nothing but love, and there is NO judgment. His forgiveness means He is somehow ready to overlook sin. To many the cross is just an expression of God's love?

We have so sentimentalised the cross that John 3:16 no longer means anything. Christian faith should not be passive. Perhaps for those less familiar, here is the verse: 'For God so loved the world that he gave his only begotten Son, that whosoever believes in him should not perish, but have everlasting life.' Today the great proclamation is the cross equals love. But we ignore the reality that Jesus' death was a God-initiated act to deal with everyone's sin. In fact when we get down to it, even though we dismiss it, the cross was a display of God's wrath. Therefore the cross equals God's justice. Many know the verse. But we have made it read something like this:

A local city council purchases a brand new fire engine. Isn't the council loving and kind to give such a fire engine? But the fire engine is to put out the fire, not just to sit on display, but to save our lives from destruction, so we won't be destroyed in the flames. Note that the previous verse says[14] 'And as Moses lifted up the serpent in the wilderness, even so must the Son of man be lifted up'. Why, because the Israelites had been severely bitten by snakes, by vipers (a picture of sin), and they needed a remedy. They needed to look (in faith) at the serpent on the pole. So we need to be saved from sin, its guilt, its sway, its corruption, and the flames of Hell, through faith and trust in the Lord Jesus.

'In conquering of those enemies that be within, you make a conquest over the devil and hell itself. . . . And as this is the most noble conquest, so it is the most necessary conquest. You must be the death of your sins, or they will be the death of your souls. Sin is a viper that does always kill where it is not killed'—Thomas Brooks

The verse confirms the doctrine of the atonement. God so loved the world that he gave his only begotten son that whomsoever believes on Him should not *perish*. . . . Today, we make it to read something like this, 'For God so loved the world that he gave his only begotten son that whomsoever believes on him should enjoy and appreciate God's love.' We know this is not what it says, but it seems to be the new thinking nevertheless. And this is a different thing altogether.

This teaching of the cross equals love is distorting the true Christian position!

Let me prove it to you. 'In this was manifested the love of God toward us, because that God sent his only begotten Son into the world, that we might live through him. Herein is love, not that we loved God, but that he loved us, and sent his Son to **be the propitiation for our sins.**' (emphasis added) (1 John 4:9-10).

This word propitiation means appeasement, expiation, placating, atoning, the blood of a victim covering the sin of the accused, the blood sprinkled to bring mercy, the blood spilt satisfies the one offended. It had to be the blood of His dear son, for as we read in Hebrews the blood of bulls and goats could never satisfy and take away sins (Heb 9:12, Heb 10:4). God no longer has to judge us, because He made his one and only son a substitution for us. Jesus' death appeased God.

The church no longer preaches the gospel of the Kingdom, but the gospel of the Beatles, love love love; love is all you need.

In the psalms we read mercy and truth have met together righteousness and peace have kissed each other (Ps 85:10).

The key thought is we must be reconciled to God. We must repent, turn from sin and serve Him.

But instead we have Hillsong's teaching aligning dangerously close to the deceptive novel *The Shack*. The teaching is along these lines of *God will never judge people for their sins. God forgave all of humanity on the cross, whether they repent or not. Some may choose a relationship with Him, but He forgives them regardless.*

In his book *The Chief End of Man*, A W Tozer writes, 'Samaritan Worship is heretical worship in the correct meaning of the term' (*The Chief End of Man*, sermon #3, Toronto, 1962).

In other words, it so easy to have correct theology. The modern heretic is not one who denies all of the truth but is selective in his orthodoxy, a belief system based on picking and choosing what he likes and dislikes, and discarding the rest. The reality is this is heresy, taking what I like and rejecting what I don't like, which is an awful indictment on our present age. In other words, if our worship is tainted, it then falls into the category of error and idolatry.

Some mistake the music of religion for worship.

The point I have sought to highlight is the most important and foundational principle found in our often-neglected Old Testament: you cannot worship God just as you please. We must remember that Cain had an experience with God, but for him, there was no saving faith.

God wants and desires worship on his terms. Not all worship is accepted by God even though we might label it worship.

A young woman suggested that there is nothing wrong with dancing, singing and having a party to praise Jesus. She went onto say, 'I don't think God has a problem with people partying and getting excited and happy if they are doing it for Him.'

This is the error of Israel wrapped in modern thinking and sophistication. The Israelites danced around the golden calf, and thought they were worshipping YHWH, and today's worshippers party, thinking that in their concerts and conferences they are worshipping Jesus.

And they rose up to play.

This is a tasteful way to speak of debauchery and immorality. The worship of the Israelites included eating, drinking, sexual immorality, and orgies. Like god, like worship. Being *vain in their imaginations*, they became vain in their worship. So great was their vanity.

Israel had journeyed to the great mountain. They had heard the voice of God Himself thunder from heaven. They had seen the smoke and fire billow from the holy mount. But none of this did anything to change their hearts. It had the opposite effect. It made many of them desire a *less-demanding* God.[5]

The calf was the perfect compromise to keep the people from defecting totally. It was visual, it was spectacular, it had natural appeal, it had glitz and glamour, and it was sensual, familiar, simple to grasp. Their calf was accommodating, and it demanded little in respect to conduct or right living. A golden calf made from the hand of men. The golden calf for us

is the party god who will let us have religion on our terms. In fact, the religion of the calf amplifies our natural appetites and desires. Isn't this modern-day Christianity to a tee? The church delights in their party god!

I have quoted A W Tozer, but I do again because he decried the abuse of this man-manipulated system in the use of entertainment more than any other in our time:

This great Egyptian god has grown into a veritable religion which holds its devotees with a strange fascination... For centuries the Church stood solidly against every form of worldly entertainment recognizing it for what it was—a device for wasting time, a refuge from the disturbing voice of conscience, a scheme to divert attention from moral accountability.[6]

Tozer appealed time and again to the church but largely went unheeded. His desire was to see the practice of biblical separation remain. But this has fallen completely out of vogue among evangelicals and charismatics today. Fundamentalists are known for their strong separation, but today this is seen as largely negative. The new evangelicals are opposed to the concept of separation, and consequently to their shame, they are laden down with worldliness. Most disagree and dismiss separation as unbiblical and not politically correct.

But the Bible commands Christians to separation, to stand against the world, the flesh, and the devil. Yet these three are accommodated and even embraced by most Christian 'evan-jellyfish'. We no longer fight the good fight of faith, but we enjoy the great god entertainment and join forces to market the church. Religious entertainment is now the mainstay of church life and is 'crowding out the serious things of God.'

God's word is NOT silent when it comes to principles and pieces of evidence of biblical music! Who, after all, is supposed to be the focus in worshipful music? God!

Here are just a few passages to show this is obvious:

And they sang together by course in praising and giving thanks unto the Lord; because he is good, for his mercy endureth for ever toward Israel. And all the people shouted with a great shout, when they praised the Lord, because the foundation of the house of the Lord was laid. (Ezra 3:11)

Sing to the LORD, For He has done excellent things; This is known in all the earth. (Isa. 12:5, see also 2 Chron. 20:21)

What principles do you see? Music should speak of God's holy character. Music should communicate who God is and what He is like.

Who should be exalted in words of song? Again, God.

But not in the seeker-sensitive emergent evangelical hybrid megachurch!

Notice that Moses knew right away that the music that he was hearing from down in the valley was **NOT** associated with worship to YHWH. Joshua wasn't so sure, but Moses knew it was music associated with pagan worship. It's the same today. There are certain types of music that are associated with the world and are in outright rebellion against God. It's because leaders have not sought God on the mountaintop, that they have established churches on the basis of the wisdom of the valley, on the philosophy of men.

Can you envisage the Rolling Stones song 'Start Me Up' made into some sort of makeshift Christian anthem? The idea is monstrous!

No greater crime has been meted out by the evangelical church than a god that is malleable and conforms to our choices, wants, and desires. The God of Abraham, Isaac, and Jacob, shaped and molded by modern-day culture, the worship of the eternal God, marketed through worldly concepts.

Charles H. Spurgeon once said, 'The devil has seldom done a cleverer thing than hinting to the Church that part of their mission is to provide entertainment for the people, with a view to winning them. From speaking out as the Puritans did, the Church has gradually toned down her testimony, then winked at and excused the frivolities of the day. Then she tolerated them in her borders. Now she has adopted them under the plea of reaching the masses.'[7]

Rock music, chart-topping hits, multimedia, and charismatic Cirque du Soleil* are common place in the house of God on any given Sunday in this present godless era.

The current 'ministers' in God's house cry out, 'These be your gods, O Israel' and happily the people rise up to play.

Footnote

• https://en.wikipedia.org/wiki/Cirque_du_Soleil

Cirque du Soleil (pronounced: [siʁk dy sɔ.lɛj], "Circus of the Sun") is a Canadian entertainment company. It is the largest theatrical producer in the world.[2] Based in Montreal, Quebec, Canada, and located in the inner-city area of Saint-Michel, it was founded inBaie-Saint-Paul in 1984 by two former street performers, Guy Laliberté and Gilles Ste-Croix.[3] It is self-described as a dramatic mix of circus arts and street entertainment. Each show is a synthesis of circus styles from around the world, with its own central theme and storyline. Shows employ continuous live music, with performers rather than stagehands changing the props*

30

I HEARD IT THROUGH
THE GRAPEVINE

The kingdom of God is at hand: repent ye, and believe the gospel.

—Mk. 1:15

Oh, our great need of repentance today!

The gospel of Mark points out to us the fact that our Lord opened his lips at the beginning of His ministry with these words: *repent* and believe the gospel.

Yet repentance has become almost a forgotten word, a byword, like an old lamp relegated to obsolescence. It's missing from Christian vocabulary and in Christian living.

For Rick Warren, repentance means a conformity or change of the mind. Though Warren might not have explicitly articulated it in his famous book *The Purpose-Driven Life*, the idea was present throughout the entire book.

Warren, who started preaching at 16, explained that 'some people view repentance as a change in behaviour. But such a change [in behaviour] is not the root; it is rather the fruit of repentance'. In layman's terms, that translates to change (that's repentance) is not the root. A change of behaviour (repentance) is the fruit of repentance.

So much for evangelical theology!

However, scripture tells us that the root and the fruit are both part of the same tree!

Either make the tree good and his fruit good, or else, make the tree corrupt and his fruit corrupt, for the tree is known by his fruit (Matt. 12:33).

'Bring forth therefore "fruits worthy of repentance", and begin not to say within yourselves, we have Abraham to our father: for I say unto you, That God is able of these stones to raise up children unto Abraham. And now also the axe is laid unto the root of the trees: every tree therefore which brings not forth good fruit is hewn down, and cast into the fire' (Lk. 3:8–9).

Strictly speaking, the phrase *fruit of repentance* isn't found in the Bible. The phrases *fruits of righteousness* and *fruit unto holiness* are (see Phil. 1:11 and Rom. 6:22).

Rather than *fruit of repentance*, the scriptural meaning contained in the above verse is fruit from repentance i.e. that which results from repentance.

The doctrine of repentance in the scriptures is very prominent. The word *repent* is taken from the Hebrew word *shuwb* (בוּש) (pronounced Shüv, Strongs H7725) which means to turn or to return. Teshuvah is the act of returning as in the example of a soldier told to turn back to his newly built house and to withdraw from active duty (see Deut. 20:5).

Repentance is at the heart of saving faith. In the New Testament, the word translated as *repentance* is the Greek word *metanoia* (μετάνοια) (Strongs G3341). *Metanoia* literally means to think after, a transformative change of heart, especially a spiritual conversion. The term derives from the Ancient Greek words μετά (*metá*) (meaning *beyond* or *after*) and νόος (*noeō*) (meaning *perception* or *understanding* or *mind*) and has different meanings in different contexts.[4]

It implies a change of mind, so in this basic meaning, Rick Warren is correct. But the word means far more than that.

The understanding from the scriptures is that repentance is the recognition of our sinfulness, our depravity, our opposition to God's ways. So it requires a turning from self to God (cf. 1 Thess. 1:9). A change of mind is not like the whimsical decision to wear a different-coloured shirt one morning but instead involves an inward working on the heart, incorporating moral choices. It's not a change of opinion, but rather, it is the development and transformation of core values.

To illustrate this, Jesus told a wonderful parable of two sons in Matthew's gospel. One son said he would go and work in the field and then failed to do so, and the other son although saying no, did what his Father asked (Matt. 21:28–32).

Another English word, *metamorphosis*—Greek μεταμόρφωσις from μετα- (*meta-*) = *change* + μορφή (*morphe*), *form*—carries with it the same idea of change and transformation, a complete and full change of character and/or appearance.

Paul went about declaring that people 'should repent and turn to God, and do works meet [fit] for repentance (Acts 26:20).

What did Paul preach? 'Repentance that is toward God, and faith toward our Lord Jesus Christ' (Acts 20:21).

Notice the order: repentance first. Repentance—this is the missing element in our evangelism and something we are ignoring at this present time.

'The vague and tenuous hope that God is too kind to punish the ungodly has become a deadly opiate for the consciences of millions' —A W Tozer.[1]

The idea has come in that the business of preaching is to bring people to Christ and then later on somehow they will repent.

'Repentance is a grace and must have its daily operation, as well as other graces. A true penitent must go on from faith to faith, from strength to strength; he must never stand still or turn back. True repentance is a continued spring, where the waters of godly sorrow are always flowing. 'My sin is ever before me' —Thomas Brooks.

He that turns not from every sin, turns not from any one sin. Every sin strikes at the honour, being, and the glory of God; at the heart of Christ. Therefore, a soul truly penitent, hates all sin conflicts with, and will labour to draw strength from a crucified Christ to overcome all. Again, repentance includes, not only a loathing of sin, but also a loathing of ourselves for it.[2]

Now it is no accident that the scriptures speak of a specific order, and it is very dangerous for us to change this purely for results and purely for numbers. Church history shows that the preaching of repentance has always brought a great period of revival and reawakening within the church.

Therefore, it is of no surprise that we see very little contrition for sin these days. It is very rare today to see anyone weeping, or agonising, and being conscious of sin in the presence of a holy God.

If we do not preach repentance, then the church will languish. The need of repentance is central to all that is necessary to the life of the church in this very dark day.

The first thing when we repent is we think differently about God, and then we must think differently about ourselves.

'But God be thanked, that ye were the servants of sin, but ye have obeyed from the heart that form of doctrine which was delivered you. . . . Being then made free from sin, ye became the servants of righteousness' (Rom. 6:17–18).

Contrary to Rick Warren's understanding, without the foundation (root) of repentance, there can be no righteous life produced. Repentance, by definition, happens before anything else.

In summary, we cannot show true change in our life unless we have changed (repented), which brings about manifestations of that change/repentance. The work of repentance is reflected in our behaviour and conduct. They are inseparably linked. Without true turning, there is no transformation!

In other words, the gospel, which calls for repentance, produces it (see Acts 2:37,38,41).

Rick Warren, in effect, believes in repentance, but he fails to qualify its place in the work of salvation. I have laboured this point to show Warren's diluted and deceptive use of terminology.

Pastor Brian Houston of the world-famous Hillsong Church in Sydney, Australia, spoke at Saddleback at the end of 2012.[2]

Brian had to compete at the Sunday night service with festive décor, sparklers and glow sticks, a dance off, best-dressed contest, a photo booth, and gourmet food trucks, plus a toasting of the New Year with sparkling cider and party favours.

Houston did preach. His sermon was taken from 2 Corinthians 7:8–10, a passage on godly sorrow. However, so he didn't put a dampener on the end-of-year celebrations, Houston preached from the passage that centres on repentance without even mentioning it ONCE.

How did he get away with it when the text itself talks of repentance? By switching and reading out of 'the Message' Bible, of course.

Here's how it reads in this liberal paraphrase:[8–9] 'I know I distressed you greatly with my letter. Although I felt awful at the time, I don't feel at all bad now that I see how it turned out. The letter upset you but only for a while. Now I'm glad—not that you were upset but that you were jarred into turning things around. You let the distress bring you to God, not drive you from him. The result was all gain, no loss. Distress that drives us to God does that. It turns us around. It gets us back in the way of salvation. We never regret that kind of pain. But those who let distress drive them away from God are full of regrets, end up on a deathbed of regrets' (2 Cor. 7:8–10).

When he got to verse 9, Houston switched from the NKJV to the Message and concluded that the problems at Corinth were all caused by Paul's 'angry' letter. Houston is up to his same old tricks of mangling the scriptures and preaching his humanistic heterodoxy.[3]

Notice, Houston like so many shoots the messenger.

This flip-flopping between the two versions allowed him to completely avoid the word *repentance*. Brian Houston made it out to be Paul's bad attitude, instead of realising the letter was totally necessary in the circumstances, where members of the Corinthian congregation were involved in incest. As a true pastor, Paul had no choice but to write his letters as he did. Instead Houston would rather avoid this topic, and of course we see the outworking of this among his own followers.

The verses in the 2 Corinthians 7:8–10 in the King James Version make ten references to repentance and godly sorrow, but *not* once was it preached in Houston's message. This is flagrant dishonesty at best! Paul had written in his first letter to the Corinthians correcting them openly about the immorality among them, so the letter was necessary to discipline the church. It was something that he did not like doing, but he needed to do to arrest them.

Charles Finney, 19th-century revivalist and evangelist, is the one of the clearest expositors of true and false repentance. He states that 'false repentance is founded in selfishness, which is expressed in regret'. In other words, distress and regret have nothing to do with repentance.

Finney leaves no room for debate. It may be simply a strong feeling of regret, in the mind of the individual, that he has done as he has, because he sees the evil consequences of it to himself, because it makes him miserable, or exposes him to the wrath of God, or injures his family or his friends. All this is pure selfishness. He may feel remorse of conscience-- biting, consuming REMORSE—and no true repentance.'

Godly sorrow is based on a realisation of the awfulness of sin primarily against God and then towards others. Finney qualifies that a hypocrite still loves the world and enjoys sin. Their heart is not changed. But the Christian does not love sin; it is always bitter to him (Charles Finney, *Lectures to Professing Christians*, 1837 Smith & Valentine, pp. 119–127).

Incredibly, Pastor Houston uses wishy-washy, weasel words from the new age Message Bible to avoid the clear biblical teaching of the need for repentance. Why I don't know.

Another such smooth prosperity preacher is Joseph Prince who pastors in

Lance Goodall

Singapore.

Prince takes the position that God actually made us righteous already; therefore, sanctification is seemingly unnecessary. Prince's positive thinking and positive confession paradigm are what he propagates. Joseph Prince claims that sin, law, repentance, and conviction are negative, so they are excluded and rejected from his message.

There is no such thing as first having 'positional righteousness' and then having to maintain that through 'practical righteousness' —

Joseph Prince. [4]

Joseph Prince, the man with five-star faith is giving us a 'replacement' theology of fancy catchphrases and word-of-faith metaphysics. If we are truly Christian we cannot take Christ as just our justification (legal righteousness), and leave off sanctification (practical righteousness). We need to understand there is a definite distinction between justification and sanctification, but we cannot take Christ in parts, and pick and choose our level of Christian experience.

Sanctification is an integral part of salvation, not an optional extra.

Another example of his tricky topsy-turvy theology is on page 233 of his book *Destined to Reign*. He makes this seemingly innocent comment, 'It is not the preaching of wrath, fiery indignation, and judgment that will cause people's hearts to turn back to God. It is his goodness, grace and mercy. When you catch a glimpse of that, you cannot help but be overwhelmed by all that He is, and this will lead to true repentance.'

If this were completely true—and this was all that was needed—then Paul would never have argued the following, 'Or do you despise the riches of His goodness, forbearance, and longsuffering, not knowing that the goodness of God leads you to repentance? [5] But in accordance with your hardness and your impenitent heart you are treasuring up for yourself wrath in the day of wrath and revelation of the righteous judgment of God,[6] who will render to each one according to his deeds' (Rom. 2:4–6 NKJV).

In other words, it is easy for men to take God's goodness for granted, to overlook it, and even to despise it. Even though the cross is the perfect expression of God's love, 1,900 years or more of human history clearly shows that men ignore it; and in the end, they come under the wrath of God.

'Behold therefore the goodness **and** severity of God: on them which fell, severity; but toward thee, goodness, if thou *continue* in his goodness: otherwise thou also shalt be cut off' (Rom. 11:22) (emphasis added).

Paul's method was completely contrary to Prince's: 'Knowing the terror of the Lord we persuade men' (2 Cor. 5:11)

The reason Prince is so dangerous is because of his 'designer-jean Christianity'. A Christianity that is comfortable, which stretches, moulds, and conforms to our needs, wants, and sensibilities. This message of Prince's is a synthetic blend—a combination of word-of-faith teaching, motivational victorious living, and Christian truth. This is the lie of the devil, who loves to mix in truth with lies. Prince is avoiding the unpleasantries. He is not preaching the whole counsel of God. The Bible warns of this and tells us that we must hold fast to truth and contend earnestly for the faith. I wish he would spend more time focused on his theology than he does on his wardrobe.

Of course, Prince's book was endorsed by Brian Houston.

One of the reasons for this outpouring of apostasy and skullduggery is that Hillsong has made the Message Bible their bible of choice.

The *Bible in Contemporary Language* was created by Eugene H. Peterson and published in segments from 1993 to 2002 by NavPress.

Peterson's removal of the word Lord is the most disturbing aspect. The Lord appears no less than 7,970 times in the King James Bible. The word Lord is, in fact, used more than any other noun. Of the 8,000-plus different words used in the King James Bible, the Lord ranks fourteenth among the most occurrences (number 13 is the single letter *a*). Only helper words such as *the*, *of*, *in*, *to* etc. all occur more often than the noun Lord.

In contrast the Message only mentions Lord 71 times. That's right: 71 times compared to 7,970 times! That's a ratio of 112:1.

In Eugene Peterson's rendering of the New Testament, the Lord appears only 23 times, and the Message never directly honours Jesus Christ as Lord.

The Message Bible NEVER *directly* honours Jesus Christ as Lord!

he Lord Jesus occurs 118 times in the King James Bible. The Lord Jesus Christ occurs 84 times in the King James Bible. The phrase Lord Jesus Christ or Lord Jesus is not in the Message. This outright denial of the Lord Jesus has never occurred in ANY translation.

Eugene Peterson's the Message Bible never directly honours Jesus Christ as Lord—not once!

Let us be clear: this is no accident. Houston, we have a big problem! It is interesting to note that Judas Iscariot never referred to Jesus as Lord.

'Then Judas, which betrayed Him, answered and said, Master, is it I?' (Matt. 25:26). *Master* which means *teacher* or *Rabbi.*[5]

Judas Iscariot thought if that he could bring Christ to power somehow, he would be appointed to some key role in leadership and enjoy wealth and privilege as part of the deal. However, on that fateful night, he kisses Jesus and betrays Him with thirty pieces of silver. He knew Jesus was the Messiah, so he thought, *Why don't we take the kingdom by force?* Judas had a spirit of covetousness. He secretly dipped into the treasury for himself. And because he harboured this covetousness and desire for influence, Satan was able to deceive him over time. Judas professed to follow Christ, but look how it turned out.

By their fruit, you will know them (Matt 7:20).

31
WON'T GET FOOLED AGAIN

And even as they did not like to retain God in their knowledge, God gave them over to a reprobate mind, to do those things which are not convenient; Being filled with all unrighteousness.

—Rom. 1:28

Today we have marketed the gospel but have not preached the gospel.

We all seem to have our version of what the gospel is and what the gospel is supposed to do. We have taken up the fanciful notion that we need to adapt the gospel to reach each successive generation. We say the good news needs to be relevant to each concurrent generation.

In today's Christian culture, we don't want to come to church to sing, 'Tell me the old, old story' but rather 'Let me tell you my story!'

You have your gospel and I have mine!

Paul talked of the good news being according to my gospel. But Paul was making the point that he had received the message of God's good news by revelation and not from being taught by man (Gal. 1:11,12). Therefore, our gospel should line up with his. But does it?

Wade Clark Roof, who has been studying the religious journey of baby boomers since the mid-1980s, sees a 'radical shift from an ethic of self-denial to an ethic of self-fulfilment'. This results in a religion 'functionally and spatially located in the self. . . . Individuals are free to create their own religious faith and consecrate their own sacred space'.[1]

The new Christianity is a religion based on needs, niceness, and narcissism. We have now created a 'sinner-sensitive church'. God is love and that's all that matters.

All we have done is made the sinner more comfortable sitting through our church services. We have decided that we can meet the sinner on his turf and make a wager that somehow in all our accommodation to his standards this will bring an eventual window for the gospel. But this is a cheap trick that has failed many a time in previous days. We can all invent and then 'practise' our own religion. By attempting to be relevant to our culture, have we not ruined the gospel to the extent that it's no longer, well, the gospel? Indeed, is it a false gospel that should be denounced as heresy? Paul wrote: 'But though we, or an angel from heaven, preach any other gospel unto you than that which we have preached unto you, let him be accursed' (Gal. 1:8).

This means there is only *ONE* gospel from God!

But this is what pastors are literally saying we need to do: adapt our approach to the gospel.

For example, Pastor Andy Stanley suggests we must adapt to engage with our culture. He told an Atlanta conference audience in 2013 they must be willing to challenge traditional assumptions and adjust their methodology without changing the content of the message.

Stanley told the diverse group of pastors and leaders, 'If we want to re-engage our culture with the Bible, then we have to bring our energy to the Bible and uncover the energy in the Bible.'[2]

The energy of the Bible? Oh no, not another pastor who reads the Message Bible? Energy has all the hallmarks of spiritual 'force' of the new age religion. Prayers, meditations, invocations, and rituals all create energies and has nothing at all to do with biblical power and the working of the Holy Spirit.

And this is from the man who made convoluted and misleading statements about the scripture:

'The foundation of our faith is not the Scripture. The foundation of our faith is not the infallibility of the Bible. The foundation of our faith is something that happened in history. And the issue is always—Who is Jesus? That's always the issue. The Scripture is simply a collection of ancient documents that tells us that story.'[3]

During the conference, Stanley explained that believers should remove every obstacle that hinders or distracts from the central question. 'Who is Jesus?' said Stanley, adding that a scripture verse he hangs in his office is Acts 15:19: 'It is my judgment, therefore, that we should *not* make it difficult for the Gentiles who are turning to God.' This is the verse written in such Bibles like the NIV.[4]

However, the verse has read like this for more than three centuries.

'Therefore I judge that we should not *trouble* those from among the Gentiles who are turning to God' (Acts 15:19 NKJV).

The church that began with Jewish converts saw an influx of gentile/Greek believers. The early church wasn't struggling over how to make it less difficult to become a Christian in the first century. Instead, discussion amongst the apostles in Jerusalem was to avoid the possibility of encumbering early gentile believers with certain laws such as circumcision and dietary concerns long held within the Jewish faith. They were not to be troubled over feast days and new moons. It had nothing to do with making it difficult or easy to become a Christian. The eventual outcome was that they would 'write unto them, that they abstain from pollutions of idols, and fornication, and *from* things strangled, and *from* blood. (Acts 15:20).

I would have to say this generation is a generation of generalisers.

Stanley suggested that 'we have to go back and speak the way the first century Christians did. It worked for them, and it may just work for us'.[5]

But what does he even mean by this? We make the gospel whatever we want it to be and make the Bible say whatever we want it to say! We are generation of generalisers. To say we will make it less difficult to become a Christian must set off alarm bells!

We have decided that we can meet the sinner on his turf.

We like to quote gospel phrases like the Lord Jesus's words: 'Come until to me all ye that labour and are heavy laden, and I will give you rest" (Matt. 11:28). But we quote them in a half-hearted fashion because the hearer must give up his burden and take His yoke. Sin must be forsaken, which is the ultimate burden. What happened to the verses in Matthew 7:13,14?

'Enter ye in at the strait [narrow, confined] gate: for wide is the gate, and broad is the way, that leads to destruction, and many there be which go in thereat: Because strait is the gate, and narrow [troubled, afflicted, difficult] is the way, which leads unto life, and few there be that find it.'

So much for Andy Stanley's less difficult paradigm.

Today, we say come as you are, but that doesn't mean stay as you are! Yes, come as you are without one plea: nothing but to the cross I cling.

But this 'come as you are' banner quickly becomes the lowest common denominator. Anyone who finds the trappings of Christianity attractive, anyone who is comfortable with our presentation, anyone who comes to our modern churches, can seemingly do as they please and make a commitment on *their* terms.

This philosophy is nothing new. Even Billy Graham's close friend Chuck Templeton counselled him to keep moving with the times because people no longer accepted the Bible as inspired, so he needed to learn 'the new jargon' if he was to remain successful in ministry.

To illustrate this point further, Martyn Lloyd-Jones, in a sermon during his Romans series, spoke of Woodbine Willie. Geoffrey Studdert Kennedy was a World War I Anglican chaplain who was heralded for his selflessness in the field of battle. However, to 'win some', Woodbine Willie came up with some innovative ideas, one of which was to revert to smoking the soldiers cheap brand of cigarettes (Wild Woodbine), from which he got his nickname. In addition, he took up swearing and cursing all as a means to win them to the gospel. 'But the verdict of history on this was that it was a complete failure.'[6]

In 2015, the story came to light that Hillsong NYC Church had two gay choir members, Josh Canfield and Reed Kelly, both Broadway performers.

The story of the Broadway boyfriends went viral and caused Hillsong to issue not one but two statements. They did acknowledge that, yes, the two openly gay men has been active in worship choir leadership for a number of years, but they have insisted that they were 'unaware' that they were gay and were 'completely taken by surprise" at the revelation'.[7] But this is just more 'public relations'.

'We are a gay welcoming church but we are not a church that affirms a gay lifestyle' —Brian Houston, 4 Aug 2015.[8]

A gay welcoming church means the leadership turn a blind eye. The pair were quickly demoted and stood down. But they remain regular members of the church. So the question that looms large is, what is the difference between removing them from the choir yet being allowed to remain in the church? They don't hide their relationship, they are still kissing and hugging each other on Instagram, and news is they are planning to marry each other in 2016. The fact that they were engaged some 8 months before this choir chaos surfaced seemed to be overlooked by most.[9]

We all have a deep-rooted problem. The problem, the Bible says, is within each one of us, within our own hearts and minds. Jesus said, 'For from within, out of the heart of men, proceeds evil thoughts, adultery, fornication, murder, theft, covetousness, wickedness, deceit, licentiousness, an evil eye, blasphemy, pride and foolishness' (Mk. 7:21–22).

'Thy prophets have seen vain and foolish things for thee: and they have not discovered thine iniquity, to turn away thy captivity; but have seen for thee false burdens and causes of banishment' (Lam 2:14).

Hillsong may not affirm a gay lifestyle, but they allow for a gay lifestyle.

'Know ye not that the unrighteous shall not inherit the kingdom of God? Be not deceived: neither fornicators, nor idolaters, nor adulterers, nor effeminate, nor abusers of themselves with mankind. . . . And such were some of you: but ye are washed, but ye are sanctified, but ye are justified in the name of the Lord Jesus, and by the Spirit of our God' (1 Cor. 6:9,11).

Come as you are, doesn't mean stay as you are!

But that's not the half of it.

On 16 October 2014 a news conference was held by Brian Houston at The Eventi Hotel in New York City. As reported by the New York Post and other outlets Brian at that stage was still in 'ongoing conversation' in regard to same-sex marriage.[10] The conference was primarily a way to explain statements made a week earlier at the Australian Royal Commission on child abuse.

Interestingly Reed and Canfield were on the *Survivor* reality TV show and it was known then they were the Broadway boyfriends, and this was as far back as 24 September 2014, when the hit show aired on CBS.[11]

Was this media conference with Carl Lentz and Brian Houston targeted then to cut off the flow of questions that would eventually arise from this couples public affection?

On 28 January 2015, the couple got engaged when Josh Canfield popped the question to Reed Kelly at the cabaret venue called 54 Below. Canfield was interviewed by playbill.com within hours of the announcement, and he admitted then that he found it helpful being honest including to Hillsong Church. He explained how he had only recently told family about his relationship with Reed, so that was still really fresh, but it was a time 'to be truthful with everyone.' He explains, 'I'm a part of Hillsong NYC. I'm one of their choir directors. I also sing on their worship team. They've been amazing as well. Nothing has changed there now that I'm completely out and with Reed. He sings in the choir as well.'[12]

Maybe it's a case of what happens in New York stays in New York.

To rub more salt into the wound, the website gonola.com reported back in March 2015 that the engaged couple were chosen to lead the mid-year 2015 Pride Festival in New Orleans, as celebrity grand marshalls, which they did.[10] Notice this event took place just 2 months before the Hillsong choir boys scandal.

The website reads:

The objective of the event is to create an atmosphere where lesbian, gay, bisexual, and transgender people can be proud of their sexual orientation and gender identity. New Orleans Pride is used to create unity in the communities, bringing together the straight and homosexual communities and to create events that are family friendly and acceptable to all.[13]

These are not my words. The event was to be family friendly, a bringing together, and making the event acceptable to **ALL**.

The two of them did an interview for Gonola which shows they were very comfortable being open about their relationship. Josh Canfield and Reed Kelly maybe key ambassadors of the homosexual community, but they are not ambassadors of Christ. Other 'hip' churches are beginning to take on this same stance. This is dancing with the devil through dialogue.

'For many walk, of whom I have told you often, and now tell you even weeping, *that they are* the enemies of the cross of Christ' (Phil. 3:18).

Brian Houston's church is not built on repentant believers in Christ, but instead is centred around those that submit to his 'vision.' Brian's response was to 'love them', and 'assist them on their journey', instead of confronting them about their sin, and calling them to repentance. When ministers of the gospel lust for power, wealth, and popularity, the connection between the Christian faith and the cross is lost. The kingdom of the men supplants the kingdom of Jesus Christ.

The Roman church has had a long history of allowing the pagan to flock into their church and not change their creed or worship but to bring both into the church.

In his book *The History of Romanism*, John Dowling describes this downgrade:

It is not unlikely that this policy, in its incipient stage, commenced by a mistaken, but well-intended desire of some good men, like the apostle Paul, to 'become all things to all men,' that they might 'by all means save some.' Yet this apology can by no means be admitted as an excuse for the almost entire subversion of Christianity in the Romish communion, by the adoption of these heathen rites, ceremonies, and superstitions. . . . It was a step pregnant with disaster to the cause of genuine Christianity, when, as early as the third century some advocated the necessity of admitting a portion of the ancient ceremonies to which the people had been accustomed, for the purpose of rendering Christian worship more striking and captivating to the outward senses. —the Christianity of the state—to judge from the institutions of its public worship—seemed but little else than a system of Christianised Paganism. The rites and institutions, by which the Greeks, Romans, and other nations, had formerly testified their religious veneration for fictitious deities, were now adopted, with some slight alterations, by Christian bishops, and employed in the service of the true God.[14]

Does not this not confirm the same error and subsequent corruption in our time some 17 centuries later? Complete obeisance given to the great god of Numbers, and Entertainment.

Although Hillsong Church could be branded as evangelical, it is flavoured with the doctrines and methodology of Roman Catholicism. It is well known that baptismal regeneration is a fundamental article of Rome, and in the same way, it stands as a common practice within Hillsong to baptise whoever wishes to go under the water, regardless of their lifestyle; and somehow, this act implies salvation has come to the individual's soul.

Hillsong NYC, which 'welcomes' thousands each week, remains a popular watering hole for celebrities like Justin Bieber and star athletes like Kevin Durant, both reportedly baptised by Pastor Carl Lentz.[15]

To clarify, the scriptural view of baptism is not that it communicates the new birth but that it is the appointed means of signifying and sealing that new birth where it already is established, and yet unrepentant Kelly Reed has taken the baptismal plunge.[16] God's word is clear: marriage is between a man and a woman. The writings of the apostle Paul to the universal church are also clear. The word of God does not vacillate. So why can these and others be welcomed to attend, worship, and remain at Hillsong?

Doctrine and discipline have been removed from the church.

'The Lord hath purposed to destroy the wall of the daughter of Zion: . . . Her gates are sunk into the ground; he hath destroyed and broken her bars: her king and her princes are among the Gentiles: the law is no more; her prophets also find no vision from the Lord' (Lam 2:8–9).

We have come up with this loose idea that 'welcoming' anyone and everyone, and our position of 'the cross equals love' is our way to evangelise, and so provide an atmosphere for the curious and the casual instead of providing a place for the consecrated and the crucified.

Recently, the Royal Commission on Sexual Abuse in Australia has laid down its findings that determined that Brian Houston was complicit in his dealings over the abuse by his father, Frank Houston.[17] It would seem that Brian has been walking a moral tight rope for some time now.

- A. W. Tozer had already observed these pitfalls of compromising the gospel in his time and wrote:

The NEW cross encourages a new and entirely different evangelistic approach. The Evangelist preaches not contrasts, but similarities. He seeks to key into public interest by showing that Christianity makes no unpleasant demands; rather, it offers the same thing the world does, only on a higher level.[18]

Tozer compared the old cross with the new. He observed a great shift away from the standard method. 'If anyone desires to come after me, let him take up his cross.' The old cross had the purpose of putting a man to death. We want the new cross to offer dialogue and discourse. The new cross of convenience and compromise. With the new cross comes a new method: 'come to Christ'. As part of this new evangelism is come to the savior without any understanding as to why. For the new Christian under this new regime, everything remains as it was; he still lives for his own pleasure. The new cross still allows for enjoyment, though the fun is now on a higher plane morally if not intellectually.

The old cross made no compromise with the flesh. It spared nothing. It slew the whole man completely and utterly.

In coming to Christ, we do not bring our old life to live on a higher plane; instead we like 'the corn of wheat must fall to the ground and die'.

32

STRANGE FIRE IN THE NOSTRILS
OF AN ANGRY GOD

And Nadab and Abihu, the sons of Aaron, took either of them his censer and put fire therein, and put incense thereon, and offered strange fire before the LORD, which he commanded them not. And there went out fire from the LORD, and devoured them, and they died before the LORD.

—Lev. 10:1–2

I want to take some time in this section to clarify and lay down some principles from the Word of God why there has to be a distinction in the type of music we use in church regardless of Rick Warren's seeker-sensitive subjective theology.

'And Nadab and Abihu, the sons of Aaron, took either of them his censer and put fire therein, and put incense thereon, and **offered strange fire before the LORD, which he commanded them not.** And there went out fire from the LORD, and devoured them, and they died before the LORD. Then Moses said unto Aaron, This is it that the LORD spake, saying, **I will be sanctified in them that come near me, and before all the people I will be glorified.** And Aaron held his peace' (Lev. 10:1–4 KJV) (emphasis added).

Adam Clarke affirms the need to obey God's clear instructions.

Nadab and Abihu offered strange fire before the Lord, and their destruction by the fire of Jehovah is recorded as a lasting warning to all presumptuous worshippers and to all who attempt to model his religion, according to their own caprice, and to minister in sacred things without that authority which proceeds from himself alone. The imposition of hands whether of pope, cardinal, or bishop can avail nothing here. The call and unction of God alone can qualify the minister of the gospel of Jesus Christ.[1]

Ellicott suggests the sins of Nadab and Abihu were fourfold. They used their own censer, not a sanctuary utensil. They both offered it together whereas the incense was only to be offered by one. They presumptuously encroached upon the functions of the high priest (see Lev. 16:12– 13, Num. 17:11). The ordinary priests only burnt it on the golden altar in the holy place (Exod. 30:7–8) or on the brazen altar (see Lev. 2:2–3, 2:16). They offered the incense separate from the morning and evening sacrifice.[2]

'Strange fire' represents all the ideas and activities of men in ministry that emanate from their own proud hearts and minds.

'[34]And the LORD said to Moses: "Take sweet spices, stacte and onycha and galbanum, and pure frankincense with *these* sweet spices; there shall be equal amounts of each. [35]You **shall make of these an incense,** a compound according to the art of the perfumer, **salted, pure,** *and* **holy.** [36]And you shall beat of it **very fine,** and put some of it before the Testimony in the tabernacle of meeting make; **you shall NOT make any for yourselves,** according to its composition. It shall be to you holy for the LORD. [38]Whoever makes *any* like it, to smell it, he shall be cut off from his people" (Exod. 30:34–38) (emphasis mine).

God is a God of order. His creation shows that. In his dealings with Israel, his instructions were not haphazard but specific and detailed. This was the case with the making of incense, a compound according to the art of the perfumer. It was to be salted, pure, *and* holy.

In our relationships with others, we either do things that please or displease our loved ones. If I make my wife's tea too hot or too sweet, she is not pleased. It's same when approaching God. There is a specific way.

Salt represents purity. Salt was the opposite to leaven. It preserved from putrefaction and corruption and signified the purity that was necessary in the worship of God. The grace of God by Christ Jesus is represented under the emblem of salt (see Lev. 2:13, Mk. 9:49, Eph. 4:29, Col. 4:6). Without salt,[purity] no offering, sacrifice, and religious service can be acceptable in the sight of God.

Note, in addition, the incense was to be finely beaten to a powder or dust, very fine, ground together so that it could be used (v. 36).

Incense beaten to fine, to dust. There was to be no place for pride. No place for glorying in man. Hard as the saying is we are to be a broken people. Blessed are the poor in spirit . . . a contrite heart. You will not despise. Made humble, we receive grace in time of need; and by humility, we are fit for the Master's use. Unfortunately, instead of humility, in this last half century, we have seen the rise of the House of Saul.

Saul represents those who have put their trust in man, those who trust in an institution, in man's strength, in man's initiative, and in organisation. Saul believed that he was a servant of God, yet Saul walked in the flesh as well in the spirit. The Spirit of God would come upon Saul, yet we read of Saul's fall in 1 Samuel 13:7–13.

He happily waited seven days, the time set by Samuel; but Samuel did not come, and Saul's men began to leave him to it. So Saul offered up a burnt offering. Saul takes on the role of priest, and offers unlawful sacrifices. He makes rash oaths. He spares King Agag and all the best of the animals totally against the will of God. He was a lawless man.

How much of the church today have that same spirit of lawlessness? Sadly, we see King Saul is rejected by God (see 1 Sam. 15:11).

In the same way, men must understand this key lesson that they cannot introduce their own ideas and ways into God's work. Proud and undisciplined men have introduced new ways and methods in to the church without giving it the slightest consideration of their long-term impacts. The great tragedy is that all such acts in the church and every undisciplined addition is a hindrance to revival.

Richard Owen Roberts, in his discussions on preaching that hinders revival, laments, 'In recent years an almost unbelievable host of novelties have appeared. Many of them are now accepted as if they were a part of divine revelation.'[2]

Like Saul, we offer up a few lambs and King Agag a raft of musical talent for God, yet God has not required it of us.

Why?

'Rebellion is as the sin of witchcraft!' (1 Sam. 15:23). 'To obey is better than sacrifice' (1 Sam. 15:22)

We have kept alive our musical talents and presented them to God as some wonder gift. King Agag is still alive and well in our church services. We give God the type of service, worship, and good work we think is suitable and is obedience and expect God to accept it on OUR terms. This is like putting money in the offering from the selling of our old Black Sabbath albums!

God sets the rules for obedience, and we need to do our upmost to comply. Much of what the Western church does (including Hillsong) is worldly success, fame, and fortune, a world of 'Churchianity' filled with fleshy self-promotion.

The reality is partial obedience is not obedience at all.

Saul and his men obeyed God where it suited them. In his work, *Samuel the Prophet*, F B Meyer provides this reminder: 'We are prepared to obey the Divine commands up to a certain point, and there we stay. Just as soon as "the best and choicest" begin to be touched, we draw the line and refuse further compliance.'

'Throughout the Bible Amalek stands for the flesh, having sprung from the stock of Esau, who . . . sold his birthright. To spare the best of Amalek is surely equivalent to sparing some root of evil, some plausible indulgence; some favourite sin. For us, Agag must stand for that evil propensity, which exists in all of us, for self-gratification; and to spare Agag is to be merciful to ourselves, to exonerate and palliate our failures, and to condone our besetting sin' (F. B. Meyer, *Samuel the Prophet*, pp. 128,129).[3]

Saints, the Spirit of the Lord has departed the established church. It has run to a prosperity gospel, a gospel of health and wealth, name it and claim it, the Word of Faith movement. We put faith in flaky teeth-filling testimonies in a desperate attempt to move in faith and the things of God. The church has run to politicians, to Washington, to the halls of the Vatican, and to earthly power because it has no heavenly power.

All this is in the way of Saul in a spirit of self-will and disobedience!

And we also note where the incense was to be used in the tabernacle, where God would meet with His people. It was to be most holy. The incense was not be used for them.

The incense was to be holy for the Lord!

Incense is not inwards but upwards. It is aimed at reaching God, as it were, in the most intimate way. The salt of purity and simplicity is missing from our worship. Instead, we have allowed decay to come into esteem. The religion of God shaped, formed, and smeared over with the fashion of the world. They have thrust the true God from their minds (see Acts 7:39,40) producing for us a religion of rank idolatry. We visualise God into what we think he is. Thus, the idol of our mind is the grossest of sin. We show a brazen treachery by our impatience with things invisible and the eternal. We've turned aside to a multitude of things visible and temporal to satisfy our fleshly appetites. And left to ourselves, we reduce God to more or less something like we are. We worship God, but we are really worshipping self. God is reduced to manageable and comprehendible terms. He then over time has become a complete bore to us. Like the children of Israel, God to us is a mere concept!

Nadab and Abihu made the fatal error of bringing strange fire before the Lord, wrong worship, and as consequence were devoured by the fire of God. God who changes not and demands that those who come near Him regard Him as holy and that He be glorified before all the people. They received the outpouring of fire of God's holy anger on them. Yet God vindicated the worship of Elijah and Gideon.

Nowadays, the fear of the Lord is totally absent from the lives of professing Christians. With that, certain men and women of Christian fame have no qualms replacing the fire of God with their own fire. The fire which had just before sanctified the ministry of Aaron as well pleasing to God, now brought to destruction his two eldest sons because they did not sanctify Yahweh in their hearts, but dared to perform a self-willed act of worship. The two brothers offered incense with what is here called *strange,* common, or profane fire *not* taken from the altar. (Exod. 30:9). Nadab and Abihu disregarded the solemn instruction they had been given, and filled their censers with a fire that did not originate from the holy fire of the altar of burnt offering. They entered the tabernacle unprotected.[5]

Offering one's own fire as a sacrifice and service to God rather than being guided by God's principles amounts to nothing less than the works based sacrifice of Cain and the error of Saul. And God rejected them both (see Gen. 4:3–5, 1 Sam. 15:18–26).

This solemn story of sin and punishment is connected with the preceding chapter by a simple *and.* It would seem they 'offered strange fire' immediately after the fire from Jehovah had consumed the appointed sacrifice. Their sin was aggravated by the timing of their sin. By this example of contempt, the people would end up following in their fragrant folly.[6]

This is the same error as Simon the sorcerer, and Ananias and Sapphira. Thus modern-day sons of Aaron, Nadab (evangelicals) and Abihu (Pentecostals), offer up strange fire, dismissing the commands of God. They think they can use the holy things for their own ends. The point is these men's entire purpose is to serve God for their own interests. Most of Christianity is spiritually in a drunken stupor, unable to see a difference between the holy and the unholy, the sacred and the common: and as a result they are in transgression, much like Nadab and Abihu.

So many churches are so completely void of the true fire of God that if the Holy Spirit withdrew fully from them, most wouldn't realise for months, if at all.

Lance Goodall

We may think we can play games, but God is not mocked!

33
JESUS IS JUST ALL RIGHT

[22]But Jacob, you have not called on Me, because, Israel, you have become weary of Me. You have not brought Me your sheep for burnt offerings or honoured Me with your sacrifices.

—Isa. 43:22,23

On the other hand, we have other branches of Christendom whose religious expression is nothing more than simply going through the motions. Instead of profane fire, these saints have NO fire, which is equally destitute. Jesus is just all right. Religion, but no devotion. Duty but no desire. Can we please keep things moving along?

You may remember Aaron had two other sons, Eleazar and Ithamar (Lev. 10:16–20). This tribe of believers are just like Aaron's other sons who serve in the courts of the Lord as obedient saints; but worship has become to them meaningless, boring, a duty, an obligation, just a necessary burden that they must carry out to keep God on their side. God now makes them weary.

They are what I describe as insensitive or sensual saints.

Octavius Winslow, in his book on *Personal Declension and Revival of Religion in the Soul*, writes:

A state of secret departure from God may exist in connection with an outward and rigid observation of the means of grace; and yet there shall be no spiritual use of, or enjoyment in, the means. And this, it may be, is the great lullaby of his soul. Rocked to sleep by a merely formal religion, the believer is beguiled into the delusion that his heart is right, and his soul prosperous in the sight of God. Even more than this,—a declining believer may have sunk so deeply into a state of formality, as to substitute the outward and the public means of grace for a close and secret walk with God.[1]

Is this not our great malady today, this lethargy of soul even among God's elect? We are inoculated and drip fed by the world, the flesh, and the devil to remain in this zombie state. Spiritual declension has ever followed a departure from the purity of the faith. Look at the reformed churches of Europe; they departed from the pure doctrines of the Reformation, and what and where are they now? Scattered to the four winds. We must first realise our condition. Deep self-examination is a must.

As perfume is to us, so our worship is to be a sweet and pleasant thing to God. 'Then he [Aaron] shall take a censer full of burning coals of fire from the altar before the Lord, with his hands full of sweet incense beaten fine, and bring it inside the veil. And he shall put the incense on the fire before the Lord that the cloud of incense may cover the mercy seat that is on the Testimony, lest he die' (Lev. 16:12–13).

In Leviticus 2:1–11, God also speaks of a sweet aroma.

[1]And when any will offer a meat offering unto the LORD, his offering shall be of fine flour; and he shall pour oil upon it, and put frankincense thereon: . . . to be an offering made by fire, of a sweet savour unto the

LORD: [9]And the priest shall take from the meat offering a memorial thereof, and shall burn it upon the altar: it is an offering made by fire, of a sweet savour unto the LORD. [11]No meat offering, which ye shall bring unto the LORD, shall be made with leaven: for ye shall burn no leaven, nor any honey, in any offering of the LORD made by fire. Nor any honey;

Nor any honey in any offering to the LORD made by fire—honey was not allowed as it was used after the customs of the pagans. It was not allowed because it was a favourite sacrifice to pagan deities.[2]

Kyphi (or *cyphi*) is a compound incense that was used in ancient Egypt for religious and medical purposes. All recipes for kyphi mention wine, honey, and raisins. In *Isis and Osiris*, the historian Plutarch comments that Egyptian priests burnt incense three times a day: frankincense at dawn, myrrh at midday, and kyphi at dusk.[3]

Like leaven, honey was also used for fermentation. The smooth, sweet swelling words of a preacher will always destroy the work of God, for they fail to warn, and instead conceal the truth from the hearer (Prov. 26:28, Is. 30:10, 1Thess.2:5, 2Pet. 2:15). Foolishly we allow the leaven of doctrinal error, of sin, of pride, and whatever works is good for the church. These leaders have chosen the methods of Egypt the Lord did not ordain.

Much of today's' Christian music aims at lifting up the music itself. People come away loving the music and excited about the music rather than being focused on an all-powerful and Holy God!

Isaiah 43:24 shows God's grievance: 'Neither hast thou filled me.'

These days we are casual in our worship and fail to worship God with a right spirit. Often, we have served him with our sins and wearied him with our transgressions. Yes, while many put on a show of external worship, the heart of these worshippers are far from him. God himself is neglected.

'Wherefore the Lord said, Forasmuch as this people draw near *me* with their mouth, and with their lips do honour me, but have removed their heart far from me, and their fear toward me is taught by the precept of men' (Isa. 29:13 cf. Mk 7:6).

'Ye have wearied the Lord with your words. Yet ye say, Where have we wearied him? When ye say, Everyone that does evil is good in the sight of the Lord, and he delights in them; or, Where is the God of judgment?' (Mal. 2:16,17).

'Thou hast made me to serve with thy sins' (Is. 43:24).

Christians may be weary of God but he is weary of us—by our continuing in sin. You have made your service wearisome to God, as it's only out of duty and obligation to him, or what you think you can get out of serving God.

'Then he [Aaron] shall take a censer full of burning coals of fire from the altar before the Lord, with his hands full of sweet incense beaten fine' (Lev. 16:12).

Fire then means purity, fellowship, and communion with God.

Fire, was a symbol of divinity. It is a symbol of Yahweh Himself. God manifesting Himself in physical fire could show God's favour when, for example, He came and met with Abraham; and when he burnt up the sacrifice at Solomon's Temple, the fire sent down on Mount Carmel in response to his servant Elijah.

Of course, fire can be a destructive thing as the case of Sodom and Gomorrah.

All the Old Testament prophets foretold God's people would enter into the Lord's refiner's fire.

Malachi speaks of a fire to purge the sons of Levi. 'For he is like a refiner's fire, and like fullers soap: and he shall sit as a refiner and purifier of silver: and he shall purify the sons of Levi, and purge them as gold and silver, that they may offer unto the Lord an offering in righteousness' (Mal. 3:2–3).

From the very earliest periods, precious metals had mixes of gold and silver. With the advent of coinage, methods were invented to remove the impurities from the gold and so a range of purities could be made.[4] Silver was discovered after gold and copper about 4000 BCE when it was used in jewellery and as a medium of exchange.[5] Cupellation, according to *Wikipedia*, is the refining process in metallurgy, where metals are treated under very high temperatures controlled to separate noble metals, like gold and silver, from base metals like lead, copper, and zinc present in the ore.[6]

Only God's divine fire will be able to separate the unholy from the holy. This holy fire must come to the house of God! Judgement begins in the house of the Lord! The priests and Levites are always cleansed first then the people.

Verse 6 says, 'I the LORD do not change; therefore you, O sons of Jacob, are not consumed—you are not destroyed.'

Christians must allow the fire of God to enter their lives. Rather than being destroyed by the fire, we are to be purified, corrected, and cleansed by it. God's fire then will bring forth a true love and true service. The more willing we are to be conformed to the image of Christ, the less one will fear the full furnace of God's coming judgements.

John the Baptist said that Jesus would come to baptise his followers with

Lance Goodall

the Holy Spirit and with fire.

'John answered, saying unto them all, I indeed baptize you with water; but one mightier than I cometh, the latchet of whose shoes I am not worthy to unloose: he shall baptize you with the Holy Ghost and with fire: Whose fan is in his hand, and *he will thoroughly purge his floor*, and will gather the wheat into his garner; but the chaff he will *burn with fire unquenchable*' (Lk. 3:16,17) (emphasis added).

This reference to fire is for purification of sin as the Holy Spirit does His cleansing work of sanctification in the believer.

But notice the floor was to be purged. The chaff and grain are separated, the floor cleared.

The grain was indeed gathered, but then the remaining husks were gathered and piled together and set ablaze.

Those who are purged remain, but those who are still blown around by winds of doctrine are lost. Where is our fire today? Where is the grace of God? Where is the move of God? A contrite heart is the poker that keeps the coals aflame. Repentance is the acceptable sacrifice to God.

Genuine repentance is a sweet fragrance in the nostrils of God.

'The sacrifices of God are a broken spirit: a broken and a contrite heart, O God, thou wilt not despise' (Ps. 51:17).

The following are taken from a list by Richard Owen Roberts that indicates whether our souls are backslidden, and we have lost our fire:[7]

- When God is viewed in mere human terms, then our religion has been reduced to idolatry in the truest sense (see Ps. 50:21).

- When prayer is a chore and where its necessity has dropped away, we are in a backslidden state.

- When you are content with the current knowledge of God and His word that you have, then you are undone.

- When knowledge is just knowledge and not applied inwardly to the heart or correspondingly to the life, then can we even call ourselves born again?

- When church for us is dull and even boring, we are backslidden.

- When your church has fallen into spiritual decline, and the Word of God is no longer preached with any power, and yet you are unconcerned at this, then there is a desperate need for revival.

- When the plight of the souls of men and their pending perdition remains acute, and it does not grip us, we are surely backslidden.

- When the world still has an appeal to us in whatever measure, we again are in need of revival.

This list should break your heart and set a new flame to desire to be right again in the sight of God.

Martyn Lloyd-Jones wrote that revival is our only hope;

"I never shall forget, as long as I live, a phrase I once read in a little book on Protestantism written by the late Dean Inge, of all men, the Dean of St. Paul's Cathedral in London. I have forgotten everything in the book except the first sentence, and this is it: "Every institution tends to produce its opposite."

'It is commonplace to say that every period of true revival and reawakening is nothing but a return to the condition of the book of Acts. The only hope for the church is to get back to this, and the only hope for the world that is hurtling itself to hell is that the church should again become what she was in her origin.' (Martyn Lloyd-Jones *Setting Our Affections Upon Glory* Wheaton, IL: Crossway, 2013, pp. 49-51.)

Coming before God and His Son Jesus Christ, to stand in His presence should be with reverence, we should come before Him with humility, with brokenness, with clean hands, and with a pure heart God will not despise.

But instead, we have turned our worship into self-love, self-indulgence, self-congratulation, intemperance, swayed by the power of the passions, no longer our reason.

The western church offers worship as something to give, to get.

Christ's church has become a cesspool for mosh pits, mardi gras, carousels, and cabarets.

Here lies the problem with much of today's Contemporary Christian music. God is not first! Music and man are first!

There is the beautiful story of the woman who comes to anoint Jesus with expensive perfume:

Now when Jesus was in Bethany, in the house of Simon the leper, [7]There came unto him a woman having an alabaster box of very precious ointment, and poured it on his head, as he sat at meat. [8] But when his disciples saw it, they had indignation, saying, To what purpose is this waste? [9]For this ointment might have been sold for much, and given to the poor. [10]When Jesus understood it, he said unto them, Why trouble ye the woman? for she hath wrought a good work upon me. [11]For ye have the poor always with you; but me ye have not always. For in that she hath poured this ointment on my body, she did it for my burial. [13]Verily I say unto you, wheresoever this gospel shall be preached in the whole world, there shall also this, that this woman hath done, be told for a memorial of her. (Matt. 26:6–13)

So many of God's people see worship is just a waste. They are not like this woman. They say yes, we are happy with a few of your songs, but let's just get it over with. Many Christians would rather be about doing other things. Look what is preached to the whole world: her sacrifice, love, and humility.

It seems many will be more comfortable sweeping the streets of heaven than standing enjoying the presence of God. Oh, the travesty of it all!

34
KNOCKIN' ON HEAVEN'S DOOR

Then said Jesus unto them again, Verily, verily, I say unto you, I am the door of the sheep.

—Jn. 10:7

Masonic influence in our world today is no longer just a few grey- haired old men meeting in some dark, dank, musty building, shut in behind closed doors on a weeknight. Their dark hand now overshadows the whole world and, unbelievably, the church.

At Elevation Church Masonic symbology is displayed and marketed by the church leadership, the logo is made prominent on the outside of their church buildings, at every Sunday service you see it: a suspended pyramid inside a circle, centre stage embedded in their trendy perspex pulpit. Some have suggested this silver *Star Trek* looking logo marked not with a cross but with the church's caret-like logo (^) stands for elevating Christ. The bright sunburnt orange background would seem to be inspired from Pastor Steven Furtick's early church choir days when he was dyeing his hair the same vivid colour.[1]

Notice we are using this type of symbology now. The question is, whatever happened to the cross? Is this a symbol pointing to God as suggested or the elevation of man?

So what is it? The triangle within a circle is an ancient occult symbol dating back to the ancient civilisations. This is the symbol used at Steven Furtick's Elevation Church without apology!

Just as other occult symbols and beliefs have been used and modified by the secret societies and satanic groups over the centuries, this symbol has also seen the same transformation over the ages. But many will shake their head and say that it's just a unique design that the church came up with! Maybe, but listen to the following quote from mystic and writer

Manly P Hall: 'Symbolism is the language of the Mysteries. . . . By symbols men have ever sought to communicate to each other those thoughts which transcend the limitations of language. . . . In a single figure a symbol may both reveal and conceal, for to the wise the subject of the symbol is obvious, while to the ignorant the figure remains inscrutable' (Manly P Hall, *The Secret Teachings of All Ages*, p. 20).

Often, there will be several layers of meaning.

Most commonly, we find the symbol as a circumscribed triangle, which is an equilateral triangle within and touching a circle at each vertex, but there are other occasions when the triangle is placed well inside the circle and not touching the sides. Another later addition is the introduction of an object inside the triangle, which is more often than not circular in shape and representative of the Illuminati's God, commonly known as Satan or Iblis.

The upright triangle represents solar power or, in the Hellenic tradition, the element of fire. The ancient deities that were affiliated with the sun were done so in order to convey the symbolism of strength and power (e.g. the Egyptian gods Horus and Ra, or the goddess Isis). The association of power and the sun eventually finds its way into a symbol for male power. The lunar association with the goddess is tied into the inverted triangle.[2]

"The Lucis Trust (the name is a derivative of Lucifer) was founded by prolific occult writer Alice Bailey and is an offshoot of Helena Blavatsky's worldwide cult theosophy. **They formed a subsidiary group in 1937 called 'Triangles', and encouraged people to form 3 person triangle groups for 'meditation'.** . . through which the new incoming Aquarian energies can function, the new ideas spread, and the New World Order emerge".[3] [emphasis mine]

Former president George H. W. Bush echoed that goal. 'Out of these troubled times . . . a NEW WORLD ORDER can emerge,' he told Congress in a 1990 message aptly titled 'Toward a New World Order'. Back then, the opportune crisis was the Gulf War. It helped build public acceptance for the global management system, which had already begun to replace American rights with global rules.[4]

In other writings, Alice Bailey of the Lucis Trust said the coming New World Order is best symbolised by a triangle within a circle, with a dot inside the triangle.

Bailey described the point as representing the ruler of the spirit world Sanat (anagram for Satan). She went on to say that Sanat (Satan) is the entity who at the appointed time will emerge to RULE both the earth and humanity.

To go further regarding the triangle and dot, sometimes Satan is more clearly represented, such as in the case of using the commonly known Illuminati symbol the Eye of Providence or the All-Seeing Eye. It is a symbol deeply rooted in Masonic traditions and is generally depicted as a single eye placed centrally inside a triangle, and sometimes it is enhanced using beams of light to show it is 'illuminated'. The eye itself is representative of Satan, who his worshippers believe is all-powerful, omnipresent, and has the ability to see everything.[5]

The symbol of the triangle is commonly held to have a much deeper and esoteric meaning than the basic geometric shape we common folk see. Some in the Christian faith view the three sides of the triangle as the Holy Trinity. Ancient Egyptians believed the right-sided triangle represented their form of the Trinity with the hypotenuse being the child god Horus, the upright side being the sacred feminine goddess Isis, and the base is the male Osiris.

When talking about magic, the occultists believe a single triangle can be used as a method for summoning spirits. They'll stand inside of a circle while a spirit is conjured into a triangle during rituals to allow the demons to channel through from the underworld and appear within the triangle.[6]

The number three is a number of the divine, showing the union of male and female that create a third being. It's the number of manifestation, to make something happen.

Since the triangle ties into the number 3 and solar worship, we can see in alchemical and hermetic mystery schools that the sun is symbolised with the dot inside of the circle. You've seen this in corporate logos.

Not only is the symbol of the square and compasses seen on Masonic regalia in the lodge, but master Masons proudly wear it on Masonic clothing such as Masonic shirts and ties. The square and compasses are the most often-seen Masonic symbols.[7]

A triangle is Freemasonry symbolism for a representation of the higher power: the *G* in Grand Creator (there are several supposed words that this *G* represents, including *geometry*). The trowel used in Freemasonry symbolism is also triangular while the 32nd degree initiates are symbolised with the triangle. The symbols can be explained as the duality of our purpose in life. The compass represents the spirit realm, or our soul, and this is purposefully drawn *above* the square to show its importance.[8]

So why are these symbols referenced and marketed and on every door and above the entrance of a supposed evangelical church?

To explain, the *V* and the *A* are opposites and provide that reflective aspect of the 'as above, so below'. Alchemy sought to unite spirit (male/heaven) and matter (female/earth) through a royal union to create their synthesis in homunculus hermaphrodite, or lapis.

This is an alchemical metaphor or version of the generic process of spiritual rebirth.[9]

Freemason symbols are now commonplace in all works of life. But few are told the true or full meaning. The entry-level Mason is told the following.

In the lower degrees of Masonry, the initiate is told that this letter stands for God and for *geometry*, which the supreme architect of the universe used to design this wonderful cosmos. However, Masonic authors boldly state that the symbolism of the traditional square and compass of Freemasonry represents the heterosexual sex act.

Masonic author Albert Pike explains this fact to members of the 32nd degree: 'The Compass, therefore, is the Hermetic Symbol of the Creative Deity, and the Square of the productive Earth or Universe' (*Morals and Dogma*, Consistory: XXXII. Sublime of the Royal Secret p. 851). Therefore, the Masons look at the compass as the male phallus and the square as the female vulva. As you look at the Masonic emblem, you can see this referenced.[10]

Occultist and 33rd-degree Mason Arthur Waite quotes Eliphas Levi [also 33rd degree], telling us that the letter *G* stands for Venus, and that Venus' symbol is a lingam, a stylised phallus (Arthur Edward Waite, *The Mysteries of Magic: A Digest of the Writings of Eliphas Levi*, 1909, p. 217).

Albert Pike agrees. He states on pages 631–32 in *Morals and Dogma* that the monad [number one] is male, and the duad [number two] is female. Their sexual union produces the triad [number three], which is represented by the letter *G*, the generative principle.

Therefore, the number three is the number of fertile sexual union: one and two, male and female, joined together to form a third. This is pointed out in the book *Symbols and Their Hidden Meanings* by T. A. Kenner:

> By extension to the concept of fertility and birth, three is also the number of manifestation, of making something happen. It indicates creative power, moving energy, resolving the conflict of duality, growing and developing.[11]

Amazingly, Steven Furtick Pastor of Elevation Church has a T-shirt design with this very same masonic logo!

It's a shirt that has the square and compass on it with the light-blue diamond in the middle. He has used previously for baptisms at the church. It makes no sense, except these signs are for those who have ears to hear and eyes to see.

Another quote identifies the power of the pyramid.

A proponent of the new age and the secret brotherhood's plan for a New

World Order is Robert Hieronimus. In his book *America's Secret Destiny*, he traced the spiritual vision of America's founding fathers and the plan's eventual fruition in what we call the New World Order and the new age movement (both of which are synonymous).

He gives the crucial key to the power of the pyramid or triangle:

> The pyramid exemplifies the initiation stage. . . . It is the house of initiation, in which the candidate confronts the world of darkness and enters the world of spirit. By passing the tests of the elements, the candidate is initiated into the realm of higher consciousness.' (Hieronimus, p. 92)

After successfully completing the initiation process, the candidate is reborn and joins the single eye in the pyramid.

'On the reverse of our nation's Great Seal is an unfinished pyramid to represent human society itself, imperfect and incomplete. Above floats the symbol of the esoteric orders, the radiant triangle with its all-seeing eye."

Just like in Elevation's Church logo!

There is only one possible origin for these symbols, and that is the secret societies that came to this country 150 years before the Revolutionary War. There can be no question that the Great Seal was directly inspired by these orders of the human quest and that it set forth the purpose for this nation (Manly P Hall, *The Secret Destiny of America*, pp. 174,181).

A phrase like 'as above, so below' is used by writers and astrologers alike to explain why and how the world works.

To fully show the subtle but definite overtone in this church's architecture, I submit the following. It should also be said according to gnostic thinking that;

> The journey of the soul in search of light is represented by a pyramid, the top of it being the final destination. This is why the All-Seeing Eye appears at the top of a pyramid in Freemason symbolism.
>
> To that end, we have incorporated the eye in the triangle symbol within our cosmology to represent an important creative concept: The spark of divinity within all creation. This understanding is the true foundation of trust that the universe is necessarily perfect . . . that in the end . . . all will become clear.[12]

This quote from the Masonic Lodge indeed does make it very clear! The All-Seeing Eye, like many other Masonic symbols, has been borrowed from the past from the nations of antiquity: the Egyptian god Osiris.[13]

The symbology or the logo used by Elevation Church is clearly mystical, occult, and Egyptian in origin and shows they are on a dangerous path. The divine spark in all of us as explained in these ancient texts is subverting the way of the cross for our salvation, and ultimate glorification is ONLY through God's son, our Creator who is distinct and separate from his Creation, and our mediator Christ Jesus.

Like any Masonic Lodge, all lodge members have a code or value system to follow. Although Elevation has its 'beliefs' link on its website, they are not much more than evangelical 101 written on a cheap restaurant napkin.

The Elevation code consists of ten values or codes. Or was it twelve?[14] Space doesn't allow too much comment on these edicts from Furtickville. We will discuss one or two here.

First is Jesus is the centre. It's about integrated priorities.

The above code is the first one listed on Furtick's church website. It is one of those subtle mission statements to subvert the cause of Christ and His gospel without you realising it. Why do I say that? For a start, integrated priorities is the language of the corporate or defence community. Jesus is the centre is nothing more than rhetoric, a flag, a banner, a rally call, to commit to Furtick's selfish ends. Being the centre isn't necessarily the same as being first. A mum can be the centre of the household—running the kids to school, grabbing groceries, balancing the budget, getting to work,—yet she may still not be first. Everyone in the family may take her for granted. Although my life may revolve around the Lord Jesus, he still may not be first. In other words, for the folk at Elevation, Jesus is just a point of reference, a focal point, a product, a way of directing one's own goals and aspirations.

As for integrated priorities, there is only one priority, which is to 'seek first the kingdom of God and His righteousness'. In a business setting, Pope Francis has highlighted the need for treating climate change and developmental objectives as integrated priorities.[15]

In other words, you give a little, and we will give a little. We will reduce emissions as long as there's still a market for coal, oil, and gas. Integration is a combining or coordinating of separate elements to provide a harmonious, interrelated whole. But is this Christianity? We are not in business with God. We are not a shareholder. The relationship should be one based on the lordship of Christ. It's different. We come under a clause of ownership. It's a takeover. It's His kingdom not ours. 'We have been bought with a price', it's not a synergistic partnership. There is nothing integrated about being a slave' (see 1 Cor. 6:20,7:23).

'But there were false prophets also among the people, even as there shall be false teachers among you, who privily shall bring in damnable heresies, even denying the Lord that bought them, and bring upon themselves swift destruction' (2 Pet. 2:1).

As part of promoting this code across the church, Elevation produced its very own kids' colouring book. One image depicts the Elevation congregation, looking up at Pastor Furtick onstage. The text reads, 'We are united under the visionary'; and on the bottom, it reads the even more damning quote: 'Elevation Church is built on the vision God gave Pastor Steven. We will protect our unity in supporting His Vision.' Pastor Steven preaches his propaganda to the little ones while at the same time soft peddling his 'unity' message to the adults. Brilliant!! Let me translate what was just said here. 'We are united in our unity under our prophet Pastor Furtick, and we will not question him.'

This is sounding very 'Koresh' like to me. This is the power of the Christian celebrity—a figure so highly 'elevated' that none question him, his vision, and the cult-like status he receives. This is dangerous religion. It's evangelical brainwashing. This is not Christianity but cult indoctrination. One further thing to note about this code of unity.

Steven Furtick's unity statement is the evangelical equivalent of the Vatican's own version: unity at all costs.

Elevation Church is caught up in beguiling Masonic Illuminati Satanic Symbology.

The leadership and congregation at Elevation church clearly MISS the significance.

The great symbol of Horus has been embossed into the church's perspex pulpit and is placed on the doors and entrance at Elevation Church for all to see. I ask again, where is the cross?

The above evidence is to show this church is 'marked' as one of Satan's

Lance Goodall

Masonic temples.

35
GLORIOUS RUINS

There was in the synagogue a man with an unclean spirit, and he cried out, 'What have you to do with us, Jesus of Nazareth? Have you come to destroy us? I know who you are: the Holy One of God.'

—Mk. 1:24

Hillsong Live has released their 22nd live-recorded album, *Glorious Ruins*, on 2 July 2013.

Recorded for the first time live in two locations—London, England, and Sydney, Australia—*Glorious Ruins* is consistent with Hillsong's passion to promote *themselves* around the WORLD. According to their own marketing material, the live album offers the church a NEW ERA of worship anthems that will cross multiple denominational and cultural boundaries.[1]

A new era of music from Hillsong is to be marketed around the world. There you have it in their own words: Hillsong is promoting a New World Era (order) by saturating the world with their music on the airwaves.

Brian Houston, as part of his promotion of the album at the time, said, 'Ruins can speak of crushing defeat or perhaps of something abandoned, but the good news today is that the ruins come to life,' explained senior pastor of Hillsong Church Brian Houston. 'Through Jesus Christ, what we look at is ruins that become glorious.'[2]

He made similar comments in May of that year after the devastating twisters hit parts of Oklahoma:

> This life can be so unpredictable; there is devastation and sadness wherever we turn. Yet, what this new song 'Glorious Ruins' declares is that out of the devastation, out of the heartache and pain—that when we are at the end of ourselves, we can cling to the promise of God, and find courage in His presence.[3]

The following is an outline by Brian Houston, as part of introducing or explaining the new Hillsong album *Glorious Ruins* in 2013.

BH: Still my hope will cling to your promise . . . Let my heart find strength in your presence. Let the ruins come to life.

No, he's not quoting scripture in some modern paraphrase. He's quoting from a verse in the song 'Glorious Ruins', the NEW song from the album of the same name. And isn't this half the problem, that Hillsong's doctrine is bound up in their lyrics, and not on the word of God.

BH: 'Glorious Ruins' is what this song is called.

Brian's little sermonette comes to a grand crescendo, 'And Jesus who left behind God's glory to taste death for you and I . . . [He] became "ruined glory" . . . and rather than remaining "ruined glory", Jesus became glorious ruins . . . Ah . . . Glorious ruins.'

C. S. Lewis described mankind as 'glorious ruins' because of our fallen nature, but that hardly applies to the Son of God.[4]

Listen to this description of our plight by the 17th-century English puritan John Howe:

> The stately ruins of this living temple still bear this doleful inscription over their portal—here God once dwelt. Enough still appears of the admirable form and structure of the soul of man to show that the divine presence did sometimes reside in it: more than enough of vicious deformity to proclaim that he is now retired and gone. The altar is overturned and the candlestick is broken: and in place of the sacred incense, with its clouds of rich perfumes, there is a poisonous and hellish vapour continually rising up. . . . Behold the desolation Behold the ruins of the fall! The faded glory, the darkness, the disorder, the impurity, the decayed state in all respects of this temple too plainly show that the great inhabitant is gone.[5]

There is an old hymn that exemplifies these thoughts called 'Come Ye Sinners' written by Joseph Hart (1759) (abridged):

Come, ye thirsty, come, and welcome,

God's free bounty glorify

True belief and true repentance,

Every grace that brings you nigh.

Come, ye weary, heavy-laden,

Lost and *ruined* by the fall

If you tarry till you're better,

You will never come at all.

So it makes perfect sense to consider man's state once perfect but now fallen, as glorious ruins. But the obvious question at this point is, is Brian referring to Christ's humanity or nature as fallen? We will assume he believes in the Lord Jesus as divine and move on. But the concerns is Brian is known for his blundering and off-the-cuff comments, and this is where things begin to come unstuck, just more of his presumptuous pontificating, and he gets it completely wrong.

You see God's wrath was gloriously meted out on Christ. He was bruised and beaten beyond recognition. Gloriously marred and broken, but he was never left in ruins.

BH does apply the ruins to our lives: 'Wherever you are facing ruins, believe God that when He brings the ruins to life, He won't just bring you back to where you were, but He will bring something that never was.'[6] It seems at this point, Brian seems to be back on track.

As an aside, worldwide, there seems to be a growing trend to take derelict and ruinous properties and build a new structure that rises gleaming, like a phoenix from ashes. New, comfortable, and exciting homes that arise from a heap of ruins would seem like a hopeful metaphor for our time.[7] But the point is the work of God is not taking the old and making it better. Behold all things are *new* according to biblical principles (2 Cor. 5:17).

The Lord Jesus did not experience death and decay as we mortals. We covered some of this in the previous chapter, 'The Cross and the Phoenix', dealing with the 2011 Hillsong album *Aftermath*.

The Lord Jesus wasn't raised glorious ruins but rather as the King of

Kings and Lord of Lords; why because ruins as referenced by Brian in his message is connected with sin, or 'paradise lost', which applies to our condition, not God's.

It seems the Lord Jesus is no longer the glorious king, but glorious ruins?

Verses in the Bible tell us plainly: 'And from Jesus Christ, who is the faithful witness, and the first begotten of the dead, and the prince of the kings of the earth' (Rev. 1:5).

'Fear not; I am the first and the last: [18] I am he that liveth, and was dead; and, behold, I am alive for evermore, Amen; and have the keys of hell and of death' (Rev. 1:17,18).

This church is blown around by every wind of doctrine, so no wonder our Lord is maligned and made just an example to follow, like some Marvel book hero. Jesus may as well be a man, simply a common carpenter

The Lord Jesus is the KING OF GLORY, not the King of Ruins, or even Glorious Ruins. He is the King of Kings and Lord of Lords.

Who God raised from the dead and has given a name above every name; that at the name of Jesus every knee should bow (see Phil 2:9, Eph. 1:21).

And that he was buried, and that he rose again the third day according to the scriptures (1 Cor. 15:4).

To validate my concerns, the following are some of the lyrics from the ill-fated song:

Lance Goodall

Glorious Ruins

Chorus

Let the ruins come to life

In the beauty of Your Name

Rising up from the ashes

God forever You reign[7]

What on earth is this chorus about: us or the Lord Jesus? If this is about Jesus, then they are now well and truly in dangerous waters! But I can only assume it's a reference to our lives apart from the fact that he did make reference to Jesus being glorious ruins in the introduction on the album DVD.

'For you will not leave my soul in sheol; NEITHER will you allow your Holy One to see CORRUPTION' (Ps. 16:10).

In John 11:25 we read, 'Jesus said unto her, I am the resurrection, and the life: he that believeth in me, though he were dead, yet shall he live.'

Yet this is Brian Houston's version of events: 'The most powerful example of this in the Bible is the death and resurrection of God's own Son. He emptied Himself of the glory of God, came humbly to earth, allowed his body to be beaten and killed, and 'LAY IN RUINS', until He was resurrected from the dead.'[8]

I think I know what he means. But my rebuttal is we know that Christ's body was raised to life on the *third day* according to the scriptures. This is what is glorious! The Lord's resurrection—it is not the human idea of life out of death (circle of life) but life from the dead. There is a difference.

Some would ask, why are you labouring this point? Brian didn't mean anything from this song. Maybe not, but this convoluted idea that the Lord Jesus was like Lazarus, his body left lying decaying in the grave, is odd to say the least. For it to lie in ruins (stinking and in putrefaction) means his body must have stayed in the grave for at least four days or more. Why? Because the body starts to break down and decay and decompose at this point. This goes against Jesus's own words prophesying he would raise himself up after three days. (See John 2:19)

Remember Lazarus? His body, according to his sister, would stink out the tomb because Jesus came to the entrance to the tomb on the fourth day! (See John 11:39)

So if Jesus's body did end up in the tomb left to LIE IN RUINS, left to decay, as Brian suggests, was it four days, four weeks, four months, or four years?

Hillsong's music is now contradicting the scriptural record. Glorious Ruins is a mythological fable made to sound like biblical truth.

Christ was raised up, quickened from the dead.

And so it is written, the first man Adam was made a living soul; the last Adam was made a quickening spirit (1 Cor. 15:45). A quickening spirit, not glorious ruins.

In other words, Christ is no longer flesh and blood. He wasn't just resuscitated but was raised in a whole new form. After his resurrection, He received a heavenly body, not just an earthly body brought to life. His body now dwells within a new realm. We pass over these things too lightly. Remember him showing himself to Thomas by simply appearing in the room (Jn.20:26), eating fish with the disciples (Lk. 24:38-43), walking with the disciples on the road to Emmaus (Lk. 24:30,31), and then disappearing from their sight. These facts make Brian Houston's fabled mythology all the more embarrassing. Our view of Jesus Christ is decidedly deficient, indeed we worship a mortal messiah, a dumb-downed deity.

Many an Old Testament reference makes it clear that a city or region or civilisation, when left in ruins, is often destroyed and is never rebuilt.

'Then you shall gather all its booty into the middle of its open square and burn the city and all its booty with fire as a whole burnt offering to the LORD your God; and it shall be a ruin forever. It shall never be rebuilt' (Deut. 13:16).

The Bible tells us that the city of Damascus, Syria may soon be destroyed as Isaiah 17:1and Jeremiah 49:24-27 predicts. The destruction of Damascus Syria is the next event to take place on the prophetic calendar. A Turkish led invasion into Syria, the destruction of Damascus, and a Turkish led invasion into Israel will put us on the brink of the Tribulation.

The destruction of Damascus currently played out may be a prelude to the battle of Gog and Magog!

As we close, Brian Houston should be on *Candid Camera*. His exegesis is complete tomfoolery. Hillsong should be laughed out of town and declared a cult by all of Christendom! He is too busy pleasing the crowd to notice the plethora of Pentecostal platitudes he preaches.

Hillsong, having left the Bible as its foundation long ago, now preaches a phony phoenix pagan philosophy, making it into some biblical metaphor of resurrection, hope, and life.

The idea reminds me of the monastery of Saint Benedict of Nursia in Monte Cassino, Italy. Due to its hilltop advantage, it was ordered to be bombed by the Western coalition so that German soldiers could not use it as a fortress. On 15 February 1944, the abbey was almost completely destroyed in a series of heavy American-led air raids. After the war, it was later rebuilt. When you rebuild, you clear away all the rubble and debris. A building is not raised on old ruins. Only the foundations remain.

Thus Glorious Ruins is not based on Christian theology, but an ancient idea of birthing order out of chaos.

In the occult world, the phoenix bird is a representation of Lucifer and his Antichrist.

Interestingly, Luciferians describe their future world leader in similar 'copycat' terms to the biblical picture of the Lord Jesus. The Antichrist is portrayed as someone who seemingly rises from the ashes of death and defeat. I find it disturbing that this album Glorious Ruins is their (22) twenty-second release.

If you know anything about numbers and the occult, then you will know. Houston, we have a problem!

36

HOUSTON, WE HAVE A PROBLEM!

For my people have committed two evils; they have forsaken me the fountain of living waters, and hewed them out cisterns, broken cisterns, that can hold no water.

—Jer. 2:13

There is an old saying 'ALL Publicity is good publicity', which must be the premise that drives Brian Houston when he spoke in 2014 and aligned the God of the Bible with Islam's Allah.

Brian Houston addressed his congregation with these words in March 2014:

> How do you view God? In a desert there's two types of birds: there's vultures and there's hummingbirds. One lives off dead carcasses, rotting meat. The other lives off the beautiful, sweet nectar in a particular flower on a particular desert plant. In the same desert, they both find what they're looking for.
>
> Do you know take it all the way back into the Old Testament and the Muslim and you, <u>we actually serve</u>

the same God. Allah to a Muslim, to us Abba Father God. And of course through history, those views have changed greatly. But lets make sure that we view God through the eyes of Jesus, the grace of the Lord Jesus Christ, the beauty of a Saviour, the loving open inclusive arms of a loving God. And that way we'll lead out of that and you'll be purposeful about your leadership and you'll draw people just like the Lord Jesus always does through the power of the Holy Spirit.[1]

Just so we don't miss what Brian Houston said, here it is again:

'We actually serve the same God. Allah to a Muslim, to us Abba Father God.'

Much of the following section is taken from a well-written article by Christine Pasciuti, although I had written on the issues with Rick Warren and Chrislam back in August 2013 in a two-part article called 'Desiring God or Desiring Influence'.[2]

A number of Christian leaders today are attempting to bridge the gap between Muslims and Christians. While perhaps well intentioned, the foundation of this new mantra, often called Chrislam, is that we all worship the same God.[3]

At President Obama's inaugural invocation in 2009, Pastor of Orange County, California's Saddleback Church Rick Warren cited several names for Jesus when leading the audience into the Lord's Prayer: 'I humbly ask this in the name of the one who changed my life, Yeshua, Isa, Jesus [Spanish pronunciation], Jesus, who taught us to pray.'

While the context of Rick Warren's comments suggest he was attempting to bridge the gap of different names used for Jesus, his efforts show how easy it is for our words to cause confusion. To the Muslim, Isa of the Quran is very different than the Jesus of the Bible. The Quran's Isa is not an historical figure. His identity and role as a prophet of Islam is based solely on supposed revelations to Muhammad over half a millennium after the Jesus of history lived and died.

Islam's Quran does not portray the divinity of Jesus Christ or claim Him to be the only begotten Son of God, Messiah, God in human flesh. It does not state that Jesus died on the cross for our sins and resurrected from the dead. Islam denies the true gospel of Christianity—the core reason Jesus came to earth. This fundamental gap between Christians and Muslims cannot and should not be bridged or smoothed over with a watered-down doctrine for the sake of 'brotherly love'.

The Quran's Isa is not an historical figure. His identity and role as a prophet of Islam is based solely on supposed revelations of Muhammad!

We increasingly hear that Christianity and Islam 'share' Jesus, that he belongs to both religions. So also with Abraham. There is talk of the West's 'Abrahamic civilization' where once people spoke of Judeo-Christian civilization. This shift of thinking reflects the growing influence of Islam.

Islam regards itself not as a subsequent faith to Judaism and Christianity but as the primordial religion, the faith from which Judaism and Christianity are subsequent developments. In the Quran, we read that Abraham 'was not a Jew, nor a Christian, but he was a monotheist, a Muslim' (Âl 'Imran 3:66). So it is Muslims and not Christians or Jews who are the true representatives of the faith of Abraham to the world today (Al-Baqarah 2:135).

While housing the offices for Christians and Muslims for Peace, Robert Schuller, pastor of Crystal Cathedral, began the movement towards softening the well-known words of Jesus in John 14:6: 'I am the way, the truth, and the life. No one comes to the Father except through Me.'

He told an imam of the Muslim American Society that 'if he came back in 100 years and found his descendants Muslims, it wouldn't bother him'.[4]

Brian McLaren—founding pastor of non-denominational Cedar Ridge Community Church in Baltimore, Washington—encouraged his congregation and other Christians through his blog to participate with Muslims in a Ramadan fast, which celebrates the month the Quran was supposed to be sent down.

Another leader in the emerging church movement, Dr Tony Campolo, says he is not convinced that Jesus lives only in Christians, reasoning that an Islamic brother who has fed the hungry and clothed the naked clearly has a personal relationship with Christ. Only he doesn't know it.

Ironically, a side-by-side comparison of the Bible and the Quran would show that the two faiths are the exact opposite.[5]

But whatever Islam claims, it does not believe in the Lord Jesus.

It asserts that Jesus was only one of God's endless prophets or messengers and not God's only begotten Son. Muslims adamantly reject the idea that Jesus is the Son of God. The Quran repeatedly emphasises that Jesus Christ is not the literal Son of God:

> Certainly they disbelieve who say: Surely Allah is the third (person) of the three; and there is no god but the one Allah, and if they desist not from what they say, a painful chastisement shall befall those among them who

disbelieve. (Quran 5:73)

They say: Allah hath begotten a son! Glory be to Him! He is self-sufficient! His are all things in the heaven and on the earth. No warrant have ye for this. Say ye about Allah what ye know not! (Quran 10:68)

Say 'Praise be to Allah', who begets no son, and has no partner in (His) dominion. Nor [needs] He any to protect Him from humiliation. Yea, magnify Him for His greatness and glory. (Quran 17:111)

Further, that He may warn those [also] who say: Allah hath begotten a son. (Quran 18:4)

It is not befitting to [the majesty of Allah] that He should be get a son. Glory be to Him when He determines a matters, He only says to it 'be' and it is. (Quran 19:35)

They say: '[Allah] Most Gracious has begotten a son!" Indeed ye have put forth a thing most monstrous! (Quran 19:88)

Thus, the Quran (Koran) emphatically denies that Jesus Christ is the Son of God—a teaching that Jesus Himself just as emphatically affirmed (Jn. 3:16–18, 10:36–38). Thus, the Christian view of Jesus Christ as God's literal Son is blasphemy to the Muslim.

Who is a liar but he that denies that Jesus is the Christ? He is antichrist, that denies the Father and the Son. Whosoever denies the Son, the same has not the Father: (but) he that acknowledges the Son has the Father also. (1 Jn. 2:21,22)

Meanwhile, Pope Francis has also been aggressively courting Muslims. The following quote from him comes from remarks that he made during his very first ecumenical meeting in 2013:

> I then greet and cordially thank you all, dear friends belonging to other religious traditions; first of all the Muslims, who worship the one God, living and merciful, and call upon Him in prayer, and all of you. I really appreciate your presence: in it I see a tangible sign of the will to grow in mutual esteem and cooperation for the common good of humanity. The Catholic Church is aware of the importance of promoting friendship and respect between men and women of different religious traditions. I wish to repeat this: promoting friendship and respect between men and women of different religious traditions—it also attests the valuable work that the Pontifical Council for interreligious dialogue performs.[6]

Did you catch that?

Apparently Pope Francis (like Houston) believes that Catholics and Muslims worship the same God. It really doesn't matter what you believe! Notice he said of religious traditions, not faiths or dogmas, because traditions can ultimately change.

More recently, Francis made the following statement about Muslims: 'We must never forget that they 'profess to hold the faith of Abraham, and together with us they adore the one, merciful God, who will judge humanity on the last day.'[7]

In a recentpapal interview given to *La Croix*, a French Catholic newspaper, Pope Francis compared the Christian Great Commission—

Jesus Christ's call for all Christians to spread the gospel—with the Islamic concept of jihad: what is interpreted (and practised) notably by the international terrorist group ISIS as the 'holy war'.

While talking about Islamophobia in the midst of the refugee crisis in Europe, the Pope – referring to ISIS – spoke of the idea of conquest in Islam, according to the *Washington Post*.

"It is true that the idea of conquest is inherent in the soul of Islam. However, it is also possible to interpret the objective in Matthew's Gospel, where Jesus sends his disciples to all nations, in terms of the same idea of conquest."[8]

This Jesuit pope showed his true colours when speaking in reference to even one of his own being massacred, a French catholic priest whose throat was slit in the name of Allah, is somehow comparable to Christian acts of violence.[9] Why is he defending ISIS?

The Jesus of the gospels is the base upon which Christianity developed. By Islamising Him and making of him a Muslim prophet who preached the Quran, Islam destroys Christianity and takes over all its history. It does the same to Judaism.

This final act of the Muslim Isa reflects Islam's apologetic strategy in relation to Christianity, which is to deny the Yeshua of history and replace him with a facsimile of Muhammad so that nothing remains but Islam.[10]

When God spoke to Moses saying; "I *am* the God of thy father, the God of Abraham, the God of Isaac, and the God of Jacob.", what was He conveying to Moses? The answer is clear that after some 400 years, Ishmael is no longer in the picture.

Rather than trying to pretend we believe the same things, a frank and honest discussion about our differences would seem to make much more sense.

It would appear that you can still watch Brian Houston's actual message in full on GOD TV.[11] Brian seems to be happy quietly endorsing these ideas from the back of the pack. Even the youngest of wolves gets to enjoy a morsel, though he does little.

I highly recommend the site called *Answering Islam* website for an honest and intelligent conversation on the key differences between the Bible and the Quran because obviously there are plenty.

We have tinkered with the truth so much in the last 70 years that most Christians have little knowledge of their Bibles and who Jesus is.

We desperately need to get back to the truth.

37
WOULD I LIE TO YOU

Who hath ascended up into heaven, or descended? Who hath gathered the wind in his fists? Who hath bound the waters in a garment? Who hath established all the ends of the earth? What is his name, and what is his son's name, if thou canst tell?

—Prov.30:4

A few days later, after the 'we worship the same god' furore blew up and exploded in Brian's face on social media, Brian explained what he meant to say or did say on Twitter, 'Recently there have been false claims on social media that I believe Muslims and Christians worship the same God. This is incorrect. Those propagating these false statements have taken one sentence from an entire message out of context.'

He continues, 'I realize that some critics WANT to believe their interpretation, but my prayer is that reasonable people will take my comment in context, accept my acknowledgement that I did not this sentence as I intended, and judge me on 40 years of pointing people to Jesus, not one sentence.'

Further down, he adds this particular clarification.

The ONE sentence that critics are drawing huge conclusions from was clearly a (clumsy) way of me explaining that though both Christians and Muslims believe they serve the God of Abraham, they are very different entities or deities in both nature and action. [1]

Ah, there you go. That is his qualification or clarification right there. What he said is correct, but it is a complete back flip from the earlier tweet, where he is suggesting that ones on social media are spreading insidious statements. No surprise really! Let's shoot the messenger.

The reason Brian Houston's statement has so many concerned is its questionable entry into a topic on purpose in the first place, a statement that has nothing whatsoever to do with his sermon.

If the sermon is about being useful for the Master's use, why even mention Allah? He had been expounding in the previous several minutes on his favourite topic: purpose. In his statement above, he explains it a lot better, but that's way too late. But to be clear, he didn't make any type of comparison in the actual sermon at the time, saying that if you are a Muslim, your view of God will be different. He only does that in the tweets as a way of clarifying, and this is a day or two later.

But is this good enough?

In Old Testament times, Nabonidus (555–539 BC), the last king of Babylon, built Tayma, Arabia, as a centre of moon god worship. Segall stated, 'South Arabia's stellar religion has always been dominated by the Moon-god in various variations.' Many scholars have also noticed that the moon god's name Sin is a part of such Arabic words as Sinai, the 'wilderness of Sin' etc. When the popularity of the moon god waned elsewhere, the Arabs remained true to their conviction that the moon god was the greatest of all gods. While they worshipped 360 gods at the kasbah in Mecca, the moon god was the chief deity. Mecca was, in fact, built as a shrine for the moon god.[2]

Islam is basically polytheistic in origin.

Muslims claim that Allah is the god of the Bible and that Islam arose from the religion of the prophets and apostles. Islam is refuted by solid overwhelming archaeological evidence. Islam is nothing more than a revival of the ancient moon-god cult. It has taken the symbols, the rites, the ceremonies, and even the name of its god from the ancient pagan religion of the moon god. As such, it is sheer idolatry and must be rejected by every born-again Christian.[3]

Here's the quote again:

'**Take** it **all** the **way** back into the Old **Testament** and the Muslim and **you, we** actually serve the same God. **Allah** to a Muslim, to us Abba Father God.' — Brian Houston

I'm sorry, but this is not misconstruing his words to say something else. They are here in black and white. This is quite different from his public relations stunt, saying as way of clarifying 'both Christians and Muslims believe they serve the God of Abraham'. But God who appeared to Moses said, 'I am the God of Abraham Isaac and Jacob.' He didn't include the name of Ishmael.

'He starts out his clarification [above], by saying there have been false claims on social media that I believe Muslims and Christians worship the same God. That is incorrect.'

Then he goes on to say it was taken out of the context of the whole message.

He seems to clarify it better in a tweet. Brian said on Twitter that what came out is not what He meant. He meant that Islam descends from one of Abraham's sons, Ishmael. Brian is clearly trying to back away from his comment made in the sermon.

The only **link** between Isaac and Ishmael is they **have** the same natural father, not the same god or centre of worship, not even the same **mother.** A big difference, **don't you** think?

And if we know our Bibles, we find that from out of the loins of righteous Lot, two separate nations came forth namely the Moabites (Gen. 19:37) and the Ammonites (Gen. 19:38). Although Lot was a nephew of Abraham, these two nations from Lot became a stumbling block to Israel later on. Instead of being blood relatives, they became sworn enemies!

It should be noted that Esau Jacob's brother also became an opposing nation, the Edomites, the Palestinian people of today. (Gen 36: Josh. 24:4)

So much for family ties!

One blogger helps to show the decline in biblical literacy. He explains:

> I have always warned against Charismatic leaders who have stopped sharing from the scriptures. One of them is Brian Houston, who is head pastor in Hillsong, Australia.
>
> When you stop sharing the scriptures, you replace the Word of God with stories. And you add human wisdom. Somehow you start to use the idea of a 'god' to fit into your own thinking and philosophies. Very often this kind of story-telling also falls short of basic historical facts related to world history. This shallow and quite fraudulent presentation of the similarities of Islam and Christianity falls into this category.

> The Koran is written 1500 years after the Hebrew Bible.
> So up to 620 A.D, there were no Muslims walking on
> the face of the Earth. Not even one.[4]

Another answer to Brian's tweet is the following.

The truth is that the term Arab designates peoples of diverse ethnic origins who are united only by the Arabic language and culture. The seed of Ishmael represents only a very small component of the genetic pool of the Arabic people. Let me explain.

In Arabic and Hebrew, the term *arab* means *nomad* (synonymous with Bedouin peoples). According to the Old Testament, the earliest inhabitants of the peninsula descended from Joktan (Gen. 10:26–29), a descendent of Shem (whence the term Semite). Later, the area was also settled by Abraham's sons through his wife Keturah (Gen. 25:1–4), the twelve sons of Ishmael (Gen. 25:13–16), and finally the sons of Esau (Gen. 36:1–19)—all descendants of Abraham (also Semitic). Clearly, Ishmael's offspring represent just a small fraction of the Arab peoples.[5]

The plain fact is Mohammed expressed his ignorance about his ancestors prior to or up to his seventeenth ancestor is another relevant aspect.

Muslims who lived in Mohammed's own time fabricated genealogies in an attempt to connect Mohammed to the descendants of Ishmael. But Mohammed himself rejected all of these false genealogies. Regarding Mohammed's own rejection of the false genealogies, Amr bin al-As an arab military commander wrote:

> Mohammed genealogized himself regarding his ancestors until he reached al-Nather bin Kinaneh, then he said, 'anyone who claimed otherwise or added further ancestors, has lied.'[6]

By his own confession, Mohammed declared that neither he nor anyone else, knew about his ancestors beyond al-Nather bin Kinaneh. Nather bin Kinaneh is the seventeenth ancestor in the genealogy Mohammed recognised as true.

When we look at the ancestors of Mohammed, it's reasonable to estimate 30 years for each generation of the seventeen ancestors of Mohammed. Therefore, we can conclude that Mohammed knew about the genealogy of his tribe as far back as about 510 years.[7]

Ibn Ishaq claims the Ishmaelites lived in Mecca during this period and gives details about their history when Mohammed himself said that nobody knew about his relatives prior to his seventeenth or twenty-first ancestor.[8]

But Mecca was not even in existence during this period.

Around the time of the Arab conquest of the Middle East and North Africa (seventh century), many of the conquered countries eventually adopted Arabic as their mother tongue, as well as Islam. There was also a certain amount of intermarriage. So the term Arab has a strictly cultural and linguistic connotation. To conclude, while some Arabs of the Arabian Peninsula may be descendants of Ishmael, most Arabs of the rest of the Arab world simply have no blood relationship to Ishmael at all.[9]

Not all Arabs are the physical descendants of Ishmael, but through Islam, they are in spiritual affinity with Ishmael's disenfranchisement from Abraham in favour of the second son Isaac, the child of God's promise. Islam nurtures the original grievance of Ishmael and Hagar his mother.

Psalm 83 also highlights that of ten nations who band together, the Ishmaelites and a subtribe called the Hagarites were sworn enemies of

Lance Goodall

Israel and God himself.

Most Arabs of the rest of the Arab world simply have no blood relationship to Ishmael at all.

Nearly every religion contains a creed and a pivotal individual who orients the believers' lives. Islam's creed *shahada* (confession/profession) is brief and explicit: 'There is no god but Allah, and Muhammad is His Prophet.' This affirms that God is a unique being and that Muhammad is God's greatest prophet. Muslims believe that Islam reached its definitive form through Muhammad.[10]

To go further, Islam 'is predicated on the belief that there is but one God, Allah the Creator of the universe and of humankind. . . . Mercy and compassion are his principal qualities."

'The first and most essential element in Islamic theology is the doctrine of God [Allah].'

a. 'True belief demands an uncompromising monotheism.'

b. Muhammad 'accuse Christians of being polytheists because of their belief in the Trinity'.

Thus, they view Jesus as simply a prophet, not the Son of God (cf. Quran 4:171; 5:73,75).[11]

'For the Father judges no man, but hath committed all judgment unto the Son: That all men should honour the Son, even as they honour the Father. He that honours not the Son honours not the Father which hath sent him' (Jn. 5:22,23).

Do you realise that Islam does not allow the Lord Jesus to be the following:

- The Son of God
- The Creator of the Universe
- The propitiation for our sins
- The mediator between God and Man
- Anything but a prophet (and not the Prophet) and certainly not God's son

The cold hard reality is Allah and Abba God cannot be the same God because Islam rejects Jesus as God's Son!

And although Brian Houston tries to use the 'I should have known better' joker card, Pope Francis very early on in his papacy authorised 'Islamic prayers and readings from the Quran' at the Vatican for the first time ever.[12]

During his visit to St Patrick's Cathedral in Manhattan on 24 September 2015, he made it very clear that he believes that Christians and Muslims worship the same God, therefore establishing the ground work for a one-world religion.[13]

The following is how he began his address:

> I would like to express two sentiments for my Muslim brothers and sisters. . . . In this moment, I give assurances of my prayers. I unite myself with you all. A prayer to almighty god, all merciful.

And then Pope Francis ended it by glorifying Mary.[14]

In Islam, one of Allah's primary titles is 'the all-merciful one'.

In recent days we have organisations like the Presbyterians of the USA allowing muslim prayer at their general assembly. And of course there was the disruption at Wheaton College when Larycia Hawkins sold out and wore a hajib and affirmed the 'same god' concept as these others. Her facebook page shows the same disappointing betrayal.

Now back to Brian, if it can be said that the phrase regarding Allah was taken out of context, it is because it shouldn't have been in Brian Houston's sermon in the first place. There was *NO* context as Brian's remark appeared out of nowhere like the iceberg in the path of the *Titanic*, full steam ahead. He needed to provide an explanation, give clarity, and perhaps give some kind of apology to anyone he may have confused or offended. But no, all we get is Brian Houston's uncommitted media statement to somehow put everyone's concerns to rest.

His clumsy reference to God and Allah is just too coincidental. As a minister of the gospel, you don't plan to say such things without giving it thought and intent. Is Brian just trying to remain in step with other religious leaders but doing a poor job of it? Is he trying to keep up with the spiritual joneses by waxing lyrical?

We would ask, what is the purpose of mentioning Allah, except to bring a marrying of two religious views under the guise of biblical orthodoxy?

As Brian Houston stated, it was just one statement. But because it was such a *significant* statement, he should have stopped and said, 'What I mean is Islam, and . . .' But he keeps right on going and sends out a cheap tweet for 'clarity'. In other words, he didn't pause but instead just ploughed on without a stutter or hesitation. Then he wonders why there is such a furore.

In a real church, Brian Houston should have been asked to provide a clear and thorough statement on how Islam and Christianity do or don't serve the same God, but it is never forthcoming. Because we have this dangerous edict today which says don't question your leader, doctrinal accuracy is an inconvenient truth, which is swept aside, for the sake of the institution.

As we close out this chapter, while churches, like Hillsong, shamelessly splash around in the shallows of Christian experience, the following should wake us up to the true spirit of Islam and its place in the hierarchy of the Illuminati system. Yes that's right, do we not see how they are being used by the grand puppeteers to bring fear and terror to the west?

The following quote should leave us in no doubt to the current state of our world as we see hordes of men in Iraq and Syria carrying a black flag, maiming and killing our Christian brothers and sisters with the sword. In Mosul near the ancient city of Nineveh, ISIS offered residents a choice: they could either convert or pay the *jizya*, the head tax levied against all people of the Book': Christians, Zoroastrians, and Jews. If they refused, they would be killed, raped, or enslaved, their wealth taken away as spoils of war.

The Order of Nobles and Mystics has origins that date back to the seventh century, apparently founded by a descendant of Mohammed.

Author Michael Howard describes the order's symbols: 'The symbol of the Order is a crescent moon, made from the claws of a Bengal tiger, engraved with a pyramid, an urn and a pentagram. The crescent is suspended from a scimitar and in the Order is a representation of the Universal Mother worshipped in ancient times as Isis. The horns of the crescent point downwards because it represents the setting moon of the old faith at the rising of the Sun of the new religion of the brotherhood of humanity' (*The Occult Conspiracy*, p. 93).***

*** Muḥammad ibn Isḥāq ibn Yasār ibn Khiyār (according to some sources, ibn Khabbār, or Kūmān, or Kūtān,[3] Arabic: محمد بن اسحاق بن یسار بن خیار, or simply ibn Isḥaq ابن اسحاق, meaning "the son of Isaac") (died 767, or 761[2]) was an Arab Muslim historian and <u>hagiographer</u>. Ibn Ishaq collected oral traditions that formed the basis of an important <u>biography</u> of the <u>Islamic prophet Muhammad</u>.

Ibn Isḥaq collected oral traditions about the life of the Islamic prophet Muhammad. These traditions, which he orally dictated to his pupils,[8]_are now known collectively as *Sīratu Rasūli l-Lāh* (<u>Arabic</u>: هللا لوسر ةريس "Life of the Messenger of God") and survive mainly in various sources: https:// en.wikipedia.org/wiki/Ibn Ishaq

38
EYES WIDE SHUT

And thou shalt grope at noonday, as the blind gropeth in darkness, and thou shalt not prosper in thy ways: and thou shalt be only oppressed and spoiled evermore, and no man shall save thee.

—Deut. 28:29

An old woman of 90 from Valdres in Norway had a vision from God in 1968. The elderly Norwegian woman prophesied that 'a lukewarmness without parallel will take hold of Christians, a falling away from true, living Christianity. Christians will not be open for penetrating preaching. They will not, like in earlier times, want to hear of sin and grace, law and gospel, repentance and restoration. There will come a substitute instead: prosperity [happiness] Christianity.'1

Hillsong has made its goal and mission 'a gospel of entertainment'— entertainment for entertainment's sake. They have, in fact, given into the culture of the day and developed a new form of media called – Christertainment. This is heralded as the successful method of evangelism.

Lance Goodall

In fact, success is the new godliness!

The vice president of Paramount was invited to Hillsong's London Conference 2013, giving him some five minutes to spruik the controversial irreligious gnostic impostor movie *Noah* loosely based on the biblical man called Noah by director Darren Aronofsky.[1]

They reached out to leaders of large congregations like Hillsong and flew the leaders in to test the film. They all gave their seal of approval on the project

Paramount was hoping that support from Christian groups would be instantaneous and they would all fall in and flock to the film, but they were hitting roadblocks when it came to word-for-word details. Paramount's *Noah* was compared against the Bible's Noah, leading to its ultimate alienation from its' faith-based audience, who rejected it at the box office.

Pastor Brian, at the church's Heart and Soul night in Sydney, gave his polite endorsement suggested before a few thousand congregants and joked, 'You'll enjoy the film—if you're not too religious.'[2]

That's an important criterion these days. Don't be too serious about your faith. Hillsong is still up to their old tricks. They were involved in a subtle form of subliminal back masking during their Hillsong Conference Sydney in 2014, their annual talkfest, in an attempt to hoodwink, if it be possible, even the very elect.

Using the popular culture of movies and art, Hillsong morphed the cult classic *2001 Space Odyssey* by Stanley Kubrick as its theme for their Sydney Conference in July 2014, this film having ancient links to evolution, pyramids, the Illuminati, and the ultimate ascent of man![3]

This is Hollywood brought into the church with popcorn and

merchandise. This is religious organisation caught up in the 'god game' marketing Christianity as a business, like used car salesmen, except this time they are using very clever marketing techniques, multimedia and group psychology.

The author and filmmaker Jay Weidner called by *Wired Magazine* an "authority on the hermetic and alchemical traditions," has proposed that legendary film director Stanley Kubrick created his masterpiece *2001: A Space Odyssey* as a visual and alchemical initiation into the ongoing transformation and evolutionary ascent of man to a so-called Star Child destiny.

Set against the backdrop of a space mission. the film is an almost surreal experience that incorporates thematic elements as well as themes of human evolution, technology, artificial intelligence and extra-terrestrial life. According to Weidner, it is a bold attempt to envision the next evolutionary step for humanity. Weidner believes Kubrick has revealed an occult agenda to launch us as a species into space where we will be able to embrace our destiny as future star children and join the greater cosmos.[4]

Another well-known movie of Kubrick's was *A Clockwork Orange*: The ultimate mind-control movie in which we see a violent rapist transformed by a disturbing brainwashing technique into a passive citizen devoid of his overall humanity.

To show the rather dark and creepy content of these movies, *Lolita,* one of Kubrick's earlier films explored the sexual relationship between an older man and an underage girl.

Stanley Kubrick was also the director, producer, and co-writer of the erotic cult thriller *Eyes Wide Shut.*[5] The movie was Kubrick's look into the world of the New York sexual underground, the bizarre rituals of a sex cult, infidelity and possible elite murder. The film is peppered with occult and Masonic visual references and hints at underage prostitution amongst New York's privileged classes.[5]

This is enough to show the negligence of those who call themselves pastors and so-called leaders to use such themes and backdrops for their conferences. The Lord Jesus is mentioned, but it's still the old lie of Satan, who promised man he can become as God.

It is noteworthy that Hillsong consistently emphasise the contrasting colours of black and white to promote their yearly conferences, which symbolizes the moral dichotomy of good and evil. This is seen in their banner advertising for each conference, including the next conference in 2017. This imagery has occurred over the last few years. In 2016, the multimedia team turned their hand to black and white spirals, reminiscent of the opening theme to the BBC series of Doctor Who of the 60s, with each having overtones of hypnosis.

Like the symbol of yin yang Hillsong are seeking to fuse together two opposites. What fellowship has righteousness with unrighteousness? What has light to do with darkness, Kubrick with Christ, Jesus and the Illuminati? (2 Cor 6:14,15).

It is my contention Hillsong is under the influence of Luciferian doctrine, the deification of man, *without* the Lord Jesus Christ, and it's all done in plain view!

To show the outright complicity of Hillsong in this matter, the 2015 conference had the theme of 'Speak, we are listening'. The Hillsong website had as its scripture for the conference, the words taken from the book of Revelation, in reference to the seven churches.

The verse was quoted from the Message Bible and reads, 'Listen to the wind words, the Spirit blowing through the churches' – Rev 2:29

Hellsong

Now let's read that as it has been read for generations.

'He who has an ear, let him hear what the Spirit says to the churches.' – Rev 2:29 NKJV

Wind words can be meaningless as evident in this quote;

Words empty as the wind are best left unsaid — Homer

Notice first of all that to hear something in scripture is different from listening. It is even more specific, to him *who has an ear*, in other words, to him who is prepared to consider and take to heart what is being said. (Prov. 8:32–36).

In case it is thought that I am dealing with semantics, the letters to the seven churches were specific warnings and words of correction to these congregations regarding error and false teachers in their midst. We need to be established in the word of God, the clear teaching of scripture, on the foundation of the apostles and prophets, and Christ as our cornerstone, not just listen to the latest thing. (Eph. 2:20-22).

> 'That we henceforth be no more children, tossed to and fro, and carried about with every wind of doctrine, by the sleight of men, and cunning craftiness, whereby they lie in wait to deceive;' - Eph. 4:14

To have words blowing through the churches is the very thing that has led to this mess in the first place. We are to learn, and value doctrine. Again notice if you paraphrase the verse used by Hillsong, in the light of the verse in Ephesians you end up with something like this.

'Listen to the words, blown here and there, carried along by every wind, from the spirit blowing through the churches.'

For the pragmatic church this is the perfect verse, this allows them to peddle the latest fad, the newest trend, some new teaching, and the happening ideas of men. To the unsuspecting, the verse quoted on Hillsong's website seems innocent enough, just another way of putting it right, but when compared with the rest of scripture the modern version says the complete opposite!

> And the prophets shall become wind, and the word is not in them: thus shall it be done unto them. — Jer 5:13

> Hear what the Spirit says to the churches;

> Because you say, 'I am rich, have become wealthy, and have need of nothing'—and do not know that you are wretched, miserable, poor, blind, and naked— 18 I counsel you to buy from Me gold refined in the fire, that you may be rich; and white garments, that you may be clothed, *that* the shame of your nakedness may not be revealed; and anoint your eyes with eye salve, that you may see. – Rev. 3:17,18

> A wonderful and horrible thing is committed in the land; The prophets prophesy falsely, and the priests bear rule by their means; and my people love to have it so: and what will ye do in the end thereof? – Jer 5:30,31

The old lady from Norway continued in her prophecy:

> The important thing will be to have success, to be something; to have material things, things that God never promised us in this way. Churches and prayer houses will be emptier and emptier. Instead of the preaching we have been used to for generations—like, to take your cross up and follow Jesus—entertainment, art

and culture will invade the churches where there should have been gatherings for repentance and revival. This will increase markedly just before the return of Jesus.[5]

Prophecy is literally being fulfilled before our eyes. The philosophy of our day is humanism, a philosophy or 'gospel' that states the end of all being is the happiness of man. The reason for man's existence is happiness. Modernist's salvation is getting all the happiness you can get. This is the new gospel!

'God did not save us to make us happy. He saved us to make us holy' — Dr Jerry Benjamin.

The gospel requires the same as the law. The gospel is not the opposite of the law but provides a higher means to establish the law. It is astonishing that many have maintained that man can aim directly at his own salvation and make his own happiness the great object of pursuit. But it is plain that God's law is different from this and requires everyone to prize God's interest supremely. Evangelicals have simply lied to themselves. There is no greater lie than lying to yourself. They quote verses like 'Believe on the Lord Jesus and you will be saved'. They think that a verbal confession is enough. They make statements like 'We believe the Bible is the wordof God! We believe in the deity of Jesus Christ!' But the overarching principle of these evangelical churches, the purpose driving these houses of worship, is humanism.

Paris Reidhead strongly censured this philosophy in his now-classic sermon 'Ten shekels and a shirt', where he spoke out against pragmatism and humanism. He stated, 'Humanism says the chief end of life is the happiness of man.'

This humanism of happiness for all now pervades every area of our lives.

'What's in it for me?' is now an epidemic, producing a spiritual cancer in our churches. This disease is so insidious, so evasive, that it is corrupting even the elect. Like leaven, it leavens the whole lump. This humanistic subjective stance is corrupting us all. Christianity is not popularity.

We want Hollywood, not wormwood; levity, not gravity; activity, not agony; not joy, but enjoyment, mirth, not myrrh; drama, not doctrine; conferences, not contrition; revival, but not repentance; programmes not prayer; morality, not Christianity; happiness, not holiness; popularity, not purity.

Isn't there a Bible verse that says, all who live godly will suffer fame, acclaim and adoration? (2 Tim.3:12)

And so when the 2014 Hillsong Women's Conference opened in London, using the neo-soul song 'Happy' written and produced by Pharrell Williams, a US rap and R&B artist, we know that we are in the last of the last days, and men and women have their eyes wide shut.

39
ANOTHER DARK HORSE

*And when he had opened the third seal, I heard the third
beast say, Come and see. And I beheld, and lo a black horse;
and he that sat on him had a pair of balances in his hand.*

—Rev. 6:5

Katy Perry (nee Hudson) completed her Prismatic World Tour down
under in the homeland of Hillsong Church.[1]

Perry's recent world tour called Prismatic just as easily could have been
called the Pyramid Tour!

**Even her stage set was arranged as a pyramid and an obelisk, the most
revered shapes in the mystery religions of Babylon and Egypt.[2]**

As you would have seen from her 'Dark Horse' video, the imagery soaked
in Egyptian mythology and Horus-Isis worship and the religious worship
of ancient gods overtone. This was the theme in her music video, with a
full stage production at the Brit Awards, which was performed during
the live broadcast on 19 February 2014.[3]

But for some reason, a few weeks earlier, during the 56th Grammy
Awards held on 26 January 2014 at Staples Centre in Los Angeles, she

mimicked a witchcraft ceremony known as the witches' Sabbath. Some suggested she had summoned Satan himself. This performance was just days before 1–2 February Candlemas and Imbolc (a.k.a. Groundhog's Day), which is one of the many Illuminati's human sacrifice nights.[4]

Typical dates for this Sabbath include the seasonal festivals of winter (2 February), spring (23 June), summer (1 August), and fall (21 December).[5]

Whether she realises or not, Katy Perry has become the tool of the global elite and the devil himself!

Coincidence or not, PRISM just happens to be a clandestine mass electronic surveillance data mining program launched in 2007 by the National Security Agency (NSA), with participation from British equivalent agency, GCHQ.

The PRISM program collects stored internet communications based on demands made to internet companies such as Google Incorporated and Apple Incorporated. In other words, most of the world's financial data and various communication traffic ultimately have everything we do tracked or monitored for when they see fit to use it.[6]

'So I looked, and behold, a black horse, and he who sat on it had a pair of scales in his hand' (Rev. 6:5).

In Revelation 6, the colours of the horses represent an aspect of God's judgement in the last days.

The horses' dark or black colour represents an ominous sign often associated with mourning or destruction. In Revelation, the rider of the black horse had scales in his hand. He cried out, 'A quart of wheat for a denarius, and three quarts of barley for a denarius; and do not harm the oil and the wine.' The black (dark) horse follows the red horse in the

extensively by these mega churches to somehow win and lure converts. These men are false apostles, deceitful workers, masquerading as apostles of Christ, transforming themselves into ministers of light.

Brian Houston and the team at Hillsong echo the words of Perry, saying 'we're all in this together', and 'we are better together'.[11] Hillsong have confirmed their new movie *Let Hope Rise* will be released on the 16th September 2016 in theatres. What hope are they expecting to rise? I have grave concerns when I see their lead singer Taya Smith on NBC's Today Show wearing a black T-shirt with a white flame motif with the inscription 'New World Order'.[12] The stage is now set. We are at a point of crisis. This world is rapidly approaching a point of no return. Like Germany in the late 1920s, that brought Hitler to power, the desire for a dictator will not happen until a real crisis and subsequent collapse occurs.

In 2016, the signs of this coming chaos are all around us. From North Korea conducting nuclear tests, to Iran who are on the brink of nuclear success and who continue to threaten Israel. From Russia, in the Middle East, working with their allies Iran and Turkey, to the South China Seas, where Chinese naval vessels are on a war footing, with a potential confrontations with the imperialist U.S. navy patrolling international waters nearby.

Although we all hope for many things, a world without wars, living in peace and harmony and prosperity for all, the world is being seduced, and prepared for a messiah type leader. Although these are wonderful goals they will be promises promoted by the soon rising antichrist.

Clearly, a New World Order is in view.

40
WALK LIKE AN EGYPTIAN

Woe to them that go down to Egypt for help; and stay on horses, and trust in chariots, . . . but they look not unto the Holy One of Israel, neither seek the Lord!

—*Isa.31:1*

Who hasn't been fascinated with enduring monuments of the pyramids of Giza just outside of Cairo? Like me, you may have dreamed of being up close, on the back of a camel, and staring skywards up at these giant edifices. As one of the original Seven Wonders of the World, and certainly the symbol of Egypt, Cairo receives some 10 million or more visitors annually.[1]

Nathan Taylor was the stage designer on the creative team at Hillsong for the United band's 2013 world tour.

Nathan said, 'They were influenced by modern architectural trends, Mount Zion is one of the most unique creative expressions over the conference to date.[2]

Modern architectural trends? I think he means ancient architectural trends from ANCIENT Egypt!

Strangely, the stage set looked uncannily like pyramids. How then did he come up with the concept of Mount Zion?

> I was playing around with shapes and experimenting with the possibility of using them on stage as a projection surface. Mount Zion came quickly after the United album and Bobbie was inspired by Isaiah 52:7, 'How beautiful on the mountains are the feet of those who bring good news, who proclaim peace, who bring good tidings, who proclaim salvation, who say to Zion, "Your God reigns!"'[3]

Of course, they needed a godly reason for such a stage layout.

But I need to ask, which mountains? Where are the tidings of good news? Is this just wishful thinking? Granted Taylor was trying to be creative and use these props as a backdrop.

When you get down to it though the stage design looks more the three pyramids of Giza. The mountain turns out to look nothing like a mountain, and therefore, the message must be nothing like the gospel.

The incredible thing was as I looked again and again at the stage props over some months, and then it hit me. I realised they had only ONE source for their stage design and their crafting of this tour theme, and it wasn't Isaiah, but rather they were shaped and moulded exactly on the colossus of Cairo's pyramids in Giza!

Hillsong had only ONE source for their stage design: the colossus of Cairo's pyramids in Giza!

I needed to see it for myself. When comparing sharp high-quality images of the pyramids and the Zion stage design angle against angle, every line matched perfectly to the pyramids on the outskirts of dusty Cairo. Apart from a few size differences and a reduction in overall scale, the stage was almost a perfect replica! Case closed.

According to one website, to the wise and adept, the pyramid is symbolic of a mountain. A square base represents the four corners of the world and the four directions. Its peak rises to the sky, connecting heaven and earth. It is a pathway between the worldly and the heavenly. The pyramids of Giza were used, among other things, to monitor solstices and equinoxes and linked to the ancient Pythagorean equation. Interestingly, inside the king's chamber, the length of the diagonals of the antechamber within the heart of the Great Pyramid is exactly **666** *pyramid inches* with the outer mantle composed of exactly 144,000 casing stones.[4]

The Egyptians were sun worshippers, reverenced the creator of the universe, the maker of all gods above and below, and even the author of himself through the luminary. The two most striking characteristic monuments which represented him on earth were the obelisk and the pyramid. [5]

These ancient monuments can be found in all corners of the world, and they remain some of the most incredible ancient structures on Earth. The Ancient Egyptians, the Chinese, Inca, Aztecs, Maya and countless other ancient cultures erected Pyramids that still exist today. No one has been able to fully understand what the real purpose of the pyramids was. The mystery regarding pyramids deepens when you realize that some like the pyramids in the Giza Plateau are astronomically aligned.

As cited previously, 'the pyramid exemplifies the initiation stage. . . . It is the house of initiation, in which the candidate confronts the world of darkness and enters the world of spirit. By passing the tests of the elements, the candidate is initiated into the realm of higher consciousness' (Hieronimus, p. 92).

Some, including Emperor Napoleon, experienced strange visions and environmental distortions while inside the Great Pyramid, particularly the king's chamber. In the 1930s, author Paul Brunton spent a night there and was assailed by visions of 'a circle of hostile creatures', which he likened to 'elemental creations, grotesque shapes, madmen, hulking and devilish apparitions'. Was this mere hallucination? [6]

So is this the gospel according to Hillsong? Illumination into a higher consciousness? Why is Hillsong dabbling in the dangerous dimensions of the pyramid?

Generally speaking, Masonic sources say that the secret society/occultists are using the eye of Horus in an effort to do what they would describe as 'illuminating' the masses so as to bring them to the 'religion of light'.[7]

To put it quite simply, the ancient great pyramids of Giza were based on elements of false satanic worship, which were built by the Nephilim hybrid giants in the time of Noah, from the pre-flood days.

In essence, a pyramid is 'a system of demonic control, and worship'.[8]

The pyramid represents the 'age of the gods' and the grand mission of the Illuminati/new age movement, which is to return to the age of the gods. It also represents the home of the dying and rising god. This figure will once day return, unlocking the full power of the mystery religions, allowing man to once again have all of the mystical knowledge to become godlike and immortal.[9]

The modern-day Illuminati Satanists are merely following the time old worship of Satan/Lucifer, the very same 'sun (g)od' of the ancient Egyptian priests and an antiquated form of true Satanic worship.[10]

At the top of the pyramid structure is always Satan because Satan is known to them as the 'sun [god] of the morning'. History is just repeating itself on a grand scale, and people had better wake up.

Once again that Hillsong United and the promoters of their albums, continue to dabble in Illuminati symbolism, mocking and laughing at the masses, who see nothing apparently off or unusual in their cover designs.

Last time we saw this inversion was with their album - *Empires*. Their new album *Dirt and Grace*, their 13th live album is based on the idea of reworking of previous songs recorded in the holy land, near Jerusalem.

In 1984, the Rothschild Foundation (Yad Hanadiv) made a formal offer to the Government of Israel to donate a permanent building for the Supreme Court. The offer was gratefully accepted and an architectural competition was held in 1986. The new Supreme Court building was dedicated on November 10, 1992.[11]

The Israeli Supreme Court building in Jerusalem, which is full of symbolism is part of the plan for the Rothschild Antichrist to rule the world. They show the journey toward illuminati status. The same families who own and control the Federal Reserve and other major financial institutions have their eyes set on the Temple Mount, and the Holy City of Jerusalem. Just as Scriptures say, the man who will be revealed as the anti-Christ will sit in that place, before the appearance of the Jewish Messiah (Yeshua HaMashiach), and many will receive him as their messiah. Just actually how this will come about remains to be seen, but one thing I am sure of is that the rabbis will not be the ones to rebuild the Temple, it will be the Illuminati.

A pyramid is imbedded in the roof of the court. In front of the Supreme Court of Israel there is another Masonic/Illuminati pyramid flanked by the pillars Jachin and Boaz, originally found in front of the Temple of

Solomon. Apparently the Rothschilds intend to place the Ark of the Covenant in Solomon's Temple in Jerusalem to legitimise their claim to be the Messiah. Inside the grounds of the court is an obelisk.[12]

Hillsong United's cover of *Dirt and Grace* has many layers of masonic symbolism in its design, including the square and compass letting us know that Jerusalem in the physical realm is moving toward the desired spiritual crescendo.

Time is running out, and as such, you will notice there is acceleration in their plans for their New World Order, which will end in utter destruction. Yet the Illuminati echelon continues to defy all logic and promulgates it's Satanic pyramid, and NWO plans with mind-numbing determination. It seems Hillsong has gone back to Egypt for its source of inspiration. This is what the Hillsong United 2013 Zion tour was all about. Their 'Egyptian jukebox' continues to pump out anthems, and illuminates the masses with Hillsong's false gospel.

They are literally casting a spell on the ignorant masses, subliminally flooding their subconscious minds with the power of their symbols for the purpose of preparing the world for the arrival of their Antichrist.[13]

41

BRIDGE OVER TROUBLED WATERS

That we henceforth be no more children, tossed to and fro, and carried about with every wind of doctrine, by the sleight of men, and cunning craftiness, whereby they lie in wait to deceive.

—Eph. 4:14

A song was playing in clothing store I was standing in some months ago, which had a clean catchy synthesizer sound and beat; and even though I was enjoying it, I realised this was not at all glorifying God. Neither was it intended to. The song was Coldplay's 'Sky Full of Stars'.

Music can have its own intoxicating power. It has the ability to create a natural high, the ability to lift your spirits even if the song and lyrics are not particularly spiritual—or maybe it is. Music has its own mystical transcendent attributes that make it so powerful.

Hillsong seems to have modelled its music after what is produced in the secular world, bringing new productions under their youth arm Young and Free. Take its recent hit 'Where You Are'. It's almost a chord-by-chord duplicate of Duke Dumont's (an English DJ, record producer and songwriter) 'Ocean Drive'. Somebody has been copying somebody? It's seems Hillsong doesn't have any problems with a little foot shuffle and dancing with the devil. And so now somehow this has become the church's new 'house' worship. The lines have become blurred.

As outlined in a previous chapter (chapter 9), you are hard-pressed to find Jesus, his name, mentioned at all in any of the new worship songs. It's *you*: you are good, you are mine, you are everything etc. At one time, it was biblical language, but now we have a sprinkling of biblical references.

This model is no more demonstrated than in the 2013 number one hit from Hillsong United—'Oceans'.[1] Born and raised on the far north coast of New South Wales, Australia, Taya Smith is a key leader in the Hillsong creative team. She is the main vocal in 'Oceans' and 'Touch the Sky' on UNITED's most recent albums, Empires and Zion.

Taya's passion was nurtured in Lismore as a part of the worship team and a youth leader. Secular singing work then led to Taya moving to Sydney in 2010, where she became a part of Hillsong Church's City Campus as a volunteer in the youth and young adults ministries, and the church creative team.[2]

'Oceans' hit number one on the Billboard Christian songs chart at the end of 2013.[3]

By the end of 2014, this song had been streamed, downloaded, or otherwise acquired over 75 million times.[4]

Plato, though dead, still speaks to our generation. He was greatly aware of the gratuitous power of music:

> The rule was to listen silently and learn; boys,

teachers, and the crowd were kept in order by threat of the stick. . . . But later, an unmusical anarchy was led by poets who had natural talent, **but were ignorant of the laws of music.** . . . Through foolishness **they deceived themselves into thinking that there was no right or wrong way in music, that it was to be judged good or bad by the pleasure it gave.** By their works and their theories they infected the masses with the presumption to think themselves adequate judges. So our theatres, once silent, grew vocal, and aristocracy of music gave way to a pernicious theocracy. . . . The criterion was not music, but a reputation for promiscuous cleverness and a spirit of law-breaking. (Plato, *Laws* 700–701a, cited in Wellesz, p. 395) (emphasis mine)

How insightful—as in Plato's day, so in ours.

The church has become infiltrated by unmusical anarchy led by those with natural talent but who are ignorant of the laws of music. In their foolishness, they deceive themselves into thinking that there is no right or wrong way in music—that it is to be judged purely by the esthetical pleasure it gives. They see there is no spiritual influence with music and that it is purely neutral.

Even in a recent 2012 Jubileum Concert with Michael W. Smith, co-hosted by Darlene Zschech, the music compilation was nothing more than a drum fest, a Jesus Rock concert, if you please. This was not worship. This is why I am concerned that these leaders are shipwrecking their own faith and those of their audiences.[5]

From the testimony of Joel Houston weird things are happening. Taya Smith, the current female lead within the Hillsong United team, is said to have gone 'crazy' in the studio, shouting at the wall. To me, this is strange, if not very disturbing.[6]

Yet one young guy parked his car after a long day, leaned back, and closed his eyes and let the opening cello carry him to heaven.[7]

Hillsong's 'Oceans' begins:

You call me out upon the waters

The great unknown, where feet may fail

And there I find You in the mystery

In oceans deep, my faith will stand

If this song is bound in mystery, then where is this young man being carried?

Then comes the bridge, and if you don't watch it, it gets stuck in your head, which is a worrying thing in itself.

> Bridge:
>
> Spirit lead me where my trust is without borders
>
> Let me walk upon the waters . . . Take me deeper than my feet could ever wander[8]

The bridge is sung at least five times.

Considering Oceans is eight minutes long, you have a mantra right there.

Jimi Hendrix spoke of this cathartic experience;

People want release any kind of way nowadays. The idea is to release in the proper form. Then they'll feel like going into another world, a clearer world. The music flows from the air; that's why I can connect with a spirit, and when they come down off this natural high, they see clearer, feel different things. (Jimi, Life Magazine's October 3, 1969)

Isn't this the euphoria that Hillsong are offering it congregants?

Someone wrote to me suggesting that Oceans is a Christian song. He suggested it is about God leading us through difficulties in life, and that we will make it through if we trust Him.

Granted the song does have that thread. But faith means trust.

Its object is always God. Biblical faith is active—possessive, not passive; objective, not subjective. In other words, faith has borders. Instead this song is full of imaginings. It is dangerous to refer to trust in this way.

Charles Spurgeon, the great preacher from the 19th century, declared, 'Faith is not a blind thing for faith begins with knowledge, it is not a speculative thing for faith believes facts of which it is sure. It's not an impractical dreaming thing for faith trusts and stakes its destiny upon the truth of God's revelation' (*The Triumph of Faith in a Believer's Life*, p. 30).

Hillsong's Ocean is conceptual not factual. We need truth for the basis of Christian lyrics, one of the basic laws that Hillsong fails to abide by.

Talking of lyrics I digress to ask what is this reference to the great unknown?

Now the world's ocean may be described in the following ways: a large stretch of sea, water covering some 75 per cent of the earth's surface, a huge quantity or expanse.[9]

So what is the great unknown? Various words related to this are the

Hellsong

following:

great beyond [10]

noun: life after death

- after life
- here after
- next world
- the great unknown

So why are Hillsong United singing about death and the afterlife?

It could quite easily mean in the context of the song that it is simply a reference to the ocean and its vast depths. But I ask, why is there a reference to the afterlife or the world beyond this one? Are they opening the door to another world, through the medium of music?

It can only be concluded that unbeknownst to the writers of Hillsong, they have formulated a song that is opening a door into the mystical.

The simple cold hard fact is it's an industry. These days worship can be defined as just about anything whether it be music, art, or experience, touch, anything that moves you in a transcendent way.

As I said to one vocal lady who sought to stick up for Hillsong's music, these types of songs are just sentimental gibberish. You couldn't sit down and come up with actual verses of scripture from these cryptic crosswords. These songs are just airbrushed with some Christian touch-up.

Yet Hillsong United took top honours (7 October 2014) at the Gospel Music Association's 45th Annual Dove Awards, winning five Doves, including Artist of the Year and Song of the Year for 'Oceans (Where Feet May Fail)'.

'The song "Oceans" has opened so many new doors and so many great opportunities to share the message of Jesus,' Hillsong United's Jonathan Douglass said backstage at the awards. 'Only by the grace of God is this song doing what it's doing.'[11]

In their endeavour to reach the world, they have become the world and accepted the world and its beliefs, sin, attitudes, likes, and dislikes, while completely forgetting what the Bible itself says. And what doors are they opening? Some are meant to stay closed.

Larry DeBruyn, in his book *Church on the Rise*, writes:

> Rock music and mysticism share something in common; both engender indescribable feelings of religious experience. In the connection between music and mysticism there exists real danger for Christian believers.

The danger is that individually and corporately, they will substitute man-made, man-centered, mechanically induced and non-rational musical experiences for genuine ones mediated by the Holy Spirit through the propositional and cognitive Word of God. (*Church on the Rise*, pp. 134–135)

This quote shines as a beacon to any wayfarer who wishes to venture out into the dangerous waters of Hillsong's music mantras.

I could quote a number of psycho-hypnotic experiences, but let's choose one.

Rob Bell is one of the fresh voices now representing the emerging church movement.

Bell recounts his experience at a U2 concert at the tender age of 16.

When they started with the song 'Where the Streets

> Have No Name' I thought I was going to spontaneously combustwith joy. This was real. This mattered. Whatever it was, I wanted more. (*Velvet Elvis*, 2005, p. 72)

With its brand of Coexist, U2 has a great influence in the emerging church and the contemporary worship movement.[12]

In simple terms, it can be stated that music is not just entertainment.

One website on occult and mystical religions offers this insight:

> Many great world religions have both inner and outer teachings. An Esoteric Christian is one who seeks through personal experience Christ, rather than through dogma and commandments. Mystery religions, sacred mysteries or simply mysteries, were religious schools of the Greco-Roman world for which participation was reserved to <u>initiates</u> [mystai].[13]

The mystery religions had little or no use for doctrine, truth, or correct belief. They were primarily concerned with the emotional dimension of their followers. As the cults continued to tone down the more objectionable features of their older practices, they began to attract greater numbers of followers.[14]

Does any of this sound familiar to you?

Mystery religions had little or no use for doctrine. Brian Houston echoes this same principle, 'We believe a basic charismatic/Pentecostal theology, but we don't build strong on theology'.[15] Yet the church is to be the pillar of the truth.

- The cults used many different means to affect the emotions and imaginations of initiates and hence bring about 'union with God'. 'Oceans' as a song is a case in point.

- The mysteries sought to welcome the initiate. Brian Houston also says, 'We make it about Jesus, about the grace of God, and we try to have a net so it's broad, not narrow.'[16]

- The immediate goal of the initiates was a mystical experience to achieve union with their god. Brian explained, 'I always wanted to have the kind of church which influenced the way people do church.' Brian Houston said, 'People may be divided on doctrine and theology and other things, but worship tends to transcend all of that.'[17] As objectionable features of the cult's older practices disappeared, it began to attract greater numbers of followers. Hillsong has become measured in its approach to such areas as speaking in tongues and miracles, Islam, and homosexuality, rarely anything that will cause controversy, to appeal to as many followers as possible.

Hillsong's enterprise must be seen in the light of the commonality with the mysteries.

Hillsong is an evangelical form of the cults.

Wikipedia defines *religious ecstasy* as 'a type of an altered state of consciousness which is characterized by greatly reduced external awareness and expanded interior mental, and spiritual awareness, frequently accompanied by visions and emotional [and sometimes physical] euphoria. Subjective perception of time, space or self may strongly change or disappear during ecstasy, sometimes called enlightenment'.[18]

Jonathan Edwards (5 October 1703–22 March 1758)—revivalist

preacher, philosopher, and Congregationalist Protestant theologian—published his influential *Treatise on Religious Affections*. In it, he argued that religious ecstasy could come from a number of sources—oneself, the devil, or God—and it was *only by observing the fruit* or changes in inner thought and behaviour that one could determine if the religious ecstasy had come from God. [19] (emphasis added)

Mickey Hart, drummer for the rock group *Grateful Dead*, saw the connection between ecstasy and religious experience:

> Grateful Dead was a ferryman, a conduit, a bridge to the spirit world, and the band provided a musical experience that offered safe passage to the other side. . . . Acoustic alchemy was necessary for the successful completion of the round trip. (Hart and Lieberman, *Spirit into Sound: The Magic of Music*, Grateful Dead Books, 1999, p. 147)

To add further to this argument, in his book *Music, the Brain, and Ecstasy*, Robert Jourdain explains that music melts away boundaries and brings a range of feelings that are 'oceanic'.

The defining trait of ecstasy is immediacy. Music seems to be the most immediate and the most ecstatic. Nevertheless, once we are engulfed in the music, we must exert every effort to resist its influence. Some 'other' has entered not just our bodies, but our intentions, taking us over (Robert Jourdain, 1997, p. 327–328).

I strongly suggest that Hillsong music is taking over but not in a good way. People are being engulfed in the music, in the experience. We have boarded a ship bound for who knows where and the name of it is the USS *Deception*.

All this clearly tells us that music is not neutral!

We can be caught up in a moment, but we need to test if it is the Holy Spirit or another spirit. Much of today's mystical influence is bound up in the popularity of pyramid worship.

To many, Jesus has become nothing but a mystical messiah.

To help bring all this together, famous experimental musician Steven Halpern relates his new age experiences about sounds, resonance, and pyramids, saying that he suddenly found himself carried along, floating in a boat, rocking around on ocean waves.[20]

Isn't this most revealing? On the ocean, out on the waters, a small floating vessel, a feeling of levitating, tuning in, and being caught up to a different plane. This sounds almost biblical—bobbing about on an ocean in a small boat.

But this is the same man who showed that words took a backseat to the music; and it was the combination of the beat, bass, and the drums that influenced us the most (Dr Steven Halpern, *Tuning the Human Instrument*, 1978, p. 14).

Another simple thing to observe is the length of the song on this occasion.

The song ran for over eight minutes. The phrase 'Take me deeper than my feet could ever wander, and my faith will be made stronger in the presence of my saviour' is a mantra that is repeated five times. The song drifts along like a boat that is engulfed in an eerie fog, caught up into another realm.

Hillsong has packaged up an 'opiate for the people'—a feel-good sensation, a set of good vibrations, a kind of narcotic for their religious audience who care little of its long-term damage to their souls. When a boat or aircraft drifts off course it must arrest its path and return to the original co-ordinates or else risk crashing into an object or being lost altogether.

'Oceans' is Hillsong's most seductive, mystical, mesmerising music yet!

This evidence is very disconcerting. Sometimes we go into error from ignorance of the scriptures, but when we fail to heed warnings, we have no one to blame but ourselves. Hillsong is dabbling in the occult world, playing around on some kind of musical Ouija board—blending sounds, mystical experience, and pyramids, all in union with what can only be the god of this world.

It is walking in the opposite direction to the will of God, stumbling into a form of 'soft magic', and has now found itself inadvertently in a spiritual maze that it can't get out of. And as for the lyric in the bridge where it makes reference to wandering, the Sûfi philosophers demonstrate the link between water and spiritual experience—the elements of the metaphor of the 'ocean of light and life'. To them, the essence of being is the *ocean without shores*.[21]

Water is the element of emotion and the unconscious. Water represents feelings, intuition, and imagination. Emotions and feelings can be very wonderful, but without being grounded in the Word of God, it leaves one open to deception.

Hillsong's worship is a never-ending giddy merry-go-round of experiences, merging the worlds of mysticism, gnosticism, and spiritism. Their music and lyrics reflect more the Buddhist path of enlightenment than Christian doxology.

The modern church has raised music to the heights that the music itself

has become a 'god', to the veiling and obscuring of the true God.

As shocking as it might seem, we have become idolaters of music. If you search back through the churches hymns over generations past, most would glorify God in the words and music. As Paul said, they were 'spiritual' hymns. In other words, doctrine put with melody.

Today we have musicians' imaginings put to music. A few biblical references thrown together hopefully with a Christian message, or some message in the end. The song 'Amazing Grace' I believe is still not outdated, as shown by Chris Tomlin's version of it.

But Hillsong's 'Oceans' is quite a different matter. The one listening to the song can make it mean anything they want. So if you want to be closer to Jesus or you want bigger faith, then great. If you just want to be able to touch something of the divine, then the song is perfect for you. Not too challenging, not too much doctrine, not too much of anything except this mystic mystery tour that we should all be very wary of.

As 20th-century occultist Manly Hall reminds us, 'symbolism is the language of the Mysteries' (Manly P Hall, *The Secret Teachings of All Ages*, p. 38).

Although most heap praise on this song, it is departing from true gospel music into new age necromancy with no strict adherence to biblical guidelines.

The song is dangerous for the following reasons:

- It repeats phrases—mantras.
- It has no clear doctrine—void of teaching.
- It is prone to mindless subjective experience—no particular focus on anything.
- The song itself 'carries' along the worshipper, not the person's

conscious engaging with the song.

And because of these aspects, the song can easily become a conduit for a false spirit.

During their 2013 tour, at a concert in LA, Joel Houston observed 'this huge crowd of people going crazy, [for them] and then you've got these two people.' He continues, 'I watched them sit through the first hour and a half of the night. . . . And I remember when we gave people the opportunity to make the decision to follow Christ, they both put their hands up and made a decision for Jesus.'[22]

This is after two hours of loud rock, and stage antics, and the backdrop of pyramids. I am sorry but a decision for Jesus, could mean anything from buying a CD, a T-shirt or just being caught up in the emotion of the concert.

When they toured in 2012, a DVD was put together *Hillsong Live in Miami* recording the full concert. It just so happened with their own promo material the band was shown backstage praying before the concert very earnestly and Joel prayed 'that their eyes would be opened'. A few frames later a young guy flashes the 'El Diablo' hand sign to Satan while queuing to get in.[23]

Then they couldn't help themselves, a few frames later as the concert progressed, they flashed a combination of both upright pyramids and inverted pyramids in subliminal fashion.[24]

In a similar way, Young and Free, on their new album *Youth Revival*, seem to be hexing their youth with subliminals in the form of a hexagram.[25]

The hexagram is a very powerful symbol to witches, magicians, and sorcerers. It is used in different kinds of witchcraft, magic, occultism, and the casting of zodiacal horoscopes. Because it has six points, and because it contains a 666, the hexagram is considered to be Satan's most powerful.

The hexagram is used to conjure up demons, making them appear in this dimension to do the bidding of the witch. Doc Marquis (former Illuminist Satanist) confirms that hexagrams are used to call forth demons to curse others. The word *hex* comes from this practice.[26]

In summary, the hexagram is [one] the most wicked and one of the most powerful of all symbols in witchcraft. It is used to call forth demons into this dimension, to communicate with the dead, to describe sex acts, and to represent false and pagan gods such as Brahma, Vishnu, and Shiva (Burns, *Masonic and Occult Symbols Illustrated*, p. 39).

As I thought more on this issue, it appeared to me that Hillsong has been drawn away like King Saul. I mentioned his disobedience in a previous chapter. But in 1 Samuel 28, Saul is found seeking the assistance of a medium, so he made contact with Samuel who had recently died. Yet God had said in Leviticus 20:6: 'And the person who turns after mediums and familiar spirits, to prostitute himself with them, I will set my face against that person and cut him off from his people.'

Yet because Saul wasn't hearing from God, he thought that this woman from Endor may help him. This is after issuing his own warning of punishment against such practises.

In the same way Houston's Hillsong has failed to heed the voice of God for years now, yet the theme of the recent 2015 Hillsong Conference was 'Speak. We're listening'. But these were the words spoken by God's servant and Prophet Samuel (1 Sam. 3:10.) Samuel actually said, 'Speak, for your *servant* is listening'. And what a difference one word can make. For to be a servant is to be in a place of abasement and humility so that those who are waiting to hear from God will, in the hearing, be ready to obey. God will not speak to the disobedient.

Saul could seek and consult the very spirit of Samuel himself, but nothing but judgement would be spoken to him, and those were the words given by Samuel. Similarly, Hillsong has been happy to obey God when it has suited them, and no amount of listening now on their part will bring God's correction except to those that God will call out in due time.

Here's what the Word of God says:

> Thus saith the Lord unto this people, Thus have they loved to wander, they have not refrained their feet, therefore the Lord doth not accept them; he will now remember their iniquity, and visit their sins. (Jer. 14:10)

> And they shall wander from sea to sea, and from the north even to the east, they shall run to and fro to seek the word of the Lord, and shall not find it. (Amos 8:12)

> Raging waves of the sea, foaming out their own shame; wandering stars, to whom is reserved the blackness of darkness forever. (Jude 1:13)

Oh, can you see it? As the United band has played this song 'Oceans' over and over, in stadium after stadium, continent after continent, with the backdrop of pyramids, bright lighting, mantras, and atmospheric choreography, Hillsong United led by Brian Houston and fronted by his son Joel is augmenting a strange global esoteric initiation.

Grasping exclusively for experience is a bridge to a false spirit to enter

the very sanctuary of God.

It is now becoming plain that Hillsong has maintained a veneer of Christian orthodoxy, but little by little, the organisation has morphed and changed like a chameleon with different shades and colours until now it takes on the appearance of a mystery cult. Hillsong is following the practices of the ancient Babylonian priesthood perfectly. We are admonished in the scripture to worship in spirit and in truth. But Hillsong has crashed through forbidden barriers and worships *only* in 'the spirit', in the mysticism of the moment.

Hillsong has transformed itself into a modern mystery cult augmenting a new global esoteric initiation. This is all part of their grand illusion, or delusion.

Paul must pull us back into line. Paul knew we are quite happy bobbing about in our little boat of mystical experiences. We think it's cool to leave all rational biblical moorings, oblivious to the danger of heretical rocks below.

'That we henceforth be no more children, tossed to and fro, and carried about with every wind of doctrine, by the sleight of men, and cunning craftiness, whereby they lie in wait to deceive; But speaking the truth in love, may grow up into him in all things, which is the head, even Christ' (Eph. 4:14,15).

We should no longer remain as children in infancy but be those who are constant in spiritual progress unto maturity. It is natural that we mature and develop, and not to do so is highly irregular. It often means a sign of disease. And yet this is the great sin of our current generation. We have brought up those who remain as babes. The church is nothing more than daddy day care. We are not to continue as children. The characteristic of children is their constant instability and their proneness to being deceived and led astray. They jump from one thing to another. They are an easy prey.

This is the great sin of our current generation: the church is nothing more than 'daddy day care'!

We have this strange aversion to development, study, learning, growth, and self-discipline. Octavius Winslow—who was one of the key evangelical preachers of the 19th century in England and America, a Baptist minister, and a contemporary of Charles Spurgeon and J C Ryle [27]—said that 'it must be admitted that character and the tendencies of the age are not favourable to deep and mature reflection upon the hidden, spiritual life of the soul'.[28]

And that was then. Wisdom tells us to hold fast to the truth, but the new motto according to Hillsong is 'entertain them to gain them'. It's music first. Doctrine, truth—well, it's in there somewhere.

And he said, Go, and tell this people, Hear ye indeed, but understand not; and see ye indeed, but perceive not. Make the heart of this people fat, and make their ears heavy, and shut their eyes; lest they see with their eyes, and hear with their ears, and understand with their heart, and convert, and be healed. (Isa. 6:9,10)

A new wind is blowing heavily upon Hillsong Church. The boat is adrift sailing into an ocean of rapidly changing currents and looming storms without a capable captain and crew at the helm. The boat is now heading into deep and troubled waters.****

Lance Goodall

**** Footnote - *Daddy Day Care* is a 2003 American family comedy film starring Eddie Murphy and co-starring Jeff Garlin. The film was released in theatres on May 9, 2003. It was produced by Revolution Studios and released by Columbia Pictures. After company downsizing, two former executives (Eddie Murphy, Jeff Garlin) decide to open a day-care centre for kids in their neighbourhood. Of course chaos ensues. https://en.wikipedia.org/wiki/DaddyDayCare

42
DAWNING OF THE AGE
OF AQUARIUS

For nothing is hidden that shall not become evident, nor anything secret that shall not be known and come to light.

—Lk. 8:17

In the Maryland area in the United States, a giant statue is buried in sand called The Awakening, created by one of the members of the elite Johnson Family.

The Awakening, J. Seward Johnson Jr.'s 15-foot-high sculpture, is of a giant struggling to emerge from the earth. The statue consists of five separate aluminium pieces buried in the ground, giving the impression of a distressed giant attempting to free himself from the ground. Although it stood for 27 years on public parkland at Hains Point, Washington DC, in the southwest section of the city, it was relocated to National Harbour, a $2 billion waterfront project under construction, in Prince George's County in Maryland.

The Awakening, which is more than 70 feet across, was installed on a specially built beach along the Potomac River as the focal point of the 300-acre development.[1]

The next long-awaited episode of the famed saga is *Star Wars: The Force Awakens,* came out December 2015. This also carries this endless reference to awakening, which bombards our modern psyche.[2]

Of course, we all have heard of various self-help books both inside and outside the church. An example is Tony Robbins, the millionaire self-help guru who offers personal motivation courses called *Unleashing the Power within.*[3]

In the church, there are books like David Jeremiah's *Life Wide Open: Unleashing the Power of a Passionate Life.*[4]

A strange coincidence then when Pastor Steven Furtick's Elevation Church released their second album on 25 November 2014 called *Wake Up the Wonder.*[5]

Throughout the ages, certain symbols have been employed to communicate hidden mystical and religious messages.

Manly P. Hall, one of the most influential occultists of the last century, wrote this of symbols, 'They are centres of a mighty force, figures pregnant with an awful power' (Manly P Hall, *Lectures on Ancient Philosophy*, p. 356).

Within the music industry, nothing is at it seems. Subliminal messages are the elite's hallmark, and it is a sure sign that a music artist like Katy Perry is bound to the elite by a strong chord.

The *Elevation* album cover is alluding to *Waking up the Wonder* (or fire within). That in itself is so new age. As Christians, there is no need to awaken anything within us. There is nothing within a human that is good. The reality is the Holy Spirit is already awake and alive and therefore He does not need to be awakened. So what are these so-called Christians who delve into this sort of spirituality really awakening? As mentioned in a previous chapter, Planetshaker conferences are all about 'awakening'.

We are commanded to quench not the spirit and to fan the flame. But we can never create or initiate the flame.

The concept of fire also encapsulates a number of ideas.

According to Alice Bailey, the famous occultist, 'fire is the most perfect and unadulterated reflection, in Heaven as on earth, of the One Flame. It is life and death, the origin and the end of every material thing. It is divine Substance' (*Secret Doctrine*, p. 146).

Hillsong's Young and Free youth band has created a new sound for the teens and young adults, the title modelled after the likes of Snoop Dogg.

> So what we get drunk/ So what we don't sleep (smoke weed) / We don't care who sees / *Living young and wild and free* ('Young, Wild and Free' by Snoop Dog and Wiz Khalifa, 2011) (emphasis added)

> We can do what we want; we can live as we choose. See there's no guarantee; we've got nothing to lose (Paul McCartney, 'New', 2013)

Hillsong Young and Free's runaway single off the album is 'Wake'.[6]

Lyrics (edited)

At break of day, in hope we rise.

We speak Your Name, we lift our eyes

Tune our hearts into Your beat.

Where we walk, there You'll be.

Lance Goodall

With fire in our eyes, our lives a-light.

Continued

You wake within me, wake within me.

Some of these lyrics are once again disturbing.

I will pick just one of them to show the 'spiritual code' embedded in this song's lyrics—that of 'fire in your eyes'.

On various websites, they talk of healing workshops that ignite the fire within—that can unleash the fire within to transform any area of our life you feel is stuck.

In her *Treatise on Cosmic Fire*, Alice Bailey has this quote:

> The Lords of Flame look on; they chant aloud: 'The time is come, that time for which we wait. Let the Flame become the FIRE and let the light shine forth.'[7]

Similar ideas were written by super group Earth, Wind, and Fire called 'Serpentine Fire'. This song is based on the new age teachings found in the Shah Kriza Yogi meditation cult.

All this sounds very freakily like Young and Free's song, don't you think?

The Lucis Trust, a United Nations entity, describes their purpose is to 'help to illuminate world thought . . . through which the new incoming Aquarian energies can function, the new ideas spread, and the New World Order emerge'.[8] Both Lucifer and Lucis come from the same root word *lucis*, being the Latin generative case meaning of *light*. But this is nothing but false light, masquerading as the true.[9]

The concept of energy is occult and is referenced in countless new age and occult publications, but it is nowhere in God's word. Yet Eugene Peterson deliberately inserts the word *energy* into the Message Bible, and of course, we find it in the lyrics and titles of the songs of these modern megachurches.

Here is one example: 'The energy you require for all that God has destined you for is of the Spirit, and it's inherent in you: That energy is God's energy, an energy deep within you, God himself willing and working at what will give him the most pleasure' (Phil. 2:13 MSG).

This is their new vocabulary. Energy, awakening, fire, unleashing—none of these have any biblical basis. Let's be clear, God's spirit is given to us. It is not inherent in is.

When fire is referenced in the Bible, it is fire that comes down, not something ignited from within(cf. 1 Kings 18:23–38, Ps. 140:10, Isa. 29:6, Matt 3:11, Acts 1:8, Acts 2:3) We can and often do quench the Spirit, but the flame of the Holy Spirit should never go out for the Christian.

No wonder Hillsong is now new age. It uses a new age Bible; and so its thinking, its culture, its motivations, as well as its music are all new age!

Here you have a simple recipe for the coming awakening: fire, mantras, and rock music, the beat being an integral part of these church's new consciousness.

Although the Bible does talk about being 'awake', it refers to ones who are in slumber and asleep. 'Wherefore he says, Awake thou that sleep, and arise from the dead, and Christ shall give thee light' (Eph. 5:14, cf. Isa. 60:1, Rom. 13:11). It's not so much the awakening of consciousness but awakening the person, arresting them to their own inaction, idleness, lethargy, passivity, and slothfulness, back to diligence and urgency.

But these churches are referring to something quite different.

The Holy Spirit will only bless (birth) what he has breathed upon. So if the music is off biblically or is trying to draw the person away from God, into an experience just from the music itself, then it will be deception and it will not lead to true conversions. The church will be left with people coming only for the entertainment. The minister or pastor then has a difficult choice to make because if the music attracted the young people in the first place, he will either have to choose to keep giving them what they want to retain them or preach true salvation, and then possibly lose them. (See Matt 13:3–23).

God uses only the gospel to save people, so what we need today more than ever are those who are filled with the power of the Holy Spirit and know the Word of God and aren't afraid to preach it.

The church may attract young people for a while through music, but its results are like my small lemon tree in my back garden: it will bear just one or two fruit.

Like the Lucis Trust, it seems quite clear that Hillsong is involved in the plan to work, and give expression, to achieve the spiritual evolution of humanity. And it appears there is no group so likely to ensure this goal as the men and women of Hillsong, who are helping to initiate action and prepare the world, especially the church for the New World Order!

43

HILLSONG AND THE COMING ANTICHRIST

This know also, that in the last days perilous times shall come. For men shall be lovers of their own selves. . . . Traitors, heady, highminded, lovers of pleasures more than lovers of God; Having a form of godliness, but denying the power thereof: from such turn away.

—2 Tim. 3:1–5

Many celebrities have accepted the idea of the Illuminati cult. It helps their music careers. Selling their soul for the chance of success and a few million.

The Illuminati has been rife with controversy and shrouded in secrecy sice its existence; but when you add Illuminati celebrities into the mix, you get a myriad of conspiracy theories, accusations, and rumours.

The Illuminati dates back to around 1 May 1776, made up of thinkers who were the antithesis to the Enlightenment. In fact, its undercurrents were even earlier with the likes of Francis Bacon and his ideas of the New Atlantis.[1]

Today, it is seen more as a secret sect that is behind all of the world's major affairs in an attempt to control the world. It is no surprise that virtually every powerful, successful celebrity has been linked to the Illuminati; and it's even stronger now with round-the-clock paparazzi, tabloids, and social networking.

In fact, some of the biggest modern superstars have been linked, including Lady Gaga, Beyoncé, Rihanna, Jay Z, Nicki Minaj, and, in recent times, artists like Katy Perry, Taylor Swift, and Mylie Cyrus.

With Beyoncé, stories have been at a fever pitch ever since she married Jay Z, who is seen as a pivotal member. Since she has been linked, many of her videos and songs have been broken down and analyzed to highlight Illuminati symbols. For example, both she and Lady Gaga produced 'Telephone' a video where people said it included elements of mind control and monarch programming, a covert, entertainment technique.[2]

In passing, Britney Spears is also a classic Disney monarch trauma victim, thrown in front of the network's bus.[3] By the way, monarch butterflies have made a regular appearance on many an album cover of artists like Taylor Swift, Miley Cyrus, and Kanye West.

Lady Gaga conspirators actually refer to her as the Illuminati puppet, which makes her one of their top targets.[4]

Conspiracy theorists say her symbolism is so blatant that it can't be denied that she is part of this mass underworld. They say everything, from her persona to her fashion to the music itself, is part of this mind control. It's a way to make her followers absent-minded and incoherent in an attempt to brainwash and control the masses. But you don't have to look too hard.[5]

Even Beyoncé's choreography is filled with Satanic meanings. Beyoncé, in a particular Instagram photo, projected a not-so-subtle metaphor. She is sitting on a ledge or platform in front of the Michelangelo painting of the *Last Supper*. Although this could be seen as just a bit of creative licence, yet on a deeper level, she is exalting herself as a Christ or a god, and what do gods assume but worship. Beyoncé just happens to be seated covering the place where the Lord Jesus resides or sits at the table. She is fulfilling biblical prophecy in making herself into a type of the great harlot, which would one day enthrone herself in the place of God, so Beyoncé has through her cheap publicity stunt committed blasphemy, usurping the place of Christ, thus becoming an Antichrist (see 2 Thess. 2:4).[6]

The Lord Jesus said there would be many false Christs (messiahs/saviours) that would come. We therefore certainly add Beyoncé to the list even if she might seem lame to many.

Yet Beyoncé's pastor Rudy Rasmus defends the singer against Christian critics who have scrutinised her explicit lyrics and videos.

Rasmus, who leads St John's United Methodist Church in downtown Houston and is a longtime friend of both Beyoncé and husband Jay Z, gave his opinion regarding the message behind Beyoncé's music without noting whether it contradicts the purity of Christianity or not.

Ramus says Beyoncé 'is tremendously gifted' and that 'the world would void an extreme talent if we silenced her or censored her.[7]

Freeman TV explains that the theme of the album *I Am… Sasha Fierce* (released 15 November 2008) revolves around the duality of opposites: black and white, good and evil, Beyoncé up and Sasha Fierce. This spiritual struggle is fought in the songs, the pictures, and the videos. Images from the album contrast the purity of Christianity and the dark side. Photos of Sasha depict her in black and white, posing with not one but two goats' heads on her black leatherette costume, one a hood ornament and the other painted in colour. 'Riding the goat is a masonic initiation where an inductee will ride a goat/tricycle contraption blindfolded while being pushed around the room by lodge members. This ritual is a watered-down version of ancient pagan goat/devil worship where coven members would copulate with a live goat or the leader of the coven, dressed as Baphomet. Songs like 'Ave Maria' and 'Halo' on the *I Am* side contain purer spiritual connotations while the tracks 'Sweet Dreams' and 'Video Phone' on the Sasha Fierce side have abundant Monarch mind control symbolism.[8]

Victims of Monarch programming often report that one of the personalities they are given is a genuine Christian who goes to church, actually believes in Christ, and is a good cover personality to detract suspicion from cult activity. Later on, the victim may be required to sacrifice an animal that has been given the same name as the Christian alter. It's hard to know for sure if Beyoncé has been in the Monarch programme since childhood or if this is a result of her fame and exposure to Jay Z.[9]

Curiously Carl Lentz has hung out with Jay Z, and openly says although probably tongue-in-cheek he had an 'illuminati meeting' with Jay-Z. He is the proud owner of Rock-a-fella records who often wears loud shirts with satanic symbols on them.[10]

Since Beyoncé released her self-titled album in December 2013, Christians and non-believers alike have criticised her videos and sexually charged lyrics. Then of course we have the demon Sasha Fierce who *inspires* and influences her theatre, as is demon-strated in the half time Superbowl 2013 and 2016 an event that showcases more than any other, the beliefs and indoctrination of the satanic ruling elite.[11]

Then you've got the wild and sensational Kesha trying to outdo the others in the Illuminati tug-of-war: 'I'm a bigger Satanist than you.' She released a single as part of her 2012 album *Warrior* called 'Dancing with the Devil', and the lyrics speak for themselves.[12]

R&B superstar Rihanna—the self-proclaimed princess of the Illuminati, the good girl gone bad—sent a bizarre tweet in which she cursed out Satan. What makes this bizarre rant even more interesting is that Rihanna has been a promoter of Satanic and occult ideas and imagery in her music and videos since the beginning of her career.

A protegé of Freemasonic and occultic rapper Jay Z, she wasted no time declaring her influence in society was going to be negative.

Rihanna's album *Good Girl Gone Bad* spells out Rihanna's transformation from a good, morally inclined young girl to a bad girl, who finds pleasure in promoting themes of sexual immorality, lust, and violence. The video for her first hit single, 'Umbrella', was heavily slanted towards occult symbolism.

At one Grammy performance, Rihanna came out wearing a temporary tattoo of Illuminati founder Adam Weishaupt.[13]

Rihanna has responded to critics by stating that she does not know anything about the Illuminati and is not a member (which seems odd in light of the tattoo). However, if through sheer ignorance she just does what she is told, she is a valuable pawn in a much bigger plan to bring in the New World Order.[14]

The symbolism used should not be understated. Manly P Hall, considered one of the greatest Masonic philosophers and an expert on the occult (in addition to being a Luciferian), said this with regard to symbolism in society: 'Symbolism is the language of the Mysteries; in fact it is the language not only of mysticism and philosophy but of all Nature. . . . In a single figure a symbol may both reveal and conceal, for to the wise the subject of the symbol is obvious, while to the ignorant the figure remains inscrutable' (Manly P. Hall, *The Secret Teachings of All Ages*, p. 38).

Rihanna promoted some of these symbols in her first major video: posing naked inside of a pyramid.

The pyramid represents the age of the gods, and the grand mission of the Illuminati/new age movement is to return to this age of the gods otherwise known as the New World Order!

The 33rd-degree Freemason and author George Steinmetz wrote in his book *Freemasonry: Its Hidden Meaning* that the pyramid 'symbolizes the perfect or divine man' (p. 63).

Steinmetz goes on to wrongly quote the Bible to promote this man-as-god heresy: "Be still—and know that I am God. . . . That *I* AM GOD—the final recognition of the All in All, the unity of the Self with the Cosmos—the cognition of *the DIVINITY OF THE SELF!* (Steinmetz, *The Lost Keys of Freemasonry*, p. 92).

This, of course, is blasphemy against God and nothing but the Satanic deception that outplayed and was offered to Adam and Eve in the Garden of Eden.

Alexander Hislop, in his book *The Two Babylons*, gives insight on this often murky history:

> When it is intended to assert the Unity of the Godhead in the strongest possible manner, the Babylonians used the term 'Adad.' Macrobii Saturnalia. In the unity of that one Only God of the Babylonians, there were three persons, and to symbolise that doctrine of the Trinity, they employed, as the discoveries of Layard prove, the

equilateral triangle, just as it is well known the Romish Church does at this day.

The Egyptians also used the triangle as a symbol of their 'tri-form divinity'. In both cases such a comparison is most degrading to the King Eternal, and is fitted utterly to pervert the minds of those who contemplate it, as if there was or could be any similitude between such a figure and Him who hath said, 'To whom will ye liken God, and what likeness will ye compare unto Him?'

The Papacy has in some of its churches, as, for instance, in the monastery of the so-called Trinitarians of Madrid, an image of the Triune God, with three heads on one body.[15]

Humans are created beings, and God alone is the Creator. We will never be God and, in fact, are all sinners in God's eyes.

From the Bible's standpoint, the Illuminati's plan is nothing more than a desire to return to the time of Noah. During this period, fallen angels interacted with humanity and, in disobedience, took women as wives (referred to in occult circles as the fusion of opposites) and created superhuman offspring called the Nephilim, or giants. The pyramid (triangle) marks the return to that age and the plan to achieve it, with its capstone, often referred to as the eye of Horus or eye of Lucifer, representing the final piece to bring that era into being.

One of the more popular uses of the pyramid symbol is on the back of the U.S. one-dollar bill.

The pyramid without its capstone represents the unfinished plan of the New World Order.

The new order, also known as the New World Order, is the one- world governmental system that the Bible prophesies will be led by the Antichrist in the few remaining years before the second coming of Christ. The date of 1776 in Roman numerals is synonymous with the founding of the original order of the Illuminati (1 May 1776) and the _he_ that is referred to is not the God of the Bible, but the All-Seeing Eye of Lucifer. If all this seems like it may be reading too much into things, ask yourself: why is this symbol on the US dollar bill to begin with?

If you are a born- again Christian, it should be clear that there are forces at work that seem to be promoting sin and all sorts of Satanic agendas in a major way.

Sin is what separates us from God, and without His redemption through Jesus Christ, then we all end up in hell. But Jesus Christ provides forgiveness. It all comes down to choice. We choose to sin. We choose to rebel. We choose to live our own lives. We choose to elevate both pop and church celebrities to **godlike** status, and let Satan delude us into thinking we can behave however we want with no fear of God. And so we must choose to recognise our sin, repent (turn and reject it), and seek forgiveness from the real and true and living God who is in heaven.

And for those who are Christians, repent of supporting this music and pray these artists, and the church will realise that God is ready and waiting to forgive them as well. But time is short.

We must see that the time to repent is now!

Theosophist Alice Bailey (1880–1949) states the evil agenda of Freemasonry is to corrupt the churches by infiltration.

> There is no question therefore that the work to be done
> in familiarizing the general public with the nature of the

> Mysteries is of paramount importance at this time. These mysteries will be restored to outer expression through the medium of the Church and the Masonic Fraternity. . . . When the Great One [Antichrist] comes with his disciples and initiates we shall have the restoration of the Mysteries and their exoteric presentation as a consequence of the first initiation.[16]

When Alice Bailey says that the Masonic Fraternity shall hide the Mysteries, gradually teaching them to the masses of the people, so that, when the Great One appears, he may bring the hidden Mysteries to 'outer expression', she is saying that, when Antichrist arises, he shall restore Luciferian worship to public worship. This is the Plan. So is this why pop artists like Rihanna, Taylor Swift, and Katy Perry keep putting pyramids in their videos?

It seems Christian groups are being influenced by this same Antichrist spirit.

Popular worship band Jesus Culture released a dance remix album titled *Reconstructed V. 1*, which shows they too have been influenced by the Illuminati. The group's switch in music and album design shows a pyramid on the front cover of their record.

But more importantly, why does an organisation like Hillsong, which calls itself Christian, spend most of 2013 and 2014 touring across the USA, Europe, and throughout England, using this very same symbolism and so prominently in their concerts?

44

THE FALL OF EMPIRES: FAITH IN RUINS

Nevertheless when the Son of man cometh, shall he find faith on the earth?

—Lk. 18:8

Hillsong produced a recent album *Empires*, which had social media in a frenzy over the album being sent out into space, with everyone wondering what it all meant.

Of more interest to me was the actual cover design that was odd to say the least. The cover design was all upside down including the band name United and all in black-and-white stripes which had a vague throwback to the stars and stripes of the American flag. So what was it all about? Was Hillsong's album just some marketing stunt?

The Masonic checkerboard is one of the most important symbols to the Illuminati, for it is used in ritualistic ceremonies. This is the use of black and white.

The number of album covers of artists with this checkerboard or stripe pattern is almost endless, with Madonna, Katy Perry, Nicki Minaj, No

Doubt, and Michael Jackson just to name a few who have used the formula. As proof of this setup, in 2010 Megan Fox posed with a *white* porcelain-coloured nude lookalike mannequin alongside her, with Fox in a black dress, seated on a checkerboard floor. This is clear symbolism for Megan switching alters.[1]

It is also a symbol for duality or the base of consciousness. Base consciousness is important because it is where all other states of mind arise. In the same way, checkerboards can also signify celebrities being pawns in the world of our propaganda media culture. The duality—stripes as seen in checkerboards as well as zebras—are also commonly used as triggers for mind control slaves in order to reach specific alters.[2]

Some of you may be aware that the IRS headquarters in New Carrollton, Maryland, is a government-owned building. Vigilant citizen who writes about all things Illuminati exposes the symbolism of the two black-and-white striped twin pillars as ancient and refers to the core of hermeticism, the basis of secret society teachings. In short, the pillars represent duality and the union of opposites.[3]

The Masonic trowel explains that 'white is the emblem of purity and innocence'. Plato asserted that white was par excellence the colour of the gods. The Levites wore white linen garments. Among the Romans, the unblemished character of a person aspiring to public office was indicated by a toga whitened with chalk.

Black, on the other hand, embodies darkness, death, and the underworld. Black is the banner of pirates and anarchists.[4] The design, by the way is the same as the ISIS flag with the white arabic writing.

The hues of white and black are widely used to depict opposites. Visually, white and black offer a high contrast.

In Western culture, white and black traditionally symbolise the dichotomy of good and evil, metaphorically related to light and darkness and day and night. The dichotomy of light and darkness appears already in the Pythagorean table of opposites.

Wikipedia suggests, for example, Hollywood Westerns contrast the villain with a black hat while the hero will normally wear white. This is often reversed. This was the case in the movie *Return of the Jedi* where Luke Skywalker wears black during the final battle.[5]

Justin Bieber's studio album *Purpose* is again a reference to this duality that pervades our culture. The cover shows a contemplative Bieber with hands in prayer pose, and yet he's embossed with an upside-down white cross and surrounded by similar stylistic black crosses in the background.

Whether on purpose, ignorance, or another attempt at creative licence, Hillsong's *Empires* album cover has all the hallmarks of this same inversion. The cover is a pedestrian crossing pattern of black and white. Just like the Beatles, 1969 *Abbey Road* album, where the now-famous shot of the band members crossing the road, has the stripes beneath them. Another example of this black-and-white opposite is at a typical modern wedding: the bride is in white, and the groom is in a black suit.

As part of their 2015 conference teaser, Hillsong, with its subtle and not-so-subtle symbols, showed a subliminal pyramid inside a hexagon at the 1:10 minute mark, flashed across the guy's T shirt. [6]

What are they trying to do?

Simply put, Hillsong is using these videos and events and music albums to attempt to alter a person's state of consciousness through music. This makes Hillsong extremely dangerous!

There are a number of triggers in respect to music and altered states of consciousness. Music which has these qualities can be involved in this inducement.

- any frequency
- any loudness, or dynamic
- any timbre
- any character of onset or attack, and
- any rhythmic duration or in combination of rhythms

I don't know about you, but these conference videos and, of course, the actual conference events themselves show overt use of 'frequency', flashing lights, strobes, and black-and-white lines, and circles, which can all bring altered states. This 'tripping' is made more successful if other senses are involved. There are two opposite points of departure, which is exactly what they are doing!

Sensory deprivation (static) is where hallucination can occur after a short while.[7] This usually involves 'masking' the senses for example by use of eyeshades (closing the eyes) and allowing as little environmental intrusion as possible e.g. Oceans.

The big question is, why Hillsong is using this overt black-and-white dualism and inversion to the max! And why are there sixty-six black- and- white stripes conveniently hidden in their album cover? Paradoxically, those in power, in particular those controlling the media and the entertainment industry, seem to be rather aware of esoteric symbols.

Why are there sixty-six black-and-white stripes on the Hillsong United *Empires* album cover?

The number '66' is the occult number for the Perfect Government of the

Perfect Man, who is represented by the number '666'[8]

Disturbingly, symbols that have once stood for goodness and light are used by those controlling mass media, entertainment, and fashion in an inverted manner, making them therefore stand for the exact opposite meaning: control and enslave. These inverted symbols are used all around us to convey a message and to put people under the very influences these symbols draw their forces from.

The *T* in United on the album cover is thus inverted, making it a blatant heralding of the now-obvious Antichrist spirit as an upside-down cross, the expression of self, to believe in yourself, and love of self.

We are seeing a fall of empires. Europe has been turning their backs on Christianity, preferring to worship materialism and secular humanism— godless religions that require no absolute moral or ethical demands. Our society loses its moral strength, and societal disintegration follows. Outspoken atheist Richard Dawkins reluctantly acknowledged however, 'I have mixed feelings about the decline of Christianity, in so far as Christianity might be a bulwark against something worse.'[9]

Christianity has always been a bulwark—a place of strength, a road to blessing, and a preservation of moral decay in society. Europe is now in spiritual freefall given over to atheistic anarchy on one side and Islamic terrorism on the other. 'Men's hearts failing them for fear' left wondering what to do.

The United States is sitting on a similar time bomb of humanism, immigration, refugees, corruption, martial law, and economic implosion.

Interestingly, in movies like *Olympus Has Fallen*, *London Has Fallen*, and the new *Captain American: Civil War*, the message is clear.

One argument for this is that Western civilisation peaked in the 1960s and is now sliding into the abyss. Coincidentally, religion in the United States fell away in the 1960s.[10]

However, we are in the midst of what might be called the great decline. Previous declines in religion pale in comparison. Over the past 15 years, the drop in religion or spirituality has been twice as great as the decline of the 1960s and 1970s.[11] According to the Pew Research Centre's demographic study on America's changing religious landscape, 35 per cent of those aged 19–34 now identify as religiously 'unaffiliated' with young people leaving the mainline Protestant traditions with a -3.4 per cent change in the last seven years.[12] In the UK the trend is similar with 48 percent of Britain now declaring no religion.[13] Christians are being slowly forced to the margins of society, the increasing threat of government intrusion into Christian education is now obvious. The ground is shifting beneath our feet as the Judeo-Christian foundations of our society are removed, brick by brick. We need to notice these things, and be prepared for them. Even the Brexit will be used to transform the European Union into a new superstate.

As we continue this great decline in the West, many of the church are being murdered as martyrs in other regions of the world. The blood of the martyrs is the seed of the church, and yet the church in the West is grabbing for success and popularity, which is in itself an unconscious acknowledgement of spiritual decline. Our archenemy has convinced us that 'heaven is overrated'.[14]

So whatever Hillsong is spruiking as the new 'Christianity' is just a failed attempt to fill theatres. Beyond that, it is impacting diddly squat.

And although imagining it is being an influence for good, Hillsong's role is to assist in the subtle formation of a one-world inclusive Christian ethos, a moralistic maxim, with an all-inclusive spiritual head, known as the beast or Antichrist, which is just around the corner.

Lance Goodall

Is this Hillsong United album a veiled reference to the darkness now imploding on our nations? Intriguingly, *Through the Ashes of Empires* is an album produced by heavy metal band Machine Head. Of course, with the fall of empires will come the rise of a New World Order.

45
COME TOGETHER

Woe to the rebellious children, saith the Lord, that take counsel, but not of me; and that cover with a covering, but not of my spirit, that they may add sin to sin:² That walk to go down into Egypt, and have not asked at my mouth; to strengthen themselves in the strength of Pharaoh, and to trust in the shadow of Egypt!³ Therefore shall the strength of Pharaoh be your shame, and the trust in the shadow of Egypt your confusion.

—Isa.30:1–3

There is an intriguing prophecy which concerns the end of the world and is as follows: 'In the final persecution of the Holy Roman Church there will reign Peter the Roman, who will feed his flock amid many tribulations, after which the seven-hilled city will be destroyed and the dreadful Judge will judge the people. The End.' Concerning *Petrus Romanus*, according to St. Malachy's list, this pope is to be the last. ¹

On the same day that Pope Benedict XVI announced his resignation, a lightning bolt struck St. Peter's Basilica at the Vatican that night. Filippo Monteforte, a photographer with Agence France Press, was rewarded for his patience with not one, but two bolts.[2]

Could this be a sign that the Malachy prophecy will be fulfilled in Pope Francis? Others suggest that another will come in his place to fulfil the Malachy prophecy, and that Francis will abdicate his role as official pope soon as well.

Pope Francis born in Buenos Aires, Argentina, is the first Jesuit pope, the first from the Americas, the first from the Southern Hemisphere and the first non-European pope since the Syrian Gregory III, who died in 741. Before seminary he was both a chemical technologist and nightclub bouncer. He was ordained a Catholic priest in 1969, and from 1973 to 1979 was Argentina's provincial superior of the Society of Jesus.[3]

As Francis reviews the role of women, defends Islam, continues to tout socialist ideals, and egocentric environmentalism, are we seeing the beginning of the dissolution of the Roman Catholic Church, and it's dissolving into ashes? Will this in time give way to a phoenix type rising into a new religious institution?

Don Moen, formerly the leader of Integrity Music, one of the biggest distributors of contemporary worship music, said in an interview with *Christianity Today* in 2003, 'I've discovered that worship music is trans-denominational, trans-cultural. It bridges any denomination. Twenty years ago there were many huge divisions between denominations. Today the walls are coming down.'[4]

John Styll, the publisher of *Worship Leader* magazine, made the following telling observation, 'You can have a pretty straight-laced but theologically liberal Presbyterian church using the same songs that are being sung at a wild and crazy charismatic church, but they use different arrangements and adapt the songs to their unique settings' (Steve Rabey, 'The Profits of Praise', *Christianity Today*, 12 Jul 1999).[5]

Hellsong

Brian Houston of Hillsong makes the same comparison, which he proudly links to success for him and his church.

'I always wanted to have the kind of church which influenced the way people do church,' Brian Houston said. **'People may be divided** on doctrine and theology and other things, but worship tends to transcend **all of that.'**[6] [emphasis added]

These ministries are, of course, actively targeting the more conservative, old-fashioned churches to move them into the broader church.

David Cloud, of Fundamental Baptist Information Service, who has written much and has been the most outspoken on this topic, makes some very important and crucial points for all Christians to consider.

There are transition songs and bridge songs designed to move 'traditional' churches along the contemporary path towards Christian rock. From the perspective of the CCM artists involved in this, they aren't doing anything sinister. They are simply trying to feed the broader church.[7]

The concept is to draw old-fashioned Bible churches into the contemporary style. The adaptation of contemporary worship music is certainly not the only factor in these dramatic transformations but it is at the very heart and soul of the changes we have seen in the church in the last three to four decades.

Now the piper's tune is an unbiblical world view, preaching a doctrine of license under the guise of grace.

This Christianity of contemporary Christian music is taking a whole generation back to the spirit and licentiousness of ancient Babylon!

Recently (July 2015), both Don Moen and Australian worship leader Darlene Zschech joined Pope Francis in an ecumenical event in St

Peter's Square, and she called it 'an amazing day for the Body of Christ'.[8]

Doesn't Zschech mean a great day for the Church of Rome? But this is no surprise as she proudly spruiked the 2008 World Youth Day in Sydney, Australia, by stating, 'We see WYD08 as a great opportunity to serve the Catholic Church in its vision to present the gospel and reach out to our city, our nation and our world in unity.'[9] How can we be serving Rome's vision?

Don Moen, re-echoing his mantra of unity, said, 'This ecumenical event brings Protestants, Catholics, and Jews together as we pray for our brothers and sisters in Christ who are being martyred and persecuted all over the world today. Although there are many denominational differences throughout the church worldwide, I have seen firsthand how coming together in worship and prayer promotes unity.'[10]

Coming together, is not the same as being fitly framed together. (Eph. 2:21).

Strangely as I write this, the WYD 2016 has opened in Krakow Poland, the homeland of previous Pope, John Paul II. Pope Francis is there and invited guests, at the event known as Catholic Woodstock. The youth event with some one million gathered is where they unite as one in their walk of faith over that week. The emblem or coat of arms of Poland is a veiled phoenix bird. The Egyptian version of the phoenix, is said to be the soul of the Sun-God Ra.[11]

This same theme was promoted in a July 2016 event Together 2016. Some of the guest speakers and artists include: Hillsong United, Kari Jobe, Francis Chan, Lecrae, Nick Hall, Passion, Crowder, Kirk Franklin, Ravi Zacharias, Jeremy Camp, Andy Mineo, Michael W Smith, Lauren Daigle, Christine Caine, Josh McDowell, and Luis Palau.[12]

According to his own Pulse website, Nick Hall, who organised the Washington DC Jamfest, sits on the leadership teams for the US Lausanne Committee, the National Association of Evangelicals, and the student advisory team for the Billy Graham Evangelistic Association (BGEA). British Anglican theologian and Ecumenical advocate John Stott was the chief architect of the 1974 Lausanne Covenant.[13]

Nick Hall met with Pope Francis in June. The pope will make a guest appearance via video at the Together 2016 event. Incidentally, this is all in front of the great obelisk on the National Mall in Washington DC. Obelisks are phallic symbols related to the Egyptian sun god, Ra. At ground level, each side measures just happens to be 55.5 feet long, which is equal to 666 inches. The height of the obelisk is 555.5 feet, which is incidentally equal to 6,666 inches to the nearest inch, the number of the beast Antichrist system.[14]

All this unity in the shadow of the shaft of Baal.

Of course an obelisk is smack bang in the middle of St. Peter's square in Rome, and not just any old obelisk, but a genuine Egyptian obelisk shipped from Heliopolis to Rome by the Roman emperor Caligula.[15]

Both the basilica in Rome and the capitol building in Washington DC have domes which represent the womb and face the phallus (obelisk). As mentioned in a previous chapter, Albert Pike explained that the 'compass, is the Hermetic Symbol of the Creative Deity, and the Square of the productive Earth [female] or Universe'. Therefore, the Masons look at the compass as the male phallus and the square as the female. As you look down from above upon the National Mall, this Masonic emblem is clearly exemplified. And then there is their catchcry 'Jesus *changes* everything' with the word *changes* written backwards.

The connections don't stop there. Capitol Hill in Washington DC was designed to mirror Capitoline Hill in Rome. Pope Pius IX even provided a memorial stone for the monument known as the Pope's Stone, a gift from the pope and the Vatican. The three-foot slab of 'costly variegated marbles' was originally from the ruins of the Temple of Concord in Rome, built in 366 BC. Engraved on the face of the stone were the words *From Rome*.[16] As you can see, this ecumenical event is layered with an intriguing array of both physical and metaphysical *union*. Another thing that ties into this matrix is the date of *Together 2016*. It was held on the 16 July 2016 a date linked to the number 7. Could this mean that the promise of the coming Antichrist is consummated and we see its fulfilment sometime in this current period? 777 is a trifecta number that speaks of spiritual growth and transformation.

On one of the main banners on the website, they suggest that 'Jesus said that we might be together'. What Jesus actually prayed in John 17 was that we may be *one*, which is not quite the same. His prayer was that our unity would be based on truth.

Think about it: they are *not* the same.

'I love the name *together*,' Joel Houston of Hillsong United said in a statement. **'There's a power in unity and a blessing that comes when people put aside their differences and gather together for one purpose.** Our prayer is for this to be a reset for us as a generation of the church— in America and beyond' (emphasis added).

Worship leader Matt Maher, a Roman Catholic, has outlined at other ecumenical events that he believes it is his calling to work towards to the unification of Christians and Catholics.[16]

In addition to Hall, 'Charismania' leader Mike Bickle, who heads International House of Prayer Kansas City (IHOPKC), and Bethel Church was there, speaking with the pope for two hours. Also World

Evangelical Alliance (WEA) head Geoff Tunnicliffe was back.[17]

These leaders may be well meaning, but these types of events all end up in the wastepaper bin of ecumenical compromise.

Is unity that easy that all you need to do is to turn up to a worship and prayer event? By doing so, we trod all over the blood of precious saints (as Rome has always done) and use it to bring unified apostasy. Do these 'evan-jackal' leaders not consider history? What of John Wycliffe, Hugh Latimer, William Tyndale, Nicholas Ridley, Martin Luther, John Hus, John Knox, John Calvin, Huldrych Zwingli, the Waldenses, and others who were either hunted, persecuted, or burnt at the stake by Rome.

And what of the numerous doctrines of devils that Roman Catholics still adhere to? [18]

- The belief in truth revealed in scripture and the importance of tradition
- The Roman Catholic church claims the right to alter doctrines and practices by virtue of her infallible authority
- Creation versus evolution theory
- The Eucharist or the mass, the literal body of Christ, called transubstantiation
- The seven sacraments, one being penance
- Purgatory, atoning for your own sins
- Prayers for the dead
- 'No salvation outside the church'
- The assumption of Mary and as co-redemptrix
- The pope, as the Vicar of Christ, one who serves in the place of, assuming the position in the office of another i.e. Christ veiled in flesh

How can any evangelical hold to these tenets of Catholic faith?

Does anyone remember the reformation? Does the Council of Trent mean anything to these leaders and their 'sheeple' that blindly follow them by the busload?

In 1540, a former Spanish soldier by the name of Ignatius Loyola headed up a new order who established with the pope's approval the Society of Jesus (the Jesuits) who set about to reverse in time the fire of the reformation. By the way, the society is consecrated to the Blessed Virgin Mary. Their chief aim was to set up a counter reformation by denying the work of the reformers and bring the world back under the authority of the pope. It was to be the conversion of Protestants. The Jesuits accursed everything that the Reformers were preaching.

The Council of Trent was held between 1545 and 1563. Four hundred years later, Pope John XXIII affirmed the decrees it had issued. It consisted of twenty-five sessions. Those sessions accurse and condemn all the doctrines of the Reformationin the fourth session, which is probably the most concerning. The Jesuits condemn freedom of speech, freedom of the press, and freedom of conscience.[19]

Going back to an earlier period, the following is a decree of Pope Lucius III in 1181 against the Christians within his realm:

> To abolish the malignity of diverse heresies which are lately sprung up in most parts of the world, it is but fitting that the power committed to the church should be awakened, that by the concurring assistance of the Imperial strength, both the insolence and mal-pertness of the heretics in their false designs may be crushed, and the truth of Catholic simplicity shining forth in the holy church, may demonstrate her pure and free from the

execrableness of their false doctrines.[20]

Just to show you we aren't talking about the murky history of the dark ages, in 2010 Pope Benedict established the Pontifical Council for New Evangelisation and announced a Synod of Bishops to be held in Rome in October 2012 on the theme 'The New Evangelisation for the Transmission of the Christian Faith'.[21] Pope Francis' recent Apostolic exhortation summed up the work of the synod and enhanced it with further considerations of his own.[22]

The term new evangelisation was all about 'classic' methods not working; John XXIII, in announcing the council in 1959, spoke about opening the windows to let in some fresh air. The truths of faith remain the same, he said; but the church's style, discipline, and worship, the presentation of her teaching were to be modernised to communicate better with the modern world and to spread the gospel. He also wanted the council to help bring about unity among Christians.[23]

Where have we heard that before? In other words, even though we haven't changed one thing, let's try to mirror the evangelicals so they may warm to us. 'Groovy, baby' Even Pope Francis calls the Church herself a missionary disciple.[24]

Speaking of evangelicals, Rick Warren is also helping to breathe fresh air into this same ecumenical house.

One revelation that came out was in an interview on 11 April 2014. Warren hosted a delegation from Rome to discuss the new evangelisation program at his very own Saddleback Church. They came to observe the Saddleback Purpose-Driven Program to gain ideas and insights for the Roman plan initiated by Pope John Paul II and continued on by Pope Benedict and Pope Francis.

The new evangelisation may sound like it's all about winning converts to

Christ, but when has Rome ever preached the true gospel? Rome's new evangelisation program is dedicated to win converts to the Roman Catholic 'Eucharistic Christ' and obedience to the sacraments of the church.

This platform for evangelisation is nothing more than centralisation.

Interviewer Raymond Arroyo asked Warren about the Vatican delegation, adding, 'This is a sizable group'

Warren's response:

> It was. They were about 30 bishops from Europe. One of the men had been actually trained and mentored by Jean Vanier, which is an interesting thing because we have a retreat centre here and my spiritual director, who grew up at Saddleback, actually went and trained under Jean Vanier too. So I am very excited about that.[25]

Warren's frank admission provides conclusive evidence of his endorsement of Roman Catholic monastic mysticism and his warm affiliation with Rome, something not seen since the days of Billy Graham.

In this same interview, Rick Warren hailed Pope Francis, saying, Well, the main thing is love always reaches people. And as our new pope he was very, very symbolic. This authenticity, this humility, the caring for the poor, this is what the whole world expects us Christians to do. . . . In fact there was a headline here in Orange County—and I love the headline. It said, 'if you love Pope Francis, you'll love Jesus.' [26]

Can anything be clearer? Warren, speaking for himself and others, calls Francis 'our pope'. And he affirms this blasphemy by essentially saying if you've seen the pope, you've seen Jesus. Seemingly for Warren, the pope is near enough to Jesus.[27]

The way is becoming broader. Like it or not, all roads lead to Rome. The Jesuit plan is to bring the 'separated brethren' back home to Rome. Those who refuse to follow will eventually be singled out as heretics, or resisters, or agitators. It is already being spoken in these terms.[28]

And yet Joel Osteen, the pastor of Houston's Lakewood Church, had his turn to meet with Pope Francis at the Vatican in June of 2014.

Osteen said it was a great honour to represent the pastors of America in the meeting with the pontiff, whom he described as warm, personable, and full of joy.[29]

According to reports, Osteen was part of a delegation organised by the International Foundation in an effort to encourage interfaith relations and ecumenism.

'I just felt very honoured and very humbled,' Osteen told local television station Click 2 Houston.[30]

Osteen attended mass in St Peter's Square prior to the meeting in the midst of a crowd of 100,000 people.[31]

Osteen told reporters, **'I love the fact that's he's made the Church more inclusive,"** he said. "Not trying to make it smaller, but to try to make it larger—to take everybody in. **So, that just resonates with me'**[32] (emphasis added).

James Robison and Kenneth Copeland were among others who met with Pope Francis in Rome to talk about unity during that same period. Robison said Francis talked about diversity and Christians could work together without compromising their beliefs. Bishop Tony Palmer, a friend of the pope's (now deceased) had assisted in the meeting.[33] Palmer died mysteriously in a motorcycle accident. His mission was to unite the Christian evangelicals with the Roman Catholic Church. He said that it was time for 'Christians to come home to Rome'. As a bridge between Pope Francis and Kenneth Copeland (friends of both), it seems Palmer was 'pulled'.

In February 2016, Pope Francis met with Patriarch Kirill in Cuba, the head of the Russian Orthodox Church after nearly 1,000 years. "Finally!" Francis exclaimed as he embraced Kirill in Havana's airport, "We are brothers," Francis added.[34] The pope's title of **Pontifex Maximus** (Latin, literally 'greatest pontiff' or 'greatest bridge builder') is no longer a mystery as to why this is a fulfilment of prophetic significance.[35] Indeed Pope Francis is the greatest builder of bridges among Christian denominations that we have seen.

In a whirlwind visit to Armenia on the 24–26 June 2016, Francis met to with the leaders of the Orthodox Church. He outlined how 'with great joy, we are walking together on a journey that has already taken us far, and we look confidently towards the day when by God's help we shall be united around the altar of Christ's sacrifice in the fullness of Eucharistic communion.'[36]

Happily the Bible-believing fundamentalists are joining together with the compromised neo-evangelicals, who in turn are reaching out to the neo-orthodox, whose hands are outstretched to the Christ-rejecting liberals, who in turn are embracing the Devil.

With his talks in 2014 Tony Palmer declared Martin Luther's protest to be over. Faith alone sufficient to save was the great rallying cry of the Protestant reformation. Has justification by faith alone, by grace alone, become unimportant now? Has it lost its meaning? How shall we escape if we neglect such a great salvation?

Others in the Southern Baptist camp like Beth Moore have been running with the ecumenical baton for a while, being influenced by Catholic mystic the late Brennan Manning as she admits in her book *When Godly People Do Ungodly Things.* In 2010, *Christianity Today* identified her as part of the contemplative prayer movement. Moore spoke at James Robison's Awake Now Conference in February 2014. She expressed her belief that God showed her there was a great spiritual awakening coming.

Interestingly, Moore warned about those who would question this coming awakening and 'downpour'.[37] *Spiritual awakening* is being used within evangelical circles today. Terms like *one, awaken, awake.* How can leaders who embrace a mystic spirituality and religious deception bring about a true revival? How does this unity automatically equate to this coming downpour? It is like saying the Jewish leaders and the early believers at the time of our Lord were required to patch up their differences before the Holy Spirit would be outpoured at Pentecost. This kind of unity will turn out to be a religious train wreck! Moore's revival will be nothing more than a revival of Rome!

While Beth Moore and others are closing the gap between Christianity and Catholicism, we should remember the saints who went before us and who paid with their blood when they stood faithfully for the gospel.

As we close out this chapter, here are some solemn reminders.

In the year 1209, a formidable army of cross-bearers, of 40 days' service, was put into motion, destined to destroy all heretics. The cruelties of these Crusaders appear to have had no parallel; in a few months, there were sacrificed about two hundred thousand lives, and barbarities practised, before unheard of, all which met the approbation of Innocent III.

Two large cities, Beziers and Carcassonne, were reduced to ashes; and thousands of others, driven from their burning houses, were wandering in the woods and mountains, sinking daily under the pressure of want (Orchard, *Concise History of the Baptists*, p. 211).

Referring to the Waldenses and Albigenses, William Jones writes in his *History of the Church*, 'They have so long before us, with an exemplary courage laboured to preserve the Christian religion in its ancient purity . . . which the Church of Rome all this while has endeavoured to abolish.'[38]

And this is the Rome Moen, Zschech, Moore, Osteen, and Warren are beckoning us to join with?

Rome's vengeance was particularly against the principle that all Christians should have access and be able to read the scriptures.

Know also that in the last days perilous times shall come (see 2 Tim. 3:1–7). The sad fact is the great evangelical heresy is happening before our eyes. The abandonment of the truth, once and for all delivered to the saints, is now being cast headlong like a millstone to the bottom of the sea.

High-ranking occultist Eliphas Levi said in 1862:

> A day will come when the pope . . . will declare that all the excommunications are lifted and all the anathemas are retracted, when all the Christians will be united within the Church, when the Jews and Moslems will be blessed and called back to her. . . . She will permit all sects to approach her by degrees and will embrace all mankind in the communion of her love and prayers. Then, *Protestants will no longer exist*. Against what will they be able to protest? The sovereign pontiff will then be truly king of the religious world, and he will do

whatever he wishes with all the nations of the earth[39] (emphasis added)

This is, of course, the great plan of Masonry, they are the ones driving this amalgamation and yet Christian leaders are leading us down the primrose path of celestial insanity!

In the book of Revelation, we find there are two lambs—the Lamb of God and another having two horns like a lamb—but he spoke like a dragon (See Rev. 13: 8,11). The dragon is speaking but with the voice of a lamb. The papacy is no longer using the tactics of rape, murder, torture, burnings, and dismemberment but of reform, unity, brotherhood, and fellowship. Timothy Leary was a 60s psychologist who became famous for experimenting with LSD as his way to promote social interaction and raise consciousness. In 1969, Leary decided to run for Governor of California, and asked The Beatles member John Lennon to write a song for him. 'Come Together, Join the Party' was Leary's campaign slogan (really a reference to the drug culture) and became the original title of the song. Leary never had much of a campaign, but the slogan gave Lennon an idea.[40] John Lennon was quoted as saying, 'Now I understand what you have to do. Put your political message across with a little honey.' This seems to be the new strategy within the corridors of the Vatican.[41]

Pope Francis wants us all to be dreamers, and imagine that we *will live as one*. The tide is now turning, and the great power committed to the dragon has been awakened that the insolence of the 'heretics' in their false designs may be crushed and the truth of Catholic simplicity may shine forth in the holy church once more.

46
WE BUILT THIS CITY

For here have we no continuing city, but we seek one to come.

—Heb. 13:14

There will not be any disassociation between the Universal church, the Sacred Lodge of all true Masons, and the inner circles of the esoteric societies. . . . In this way, the goals and work of the United Nations hall be solidified and a new Church of God, led by all the religions and by all the spiritual groups, shall put an end to the great heresy of separateness.

—Alice Bailey 1

Zion is the third studio album by Australian contemporary Christian band Hillsong United. Production for the album began in March 2011 in Sydney, Australia. The album was released on 22 February 2013 for Australia and was released by 26 February 2013 internationally.[2]

The irony is 'Zion' is a single listed in ninth spot on the album and instead of it being the main track as you would anticipate, it is an

Any event or thing assigned with the number 11 aids in the raising of the Antichrist.

In Latin, the devil's name is LVX, which translates as 50 + 5 + 10 = 65 = 6+5 =11.

Armistice Day/Remembrance Day is November 11 at 11:11.[10]

The upright columns before the entrance of every mystery temple, Masonic included, are synonymous of the power and purpose of 11.[11]

It cannot be brushed aside that there is great significance attached to the release date chosen for Hillsong for *Zion* in Australia, incorporating the 'holy' master number of 22 and the karmic number 13. Again the dates of the production for the album began in March 2011 in Sydney, Australia. The album was released on 22 February 2013 for Australia and was released by 26 February 2013 internationally.

As way of reference to show this occult signature in current events, here are a couple of examples.

President John F Kennedy was assassinated on 22 November 1963 in a public square that had been home to a Masonic Lodge and that has an obelisk in its centre. November is month number 11, and the day of the murder was the 22nd. Numbers 11 and 22 are sacred primary occult numbers.[12]If you remember it was on the morning of 22 March 2016, three coordinated bombings occurred in Belgium: two at Brussels Airport in Zaventem, and one at Maalbeek metro station in Brussels.

Finally, the master number 33 combines the most proficient powers of expression (the 3) with the teacher and caregiver par excellence: the 6. Its true essence is the final word in spiritual evolution: the master teacher.[13]

Similarly, it must be said that the international date for Hillsong's album release, 26 February 2013, is equally concerning, if not more so, as the numbers are 26, 2, and 13. The number 26 is divisible by the number 13, which can be written 13 + 13, or written - 13 x 2 = 26. Even 26 divided by 2 is 13.

Even the album began in March 2011, which is another key to give you the numerical combinations of 3, 11, and 13 (3+2+0+11 = 16).

None of this requires too much creative gymnastics to show a reoccurring pattern. In the presence of two or three witnesses, let the thing be established, and here we have a fait accompli of 3.

Remember, the karmic numbers are 13, 14, 16, and 19.

In relation to numbers, the 19th-century Bible scholar E W Bullinger writes:

> As to the significance of thirteen, all are aware that it has come down to us as a number of ill-omen. Many superstitions cluster around it, and various explanations are current concerning them.
>
> Unfortunately, those who go backwards to find a reason seldom go back far enough. The popular explanations do not, so far as we are aware, go further back than the Apostles. But we must go back to the first occurrence of the number thirteen in order to discover the key to its significance. It occurs first in Gen. 14:4, where we read 'Twelve years they served Chedorlaomer, and the thirteenth year they REBELLED.'

Hence every occurrence of the number thirteen, and likewise of every multiple of it, stamps that with which it stands in connection with rebellion, apostasy, defection, corruption, disintegration, revolution, or some kindred idea. [14]

In the occult thirteen (13) is deemed sacred. It was therefore no accident that Hitler chose the year 1939 to begin World War II because 39 is formed by the multiplication of 13 x 3. Thus, you can see how human history has been shaped by the occult belief in the power of numbers.[15]

Another example that is just hideous is on 6 August 1945 at 8:15 a.m. United States B-29 bomber *Enola Gay*, on mission number 13, dropped an atomic bomb called Little Boy on Hiroshima, Japan, near the 33rd

Parallel. The bombing was 169 years (13 x 13) years from America's independence. Harry Truman was a Mason.

This accusation is therefore a serious one, but it must be shown for what it is: an occultic influence that is reflected in the music and culture being marketed and sold as Christianity by Hillsong to the world.

It was on 25 April 1945, two days previous to the full moon of Taurus and the Festival of Wesak (note: the best time to recite the Great Invocation, according to Lucis Trust, as the energies of the hierarchy are in alignment with the earth), that delegates from fifty nations met in San Francisco for a conference known officially as the United Nations Conference on International Organization.[16] Of this period, the Tibetan master tells us: 'It will be a time of supreme difficulty, in which the Forces of Light will face . . . the forces of selfishness and separativeness.'[17]

It seems the dreaded UN proceeded with a spiritual undertaking in alignment with the Luciferic light to eradicate these 'selfish ones'.

There will come when

> The Religion of the future will be a general converging
> of religions in a universal Christ that will satisfy all. . . .
> In the end, it is hoped that the Christian will be a better

> Christian and each Hindu a better Hindu. (Jesuit
> theologian Father Jacques Dupuis at the 2003 interfaith
> congress 'The Future of God'*)[18]

Rick Warren once said, 'I have known many people believe in the Messiah of Jesus. Regardless of what religion they are they believe in him. It's about a relationship, not a religion.'[19]

Just as the United Nations believes that a New World Order is just around the corner, the Baha'i believe the human race is nearing the next stage in their spiritual evolution—a phase that brings us one rung higher on the evolutionary ladder towards a supposed world peace and utopia. In the Baha'i document 'A Vision of World Peace', they claim that religions of exclusivity, intolerance, and perversions of truth are the root of all evil and the cause for all of the world's social, political, and economic ills.

They blame the resurgence of 'fanatical religious fervour occurring across the globe for what they call a dying convulsion that is undermining the spiritual values which are conducive to the unity of mankind'.[20]

Are you starting to get the picture?

At this very time, Pope Francis believes that all religions are different paths to the same God, praying for his Muslim brothers and sisters and laying a foundation for the coming one-world religion. Aloft aboard the papal plane in late November 2015, the pope chatted with journalists on various issues. Commenting about the Paris attacks, he said, 'We are all God's children, we all have the same Father. . . . We need to live peacefully alongside one another develop friendships.' Even music festivals like Tomorrowland are appealing to their audience with the same message 'unite forever' under the all-seeing eye.[21]

He then went on to discuss fundamentalism within the church.

'Fundamentalism is a sickness that is in all religions,' said the pontiff.[22]

Francis said, 'Fundamentalism is always a tragedy. It is not religious, it lacks God, it is idolatrous.'[23]

Following his first visit to the Middle East as pope in May 2014, the pontiff criticised fundamentalism in Christianity, Islam, and Judaism as a form of violence.

'A fundamentalist group, even if it kills no one, even it strikes no one, is violent. The mental structure of fundamentalism is violence in the name of God.'[24]

Sadly, these comments have not gotten the attention they deserve.

One must conclude Pope Francis is against a Christianity that believes in a literal interpretation of the Bible. Nearly 2,000 years ago, the Apostle John warned us that a one-world religion would be fulfilled, and now we can see that it is coming to fruition. So what will the end result of all of this be?

The ultimate goal is to destroy and eliminate all dissenters who resist or take offence to this new community. This new one world of collective consciousness, unity, and oneness will soon see its fulfillment. Pope Francis is calling for a world of unity under the guise of a new humanity, where there are no longer borders or barriers. Soon there will be a day dawning when there will be a great world body of believers, and Hillsong will be among that grand throng. They are working toward a new world built on rock'n' roll.

They aren't called Hillsong United for nothing.

47
DANCING WITH THE DEVIL

Let no man deceive you by any means: for that day shall not come, except there come a falling away first, and that man of sin be revealed, the son of perdition; [4] *Who opposeth and exalteth himself above all that is called God, or that is worshipped; so that he as God sitteth in the temple of God, shewing himself that he is God.*

—2 Thess. 2:3,4

What we learn from history is that we don't learn from history.

I don't really know where to start with this, but this is the worst of the worst.

Hillsong London was absolutely slammed for their production of Hillsong Carols 2015 at Wembley Stadium, where they had a Vegas-style rendition of 'Silent Night', yes with 1920s flapper girls, in short-tiered fringe Charleston Gatsby dresses, which turned into none other than a sleazy night.

After pulling down the footage from YouTube and other weak responses, I don't think there was a one proper clarification, or an apology, as to the reasons behind this production.

Hellsong

Now Hillsong London has now crossed another line all in the name of entertainment, an event that not even the New Testament apostles could have predicted.

Satan has been glorified at an Easter service!

The London branch of Hillsong has done it again. They have corrupted the very sanctuary of God by seating Satan at the centre of worship in their 2016 Easter production.

Some would suggest Easter is pagan in origin, however Gary Clarke and his blind flock have staged another depraved perversion for all the world to be aghast at. This church has become the centrepiece for religious apostasy beyond the traditional sense. Not only are they denying key doctrines of the Bible, but they crucify to themselves the Son of God afresh and put *him* to an open shame, denying the very one who bought them (Heb 6:6).

By flattering themselves and glorying in their dramatic prowess, Hillsong London have put on another 'show-stopping' West End production, with sets and props, singers, and dancers —the whole gambit. But by doing so, they have allowed the very spirit of hell to be seated on the throne of God.

In all serious, when I was viewing various videos of this event, their production was like being in the pit of hell from the outset as smoke and red haze enveloped the stage area which created a gloomy and downright sinister portrayal of the crucifixion of the Lord Jesus as he went to the cross. The whole thing became an inverted betrayal of the Easter/ Passover season, with the devil and his demon hordes celebrating Christ's death, as if in victory, mocking and jeering at him, in a satanic ritual. The atmosphere was torturous, and even a few minutes of watching this disgrace on YouTube was agony.

To the innocent bystander, it may have seemed like a modern play to illustrate the cross and all the horror that Christ went through. But once more, Hillsong played the Illuminati card, and several hidden subliminal messages were thrown up on the big screen.

Seventeen minutes into the video that I watched, a large red pyramid, flashing at high-frequency, appeared. The pyramid, with an elevated capstone, moved, and then covered the image of Christ's eye.

Hillsong London's Easter event although in Christian camouflage was all about the occult.

At about the 20-minute mark, you see a variety of kaleidoscope patterns that swirl around, which then morph into very clear images of horned creatures, Baphomet, an owl, a horned bat-like creature, and, at one point, glowing red demon eyes.

And as these collage of images go from one to the next, the choir on stage sang 'Praise the Name of the Lord Our God'. As the choir sang this song, all this was playing out in the background, and a large white ziggurat structure was displayed with a pyramid and a capstone.[1]

Hillsong is mocking the cross and glorying in the devil!

Hillsong London's use of drama and music and choreography has brought their church to the very gates of hell. You literally feel the oppression in the Hillsong meeting. It is like you have landed in a druid den or witches' coven. We have become desensitised by our modern media. Discernment has completely GONE from Christians. This blind obedience to church leaders is beyond comprehension.

We are no longer talking about Hillsong's money or their music but their league with the devil!

There is even a scene where a flash of light representing the resurrection of Jesus Christ revealed among the darkness of the stage a dark-skinned man standing bare chested as some kind of 'god'. We are drowning in spiritual and moral adultery. Paganism is the spiritual benchmark. I am sorry but this is not cool.

Again, the idea is that if we present the best and most fantastic show equal to quality of the world, then the world will respect us and somehow turn to Christ.

Instead, it is prophesied our world will soon embrace a personage who fits the description of the wicked (the Antichrist).

Permit me to introduce a strange but striking figure called Antiochus Epiphanes IV. Epiphanes, *God manifest* for obvious reasons, foreshadows the future maniac who will be worshipped en masse.

Antiochus Epiphanes IV was the eighth ruler of the Seleucid empire, ruling around 175 BC. His domain made up part of Alexander the Great's previous empire 150 years prior, which stretched from Egypt all the way to Babylon and Persia into selected parts of India. Over a period of 125 years, the Seleucids and Ptolemies battled for this vast region. The former finally won in 198 B.C. when Antiochus III defeated the Egyptians and incorporated Judea into his empire. Initially, he continued to allow the Jews autonomy, but after a stinging defeat at the hands of the Romans he began a program of Hellenisation that threatened to force the Jews to abandon their monotheism for the Greeks' paganism. Antiochus backed down in the face of Jewish opposition to his effort to introduce idols in their temples; but his son, Antiochus IV, who inherited the throne in 176 B.C. resumed his father's original policy, but this time without excluding the Jews. A brief Jewish rebellion only hardened his views and led him to outlaw central tenets of Judaism.[2]

Antiochus Epiphanes is one of the most important types—or foreshadows—of the Antichrist in the Bible. He came from the line of Seleucids called the dynasty of Antiochus. There were others before him:

Antiochus I, II, III. The Jews changed his name to *Epimanus*, meaning *the mad one*.

The *Jewish Encyclopaedia* outlines that this illustrious king of Syria reigned in 175 BC and died in 164. He took possession of the Syrian throne, which rightly belonged to his nephew Demetrius. Antiochus, in rabbinical sources, is known as (the wicked). He exercised great influence upon Jewish history and the development of the Jewish religion. Antiochus combined in himself the worst of the Greeks and the Romans. His vanity and his fondness for display were to the verge of eccentricity.3

In Israel, Onias III was the high priest at the time, but a party spirit arose among the people: the struggle of the Tobiads against the conservatives who sided with Onias. Antiochus was determined to Hellenise Israel. The Jews were quickly becoming more Greek than any other time in history. A group of Jews came to Antiochus with a plan. They proposed that the high priest Onias III should be removed, and his Hellenised brother Jason should take his place. Joshua (Jason) succeeded Onias as high priest. It was during his office, he changed his name to Jason, following Greek usage.

They would set up a Greek constitution and coin Greek money. In order to ingratiate himself with the king, Jason established an arena for public games close by the Temple.

During the period of Jason and Menelaus, the Jewish religious authorities promoted Greek institutions and in so doing represented popular desires and wishes.[4]

The Greek Hellenisers took control of the government in Jerusalem, and they began to build gymnasiums within the city and encouraged the young to spend all their time there. The young priests engaged in sports. Jerusalem was filled with Greek styles, clothes, names, language, and, worst of all, the Greek religion and Greek morals.

The gymnasium was a place where the citizens of a polis (Greek city) practised athletic and cultural activities according to the Greek way of life.[5]

In Greek entertainment, there was this mixture of pagan religious philosophy and entertainment. According to historical records, the first ancient Olympic Games can be traced back to 776 BC. They were dedicated to the Olympian gods, on the ancient plains of Olympia. The Greeks erected statues and built temples in a grove dedicated to Zeus, supreme among the gods.

The ancient Greeks were highly competitive and believed in the 'contest'. The ultimate Greek goal was to be the best. It was therefore considered one of the greatest honours to win a victory at Olympia. Athletics were of prime importance to the Greeks. The education of boys concentrated on athletics and music as well as academic subjects such as philosophy. Education took place in the gymnasium and the palaestra, as well as the academy.[6]

The athletes competed in the nude in a show of sexual exhibitionism.

For both training and competitions, athletes were always nude. Their bodies, shaped by exercise, were used as models by sculptors and painters who drew inspiration for their works directly from the athletes and their movements while practising sport. The beauty of the naked body

Lance Goodall

reflected the internal beauty and illustrated the harmonious balance between body and mind. There was a gymnasium and a palaestra in every Greek city.[7]

Everything in the Greek world was diametrically opposed to the Hebrew world. The Jews believed they were made in God's image whereas the Greeks believed 'We make god in our image'. This was the underlying philosophy of the Greeks.[8]

Over time, the various elements of Greek political thought and bureaucracy took over. Jason the Priest began to encourage the diffusion among his countrymen of Greek habits and manners; Jason ignored the benefits that the Jews had obtained in the past from Greek kings, and now he approved behaviour and customs that broke the law. Second Maccabees describes in detail the decadence of the priestly class, the lack of cultural services, carelessness towards sacrifices, contempt for the Temple, and staging of theatrical shows in the gymnasium.[9]

On the other hand, some of the Hellenisers felt that things were not moving fast enough, so they convinced Antiochus to remove Jason and replace him with Menelaus who was not even a member of the priestly family.[10]

The strange thing was the compromising Tobiads, and Menelaus asked Antiochus IV for permission to build a gymnasium in Jerusalem and, having obtained it, then chose to hide their circumcision so as to look like Greeks when naked.[11]

According to II Maccabees, it was Menelaus who persuaded Antiochus to Hellenise the Jewish worship and thereby brought about the uprising of the Judeans under the guidance of the Maccabees.[12]

Upon a triumphant return from Egypt, in 168 BC, Antiochus sacked the Temple at Jerusalem and took its golden vessels Antiochus, Josephus tells us, 'came up to Jerusalem, and, pretending peace . . . led by his covetous inclination, . . . left the temple bare, and took away the golden candlesticks, and the golden altar, and table and the altar [of burnt offering]; and did not abstain from even the veils, which were made of fine linen and scarlet. He also emptied it of its secret treasures, and left nothing at all remaining' (*Antiquities of the Jews*, XII, v. 4).

The Seleucids outlawed temple sacrifices, circumcision, Sabbath and festival observance, and the reading of the scriptures. In the year 168 B.C.E., the Syrian tyrant Antiochus Epiphanes sent his soldiers to Jerusalem. They desecrated the Temple, the holiest place for Jews at that time. Altars and idols were set up for the worship of Greek gods and he offered Jews two options: conversion or death.[13]

This act stopped the commanded twice-daily sacrifices at the Temple (Exod. 29:39–42, Num. 28:4–6). This was an overt attempt to wipe out the Jewish religion with all of its doctrines.

Daniel added this in chapter 11: 'And arms shall stand on his [Antiochus'] part, and they shall pollute the sanctuary of strength [the Jewish Temple], and shall take away the daily sacrifice, and they shall place the '*abomination that makes desolate*' (vs. 31).

Now then, *what exactly* is this coming 'abomination' that will be 'set up' again? The truth—born of history—is beyond eye-opening in regard to prophecy.

The first fulfillment was not just Antiochus' armies coming into Jerusalem—an early 'treading it down' for three years until 165 BC— but the fact that those armies set up an image—a specific idol—on the Temple's altar, which *defiled* and made it *desolate*. Antiochus further polluted the Temple by offering swine's blood upon the altar.

Antiochus IV instituted idolatrous pagan worship at the Temple, and there converted the altar of burnt offering to an altar of sacrifice to Zeus. This 'desolating sacrilege on the altar of burnt offering' (1 Macc 1:54) identifies Antiochus's blasphemous sacrifices as the 'abomination of desolation' prophesied in Daniel 11:31.[14] A statue of Zeus/Antiochus was placed in the Temple above the altar. The most detestable of animals (the pig) were brought and sacrificed on the altar. This abominable act was perpetrated on Kislev 25, 168 BC.[15] And he built a statue of the god, Zeus, giving Zeus his own features. Now Zeus was a corruption of Theos in Greek. Almost the same spelling, Zeus was the corruption of Theos in Greek, meaning *god*.[16]

Antiochus had misunderstood the true character of Judaism, for his tyranny aroused both the religious and the political consciousness of the Jews, which resulted in the revolution led by the Maccabees. The Ḥasidim (pious ones), much to the surprise of the Hellenes, suffered martyrdom by the hundreds. Though many Jews had been seduced by the virtues of Hellenism, the extreme measures adopted by Antiochus helped unite the people. When a Greek official tried to force a priest named Mattathias to make a sacrifice to a pagan god, the Jews murdered the man. Predictably, Antiochus began reprisals; but in 167 BCE the Jews rose up behind Mattathias and his five sons and fought for their liberation.

The family of Mattathias became known as the *Maccabees*, from the Hebrew word for hammer, because they were said to strike hammer blows against their enemies. Jews refer to the Maccabees, but the family is more commonly known as the Hasmoneans.

Like other rulers before him, Antiochus underestimated the will and strength of his Jewish adversaries and sent a small force to put down the rebellion. When that failed, he led a more powerful army into battle only to be defeated. Mattathias the Hasmonean (the Maccabean family) organized open resistance in 167–166 BC, which, through the heroic achievements of his son, and successor Judas the Maccabee in defeating two large and well-equipped armies of Antiochus began the demise of the punishing rulership of Antiochus.[17] Jerusalem was recaptured by the Maccabees in 164 BCE. The Temple was finally purified, an event that gave birth to the holiday of Hanukkah, meaning dedication (also known as the Festival of Lights).[18]

It took more than two decades of fighting before the Maccabees forced the Seleucids to retreat from the Land of Israel. By this time Antiochus had died and his successor agreed to the Jews' demand for independence. In the year 142 BCE, after more than 500 years of subjugation, the Jews were again in control.[19]

Space does not allow for details regarding the book of Daniel, but notice Antiochus IV had an agenda to use culture and religion for political expedience to gain political control. The Antichrist will do the same thing. He will bring in a multicultural and multifaith culture, just like today in parts of Europe, e.g. London, Brussels, France, etc., and he will come in the spirit and character of Antiochus. Of course the ultimate fulfillment of the abomination of desolation is still be repeated, not only the statue, but the final leader of the religious system who enters into Jerusalem and says, "I am God."

But to understand what is happening in these last days, we need to understand and apply what happened during the days of Antiochus IV and the Maccabean wars. This is not just a history lesson.

There were the cultural elements of the Greek world that Antiochus wanted everybody to accept. He wanted to Hellenise all culture. The Hebrews went along with the cultural shift. Things were progressively banned. The problem was God's people continued to go along with it until it couldn't be stopped. The priesthood was shut down. The Jews were seduced, and eventually, things got to the point they were outlawed, but it was too late. The main problem was not the Greeks. The main problem were the Jews who collaborated and those who stood by and said nothing.[20]

Is this not the same dilemma in our time? The church has finally woken to find itself bankrupt, the treasures of power, purity, holiness, and moral persuasion stolen. The church instead finds itself accepting men's philosophy and with that the removal of Christian ethics from society and the overthrow of Christian heritage from our laws, schools, and legislature.

Antiochus IV was empowered by spiritual seduction and by Hellenising God's people—that is, using the popular culture. Riding on the back of the popular culture was a compromised morality. God's people lost their way and their identity. The church is hellenised itself to embrace the 'Greek' gods of this age in a similar fashion.

The key points prophesied in the book of Daniel:

1. Antiochus IV's war against Israel would happen during more than one Egyptian conflict (Dan. 11:29–30).
2. Antiochus would take military control of Jerusalem and the temple: "Forces from him shall appear" (v. 31a).
3. He would cause the sacrifices to cease: "Forces from him shall appear and profane the temple and fortress, and shall take away the regular burnt offering" (v. 31).
4. He would "set up the abomination that makes desolate" (v. 31b).
5. Antiochus would prefer and protect those who would "violate the covenant" (v. 32a).
6. Antiochus IV would be met with resistance (vv. 32b–33).
7. The righteous would suffer intense persecution (vv. 33–34a).

8. There would be imposters among the righteous (v. 34b).

9. These events would result in a purification of the people of God (v. 35).[21]

This is exactly what happened in the days of the Maccabees.

Antiochus IV plundered the Temple. The great truth is the New Testament calls the church "the temple" no fewer than seven times. Greek culture was more than comfortable with both homosexuality and bisexuality.[22]

The church is to be salt and light! A preserver of freedoms and rights of the innocent. She is to be light, where men love only darkness. But how can the church be salt and light in a society when the church is going along with the culture? If the church loses its holiness, when it loses its distinctiveness and does not preach the truth, then it cannot function as God intended and is good for nothing. We have been duped into looking for the Antichrist when the spirit of antichrist already pervades the whole of our world system.

The Antichrist is not just a person but the spirit of the age!

There are many trials for God's people, and at times it seems that the work of God is lost completely. Then God begins to raise up a remnant, a true remnant. Those whose lives are consistent with faith in their Lord and Master. God is wanting to send out labourers (Matt. 9:37,38). But the truth is we are not capable of reaping souls if our lives don't reflect the transforming power of the gospel we preach. Our walk with Christ should offer proof to the world that God and His word are true.

But there is still hope. The message is clear:

It's harvest time, but are we ready?

In the last days, a small group of people will arise like the Maccabees. God, in the midst of the chaos and lawlessness, is beginning to build an army that will stand up to counter the moral landslide. Notice small numbers and small groups. In this period, many joined themselves in hypocrisy. Treason was found in the ranks, but in the end, they overcome. In the end, the Maccabees won, as was prophesied by Daniel.[23]

And such as do wickedly against the covenant shall he corrupt with flatteries, but the people that do know their God shall be strong and do exploits (Dan. 11:32).

There were those at the time of Maccabean crisis who caved in to the culture and walked away from God's statutes and judgments. We are seeing this fulfilled in our day. Those who are walking away from God's covenant are instead integrating the flesh into their church services. These ones are being corrupted and deluded by the flatteries of their leaders.

Evil men and seducers waxing worse and worse, deceiving, and being deceived (1 Tim. 3:13).

Hillsong's Women's Colour Conference 2016 had its first opening in New York City. It was no surprise that once more it was a celebration of debauchery: a half-naked cowboy, the church's youth pastor no less onstage with swinging guitar (a phallic symbol) in nothing on but his boyleg underwear. The show also included a Batman and Robin, the snowman from *Frozen*, several scantily clad females who strutted around with Elvis, Spiderman, Spongebob, and a half-baked transvestite Statue of Liberty.[24]

Bobbie Houston played host, alongside Pastor Carl Lentz of the

Hellsong

Hillsong New York campus.

Every aspect of modern culture is moulding the thinking of Hillsong's leadership.

We were not made to fit in but made to stand out. (1 Pet. 1:16, 2 Pet. 3:11)

Yet there is another group. Those who know their God and stand up and who are able to achieve much in the power of God to stem the tide of the evil culture around them and bring deliverance to the lives of men. But I hear this warning from the Holy Spirit that just as there is coming a revival to bring in an end-time harvest, there is equally a false revival that has already started that deceives many. It will have signs and wonders and will be difficult to distinguish from the real thing. It will have the appearance of God, and an appearance of success.

I hear this warning from the Holy Spirit that just as there is coming a revival to bring in an end-time harvest, there is equally a false revival that will deceive many.

And of the children of Issachar, which were men that had understanding of the times, to know what Israel ought to do; the heads of them were two hundred; and all their brethren were at their commandment (1 Chron. 12:32).

The men of Issachar understood what God was about to do and would be in their day a wonderful help in establishing the new kingdom under David. God never goes for the crowds. Although we need numbers to show results, God will choose 7,000, 300, 200, or just one man—as in the case of Moses, Elijah, Gideon, David—to outwork his plan. God's people know what hour it is, what's required of them. They do not follow the status quo. They are striving for perfection and looking to be used of God to teach others in the way of salvation. The Lord is calling ones to be separate, to holiness and righteousness unto the Lord and to walk in obedience and utter submission to His will. To be free from sin, to be perfect as your Father in heaven is perfect, be dead to flesh and alive in Christ.God will use these ones to bring conviction to hearts and the truth of God's judgment on sin.

The remnant are being refined at this time and are preparing themselves now, for they are born for a time such as this.

48
HILLSONG OR HELLSONG

Who shall ascend into the hill of the Lord? or who shall stand in his holy place?[4] He that hath clean hands, and a pure heart; who hath not lifted up his soul unto vanity, nor sworn deceitfully.

—Ps. 24:3–4

We live in perilous times. Our period of history is fulfilling biblical prophecy by the hour. We live in a world of tweeters at a time when our world teeters on the precipice. We are happy with a form of religion. We have embraced a gospel of happiness instead of a gospel of holiness. Each week we go through our performance. The pulpit now is filled with puppets, prosperity, and pantomimes.

Prayer has been left for the privileged few. We have replaced the death of the cross for the delights of croissants. Yet I drive past a local temple mosque on any given night to see some fifty or more cars overflowing their carparks. Our commitment is 'I'll try to get to the meeting if I have nothing else on.'

We have a religion of no cost, no demand, and no discipline.

One of the greatest tragedies of our age is the church has given up on the gospel. Whatever method it uses now is nothing more than cotton candy to draw crowds and keep crowds. The world therefore has no understanding of the true revelation of God who will ultimately judge all men. The Lord Jesus Christ has had a 'guts full' of the so-called Christian church in the West.

It is bad enough that the world lives totally ignoring God and the statutes in His word, but when the church chooses a similar path, then I despair. The devil has done a great job of completely comatosing the world to the realities of God, his attributes, God's wrath, eternity, and the torments of hell, blinding them to even the possibility of an afterlife. And yet the devil's crowning achievement is that he has managed to do the very same thing to the church. Happiness is now the truth. Don't burden us with your old-time religion. But the renewed man is a pardoned man, a pardoned man is a holy man, and the holy man is a happy man. Happy is the man who hungers and thirsts after righteousness, for he will be filled (see Matt. 5:6).

Happiness is now the truth!

The cross is a testimony of God's judgement on sin. So if I have no claim to the cross and the cross has no claim on me, then I must stand accountable for my sin, every sin, to somehow in God's high court to defend and argue my own case.

The gospel in Jesus Christ is the dealing with God's wrath against our sin. God's anger, God's justice, was dealt with on the cross. The Law demanded perfection. Break one law and you break them all. All we can do is give the law mental ascent. You know the law is right, but we must accept our utter failure to live up to its expectations. You must be born again, or 'born from above', the power of God in regeneration must be experienced in our lives, removing the guilt of sin, and taking away condemnation, it is a gift of God, not of works (Eph. 2 8, 9).

Would you go to court without taking a very good lawyer? Then why would you go to the supreme court of God on the day of judgement without sufficient defence? Would you even risk your verdict being read out as guilty? There is no retrial here, no parole, no double jeopardy, no cold case. All is open and revealed on that day. You need to come clothed, not naked, your name written down in the Lamb's book of life, not coming with good deeds, expecting this will help, when no one has any merit before a holy God.

The thing that cuts me to the heart is so many people simply drift through this life, including professing Christians without the slightest thought, consideration or preparation for the next life.

Can avoidance be equated with prudence?

The whole world is now under God's wrath, and those who follow God with their whole heart will come through this period refined and ready for the marriage supper of the Lamb without spot wrinkle or blemish.

Whose fan *is* in his hand, and he will thoroughly purge his floor and gather his wheat into the garner, but he will burn up the chaff with unquenchable fire (Matt. 3:12).

The chaff includes those who have only a profession of faith.

When the church makes friends with the world, to impress them, welcome them, accept them, and to show them that Christians are just like them, then the church is in deep trouble. The Bible clearly says when we make friends with the world, then we are an enemy of God. Hillsong and others continually show themselves to be lovers of worldly things more than God. Hillsong in America is a sham. It's a playhouse for people who want a form of spirituality without having to give up their sins.

God's truth has so been distorted to suit modern Christians and their lust for sin. It is Satan's perfect game plan. Hillsong prides itself on being able to reach the rich and famous and loves having all sorts of ungodly people in their midst to show how accepting, loving, kind, and amazing they are. But all they are doing is accepting and loving these people and flaunting them to the flock without disciplining them, leaving them to remain under the judgement of God.

Hillsong is still missing the mark, rejecting God's word, which is evident by the way the 'gay' fiasco at Hillsong New York went down and the creeping compromise. The revelation has come out that a homosexual couple at Hillsong had been involved in their music ministry.[1]

It is important we recognise the need for purity and holiness and remaining in repentance, and forsaking our wicked ways. This is challenging, and yet the call of God to us is to repent and be ready.

I was previously in a church that was very influenced and shaped by the culture and music of Hillsong. In fact, it was a mini-Hillsong. Anyway, Hillsong music is now off the menu and does nothing for me spiritually now, except for some of the old ones. It's like eating a TV dinner and having a good home-cooked meal. It doesn't compare.

On the whole Hillsong music is manufactured, trite, common, and fails to meet the following criteria:

1. Foremost, does it contain clear biblical doctrine that lines up with the core doctrines of the Christian faith?
2. Does it teach us about God and his character?
3. Does it show or remind us of the condition of man in the light of who God is?

4. Does the song give the gospel, talk of salvation themes like sin, corruption, man's blindness, the cross, the blood, the resurrection, and hope of eternal life?

5. Does the melody distract or induce worship?

6. Does the music/musicians play for entertainment, for themselves, or for God's glory?

7. Does the whole thing ring true, or is it just making noise? Are we caught up in the volume of sound, and euphoria of the moment, instead of the simplicity of worship?

8. Is the beat dominating and creating a barrier to worship in the proper sense?

The trouble with the Modern Laodicean Church of this last 50 years is that we are happy with the near enough; the close enough; the religion that looks, tastes, and smells like Christianity but is completely artificial; and holds to nothing of the genuine. But it suits our needs, and our wants. We are comfortable in our comfort, basking in our blindness, promoting our powerlessness, and being proud of our professionalism.

May I say, we are actually happy with the counterfeit!

In a popular photo of Hillsong United's tour, as part of the stage set, there is a circular ring that encompasses the area above the stage. Joel Houston's face is literally projected up inside the pyramid. AGAIN, this is nothing more than the 'deification of man'.

In one of the YouTube clips I have placed on my website, you see there is a plastic man, a lava like bubble man bobbing up and down and moving around inside the pyramid/triangle. This is while the 'worship' is taking place.

What has this to do with Christ?

J C Ryle lamented our current crowd of Disneyland 'day pass' professors of faith, 'I must honestly declare my conviction that, since the days of the Reformation, there never has been so much profession of religion without practice, so much talking about God without walking with Him, so much hearing God's words without doing them.'

Today 'believers' are defiant, dismissive disciples, denying the very truth that's meant to save them!

In Hillsong's 2012 conference, they wanted to know nothing except Jesus Christ and Him being crucified (supposedly). But now it's nothing but Egyptian occult mystery with religious window dressing!

When I was a lot younger, I used to hear a song on the radio called 'I'd Rather Have Jesus' sung by Jim Reeves. [2]

Lyrics (Abridged)

I'd rather have Jesus than silver or gold

I'd rather be His than have riches untold

I'd rather have Jesus than houses or land

I'd rather be led by His nail pierced hands

I'd rather have Jesus than worldly applause

I'd rather be faithful to His dear cause

I'd rather have Jesus than world-wide fame

Yes, I'd rather be true to His holy name

This song, which I remembered from my youth and which I have added to my music collection, is a complete slap in the face to the values and culture of Hillsong!

Let no man deceive you by any means: for that day shall not come, except there come a falling away first, and that man of sin be revealed, the son of perdition; 4 Who opposes and exalts himself above all that is called God, or that is worshipped; so that he as God sits in the temple of God, showing himself that he is God. (2 Thess. 2:3–4)

And with all deceivableness of unrighteousness in them that perish; because they received not the love of the truth, that they might be saved.[11] And for this cause God shall send them strong delusion, that they should believe a lie:[12] That they all might be damned who believed not the truth, but had pleasure in unrighteousness. (2 Thess. 2:10–12)

They are without excuse. (Rom. 1:20)

It is my firm opinion that Hillsong has played the harlot long enough. God will give individuals within the cult time to come out, but the organisation and its leadership are clearly deluded and under God's judgement.

There is simply no turning back!

They have suppressed and withheld the truth in unrighteousness long enough. This fall from grace has been going on for years, and now they worship the same gods as the world.

They will not be able to recognise the coming Antichrist because they are helping to prepare the way for the man of sin! They are making the way straight for the coming FALSE CHRIST!

Therefore, God has given them over to this deception of loving the world all in the name of Christ!

'Little children, it is the last time: and as ye have heard that antichrist shall come, even now are there many antichrists; whereby we know that it is the last time' —1 Jn. 2:18

49
EPILOGUE

Blow ye the trumpet in Zion, and sound an alarm in my holy mountain: let all the inhabitants of the land tremble: for the day of the LORD cometh, for it is nigh at hand.

—Joel 2:1

So there you have it, Christians giving the world our version of their music. We have conned ourselves into believing a lie that we can serve and save the world through a relevant message, and a guitar solo.

Way back in 1968, Colin Chapman made this prophetic statement, 'The [rock] medium is so anti-Christian in its ethos—libertarian, anti-authoritarian, equating infatuation and sexual attraction with love, and on the drug-culture fringe—that when Christians assume that ethos to communicate the message of self-denial, cross-bearing and following Christ then it utterly mangles the message' (Colin Chapman, 'Modern Music and Evangelism', *Background to the Task*, Evangelical Alliance Commission on Evangelism, 1968).

But this is exactly what we have attempted to do over the last five decades, something that even the world doesn't believe, and all we have done is pollute the church of God by this error to its very core. An alarm must go out because some one hundred and fifty years ago the church caved into modernism and never recovered. Now the giant of pragmatism is waiting to bring the same ruin. I am concerned that those who are of God's house are being swept along by this error, for Satan is not passive in his desire to destroy the faith of many in this movement.

The message is to simply add Jesus to your life. Receive Christ—come to Christ. But we have made salvation like a booby prize, the Son of God a consolation prize to all the other trinkets one can acquire. In order for you to be saved from hell, and to receive God's gift of everlasting life, you must admit that you are a sinner, acknowledge and repent of your sin and receive the Lord Jesus Christ as your personal Lord and Saviour by faith alone for your eternal salvation (Luke 3:3; John 14:6; Acts 4:12; Acts 20:21; Romans 5:1; Romans 10:9–10).

We are generation of Esaus!

The gospel now has become nothing more than an introduction to Jesus as you would be introduced to the prime minister or the president. This is an easy believism, where involvement is like signing up for membership at a golf club or community group.

This belief has led to several Christians entering talent quests like *Idol* all in the name of Jesus. These Christians run around in the name of kingdom now when all it is, is the going after earthly rewards, with little concern or impact for the kingdom of God. Then we are surprised when our Christian pop idols walk away from the faith.

We have sold the idea to ourselves that we can invest in double digit dominionism!

'Hear what the Spirit is saying to the churches!

Come out of her my people, that you be not partakers of her sins!' (Rev. 18:5).

Yes, I know you've heard it before. But....

> How is the faithful city become an harlot! It was full of judgment; righteousness lodged in it; but now murderers.[22] Thy silver is become dross, thy wine mixed with water: [23]Thy princes are rebellious, and companions of thieves: every one loveth gifts, and followeth after rewards: they judge not the fatherless, neither doth the cause of the widow come unto them.
>
> [24]Therefore saith the Lord, the Lord of hosts, the mighty One of Israel, Ah, I will ease me of mine adversaries, and avenge me of mine enemies:
>
> [25]And I will turn my hand upon thee, and purely purge away thy dross, and take away all thy tin:
>
> [26]And I will restore thy judges as at the first, and thy counsellors as at the beginning: afterward thou shalt be called, the city of righteousness, the faithful city.
>
> [27]Zion shall be redeemed with judgment, and her converts with righteousness. [28] And the destruction of the transgressors and of the sinners shall be together, and they that forsake the Lord shall be consumed. (Isa. 1:21–27)

Again in Isaiah:

> And it shall come to pass, that he that is left in Zion, and he that remaineth in Jerusalem, shall be called holy, even every one that is written among the living in

Jerusalem: When the Lord shall have washed away the filth of the daughters of Zion, and shall have purged the blood of Jerusalem from the midst thereof by the spirit of judgment, and by the spirit of burning. (Isa. 4:3,4)

The fire of God's wrath, will prove and purify his people; gathering them up, in order to separate the dross from the silver, the bad from the good, the wheat from the chaff. The severity of God's judgments, will come upon his servants. (See Ezek. 22:18–22; Mal. 3:2,3).

These are last-day prophecies! The church will be a remnant, not a broad way for a bunch of brazen believers! Notice it says those who are left in Zion!

And said unto them, Hear me, ye Levites, sanctify now yourselves, and sanctify the house of the LORD God of your fathers, and carry forth the filthiness out of the holy place. ⁶For our fathers have trespassed, and done that which was evil in the eyes of the LORD our God, and have *forsaken Him*, and have turned away their faces from the habitation of the LORD, and turned their backs. (2 Chron. 29:5,6)

²⁵I, even I, am he that blots out thy transgressions for mine own sake, and will not remember thy sins. ²⁶Put me in remembrance: let us plead together: declare thou [*your sin*], that thou may be justified. ²⁷Your first father has sinned, and thy teachers have transgressed against me. ²⁸Therefore I have profaned the princes of the sanctuary, and have given Jacob to the curse, and Israel to reproaches (Isa. 43:25–28)

²⁵There is a conspiracy of her prophets in the midst thereof, like a roaring lion ravening the prey; they have devoured souls; they have taken the treasure and precious things; they have made her many widows in the midst there of. ²⁶Her priests have violated my law, and have profaned mine holy things: they have put no difference between the holy and profane, neither have they shewed difference between the unclean and the clean, and have hid their eyes from my sabbaths, and I am profaned among them. ²⁷Her princes in the midst thereof are like wolves ravening the prey, to shed blood, and to destroy souls, to get dishonest gain. ²⁸And her prophets have daubed them with untempered morter, seeing vanity, and divining lies unto them, saying, Thus saith the Lord God, when the Lord hath not spoken. ²⁹The people of the land have used oppression, and exercised robbery, and have vexed the poor and needy: yea, they have oppressed the stranger wrongfully. ³⁰And I sought for a man among them, that should make up the hedge, and stand in the gap before me for the land, that I should not destroy it: but I found none. (Ezek. 22:25–30)

Woe to her that is filthy and polluted, to the oppressing city! ²She obeyed not the voice; she received not correction; she trusted not in the Lord; she drew notnear to her God. ³ Her princes within her are roaring lions; her judges are evening wolves; they gnaw not the bones till the morrow.⁴Her prophets are light and treacherous persons: her priests have polluted the sanctuary, they have done violence to the law. (Zeph. 3:1–4)

God's judgement is looming. World War 3 is just around the corner.

Almighty God is about to consume both man and beast from off the earth (Zeph. 1:3). At the same time sin and sinners shall be purged from the church, (Zeph. 3:11). God will take them away. *I will take away out of the midst of thee,* not only the profane, who are a shame to the land, but the hypocrites, who appear beautiful on the outside, and rejoice in pride, in the holy city, the holy house. Their pride is in the house, in the temple, the house itself, but not the God of the temple. They have made this their pride, they have relied on their success, their music; these are their righteousness and strength, boasting of *the temple, the temple of the Lord* (Jer. 7:4). God will remove the haughty from his holy mountain. Those who are conceited, caught up in church programmes, men's pride, and growth, the foundation and ground of their security. But what is most offensive to God are those carried along by the pretensions of holiness, God will silence and take away.

> For, behold, the day cometh, that shall burn as an oven; and all the proud, yea, and all that do wickedly, shall be stubble: and the day that cometh shall burn them up, saith the Lord of hosts, that it shall leave them neither root nor branch. (Mal 4:1)

> Seek ye the Lord, all ye meek of the earth, which have wrought his judgment; seek righteousness, seek meekness: it may be ye shall be hid in the day of the Lord's anger. (Zeph 2:3)

> For if you turn again to the LORD, your brothers and your children shall find compassion before them that lead them captive, so that they shall come again into this land: for the LORD your God is gracious and merciful, and will not turn away his face from you, *if you return to Him.* (2 Chron. 30:9 AKJV)

In closing, I am saying the Lord Jesus will forgive you as you come to realise the deception, the shallowness, the bankruptcy, the evil plague of your heart, the wasted time, the music, the idolatry of men, and the humanistic philosophy you have been serving and living under all this time. God will wipe away all tears, but it is all or nothing. God is the ultimate judge. I am only here to blow the trumpet in Zion.

> The question is who is on the Lord's side? As Elijah said; How long halt ye between two opinions? If the LORD *be* God, follow him: but if Baal, *then* follow him. (See 1 Kings 18:21)

> [11]And that, knowing the time, that now it is high time to awake out of sleep: for now is our salvation nearer than when we believed. The night is far spent, the day is at hand: let us therefore cast off the works of darkness, and let us put on the armour of light. Let us walk honestly, as in the day; not in rioting and drunkenness, not in chambering and wantonness, not in strife and envying. But put ye on the Lord Jesus Christ, and make not provision for the flesh, to fulfil the lusts thereof. (Rom. 13:11–14 KJV)

Time is literally running out!

We are promoting the church as the hope of the world and *not* the Lord Jesus Christ.

> For there are certain men crept in unawares, who were before of old ordained to this condemnation, ungodly men, turning the grace of our God into lasciviousness, and denying the only Lord God, and our Lord Jesus

Christ.(Jude 4)

> Be ye not unequally yoked together with unbelievers: for what fellowship hath righteousness with unrighteousness? and what communion hath light with darkness? And what concord hath Christ with Belial? or what part hath he that believeth with an infidel? And what agreement hath the temple of God with idols? for ye are the temple of the living God; as God hath said, I will dwell in them, and walk in *them*; and I will be their God, and they shall be my people. Wherefore come out from among them, and be ye separate, saith the Lord, and touch not the unclean *thing*; and I will receive you, And will be a Father unto you, and ye shall be my sons and daughters, saith the Lord Almighty.(2 Cor. 6:14–17)

God's people have lost their way and now dance to the flute of the musician whose song is not the song of the Lord.

The love of fame and fortune has been Christianised, and an unsuspecting flock have given their allegiance to a captain who cares little if anything for their salvation.

Christianity is the denial of the praise of men for the praise of God. We cannot have both. It is a spiritual impossibility. Yet we have this amalgam of clay and iron, success, and the reproach of Christ. Friendship with the world is to be an enemy of Christ!

This cruise-ship Christianity of conferences and cocktails has brought shipwreck to the faith!

The church in the West for too long has sailed along on fair seas. The zephyr has fluttered at our sails in the height of summer and has blown comfort upon the people.

The ship has sailed below sapphire skies, the crew sleeps, while the current of the world and tides of apostasy have taken it off course, sending it adrift.

The worst of it is darkening clouds beckon on the horizon, bringing a storm of ecumenism and coming persecution with barely anyone to trim the sail of this wayward vessel.

We have corrupted our Christianity. We have gone from contemporary Christianity to cool Christianity, from convenient Christianity to compromised Christianity. We have cabaret Christianity otherwise known as corrupt Christianity. We have a counterfeit Christianity, even a Christless Christianity, a faith without Him, only a faith about Him!

Without doubt, the great falling away is well underway!

Thou, O Lord, remainest for ever; thy throne from generation to generation.

Wherefore dost thou forget us forever, and forsake us so long time?

Turn thou us unto thee, O Lord, and we shall be turned; renew our days as of old.

But thou hast utterly rejected us; thou art very wroth against us.

—Lam. 5:19–22 (KJV)

ENDNOTES

The following is a full list of source documents and websites from which the information for this work has been taken or gleaned. Not all hyperlinks will work instantly from the link shown below, but can still be sourced by 'copy and paste' of the same link into a search engine, or doing a similar word search.

Often the link below is a news channel which has also been reported by a number of other media outlets and can be confirmed that way.

Chapter 1 – Build it and they will come

1. http://www.couriermail.com.au/questnews/southeast/ninetythree-year-old-st-mary-magdalenes-is-closing-while-hillsong-grows-bigger-than-ever/news-story/4ee1ab704ab827c306a0212bd7af70e7

2. ibid

3. http://www.couriermail.com.au/questnews/southeast/hillsong-mt-gravatt-pays-queensland-police-to-attend-sunday-services-because-of-huge-crowds/news-story/74e48f6a67bfdcabe8bacbf90f0a5827

4. http://www.huffingtonpost.com/2013/11/05/australia-hillsong-church-influence_n_4214660.html

5. http://www.dailytelegraph.com.au/news/nsw/hillsong-church-rakes-in-100m-a-year-from-its-flock-of-34000/news-story/45e21c47b6b5221fab97ad0ba0a6f1bd

6. http://www.cbsnews.com/news/new-york-city-hillsong-mega church-draws-thousands-every-sunday/

7. http://www.huffingtonpost.com/2013/11/05/australia-hillsong-church-influence_n_4214660.html

8. https://en.wikipedia.org/wiki/Field_of_Dreams

9. https://cruxnow.com/church/2014/09/11/u-s-churches-feel-beat-of-change-more-diversity-more-drums/

Chapter 2 – Bad Blood

1. http://heavy.com/entertainment/2014/11/taylor-swift-amas-american-music-awards-2014-opening-performance-blank-space-video/

2. www.youtube.com/watch?v=nYQ90wZ9wpU

3. www.youtube.com/watch?v=tu4q3WLhOlw

4. https://www.theamas.com/2014/11/taylor-swift-dick-clark-award/

5. http://www.biography.com/people/taylor-swift-369608

6. "Taylor Swift | Bio, Pictures, Videos". Rolling Stone. RetrievedJuly 30,2012.Ann Powers (October 25, 2010). "Album review: Taylor Swift's 'Speak Now' - latimes.com". Latimesblogs.latimes.com. Retrieved July 30, 2012.

7. www.youtube.com/watch?v=Pd2VOwg2Rpg

8. http://illuminatiwatcher.com/illuminati-symbolism-2014-american-music-awards/

9. http://www.illuminati-news.com/00357.html

Chapter 3 – Everybody's Free to Feel Good

1. http://www.nytimes.com/1997/12/30/nyregion/taking-back-nightclub-gospel-spots-offer-entertainment-with-christian-flavor.html

2. http://content.time.com/time/magazine/article/0,9171,11010310 20-517740,00.html

   and https://en.wikipedia.org/wiki/Club_3_Degrees

3. http://www.thedoordallas.com/

4. http://www.russelldavidhobbs.com/

Chapter 4 – You've Gotta Right to Party

1. https://www.houstoniamag.com/articles/2014/5/16/video-church-folks-get-turnt-up-at-christian-nightclub-may-2014

2. Article Innocent Amusements by Pres .C. G. Finney. The Independent. New York, November 7, 1872

3. (The Set of the Sail, p. 35, 36) -From the book, 'Tozer on Christian Leadership', published by Wing Spread Publishers.

Chapter 5 – Give me the Night

1. https://www.youtube.com/watch?v=m8Bg47-bk5Y and http://youtu.be/YsFSDQ g9RFg

2. Keystoadeeperlife–p22AW Tozer

Chapter 6 - Dancing in the Dark

1. http://www.hillsong.com/brisbane/city

2. http://www.barsandnightclubs.com.au/brisbane/the-valley/

3. https://www.yelp.com.au/biz/the-met-fortitude-valley

4. https://coercioncode.com/2014/05/30/dancing-in-the-dark-hillsong-night-club-church/

5. http://themet.com.au/

6. http://www.hillsong.com/brisbane/city

7. http://www.hillsong.com/la

8. http://www.goldcoastbulletin.com.au/news/gold-coast/popular-pentecostal-church-hillsong-acquires-two-gold-coast-chapels-after-successful-trial-run/news-story/d65ed37daf89d46429aa7dbf81a40020

9. http://hillsong.com/goldcoast/#location

10. http://www.christianpost.com/news/hillsong-church-brian-houston-opens-16th-global-campus-sunday-arizona-157942/

11. http://hillsong.com/los-angeles/blog/2016/02/hillsong-san-francisco/#.WLfS3W996Uk

12. and http://hillsong.com/sanfrancisco/

13. http://www.christianpost.com/news/hillsong-church-tbn-launche-hillsong-channel-24-hour-worship-ministry-network-159409/

14. https://en.wikipedia.org/wiki/Irving_Plaza

15. Ibid

16. Ibid

17. http://www.cbsnews.com/news/new-york-city-hillsong-megachurch-draws-thousands-every-sunday/

Chapter 7 – California Dreamin'

1. http://www.hillsong.com/la

   https://www.youtube.com/watch?v= 0-IzFygO5eA

2. http://thebelasco.com/history/

3. http://www.partyearth.com/los-angeles/clubs/the-belasco-2/

4. https://www.youtube.com/watch?v=uK19yy1P8GM and

   www.youtube.com/watch?v=DuiPAmHjPK8/

5. http://hillsong.com/conference/nyc/

6. http://www.yelp.com/biz/hillsong-la-los-angeles-2/

7. http://hillsong.com/new-building-announcement/blog/2015/10/new-building-announcement/#.WLn2w2996Uk

8. http://www.ladowntownnews.com/news/mega-church-inks-deal-for-variety-arts-center/article_62be7fda-c61d-11e5-b84d-8fdc76880161.html

9. https://en.wikipedia.org/wiki/Friday_Morning_Club

10. http://www.ladowntownnews.com/opinion/a-comeback-for-the-variety-arts-center/article_7c715fd8-d1df-11e5-b798-434753e80b17.html

11. https://en.wikipedia.org/wiki/Interpretatio_Christiana

12. http://youtu.be/KxkqUNNMw38

Chapter 8 – I want to break Free

1. Part of the transcript from a sermon preached by Bruce Hills at Legana Church inTasmania-Easter-April 2009-DVD can be obtained by ordering from Legana Church. The meeting was held on Sunday 26th April 2009 to determine the vote from the congregation. 80% of those present agreed to have Brian & Bobbie Houston as senior pastors

2. http://www.smh.com.au/national/hillsong-on-a-mission-to-spread-the-word-north-20090510-az7o.html/

3. http://www.dailytelegraph.com.au/news/nsw/hillsong-church-rakes-in-100m-a-year-from-its-flock-of-34000/news-story/45e21c47b6b5221fab97ad0ba0a6f1bd

   Published 20/07/2015. (Accessed 21/07/2015.)

4. J. EdwinOrr, Revival is like judgement Day (Atlanta: Home Mission Board, SBC 1987) p. 14

5. Warren W. Wiersbe-The integrity Crisis (Nashville; Oliver Nelson Publishers, 1988) p.56.

6. https://www.youtube.com/watch?v=Ndlqyc-YXho

7. I personally visited the store, and viewed the books all over the shelves in the resource centre (bookshop) at Brisbane Campus. I suggest you check out any Hillsong bookshop or their website.

8. https://hillsongchurchwatch.com/tag/world-youth-day-2008/

   also

   http://www.christianpost.com/news/hillsong-conference-kicks-off-with-over-24-000-33175/

9. This "play" was performed at the Garden City, Brisbane congregation in the 10:30 am service on the11ᵗʰ October 2009."

Chapter 9 - And the beat goes on

1. https://en.wikipedia.org/wiki/Hard_rock

2. ibid

3. https://www.wayoflife.org/database/how_contemporary_praise_transforms_churches.html

4. http://www.scaruffi.com/history/cpt11.html

5. http://beginningandend.com/nebuchadnezzar-666-foreshadow-of-the-antichrist-3/

6. http://www.jesus-is-savior.com/Evils%20in%20America/CCM/nwo_images_in_ccm.htm

Chapter 10 - Worship Wars

1. http://www.encyclopedia.com/people/literature-and-arts/music-history-composers-and-performers-biographies/isaac-watts

2. https://en.wikipedia.org/wiki/Isaac_Watts

3. ibid

4. http://truthinhistory.org/isaac-watts-gods-gift-to-the-church.html/

5. http://www.encyclopedia.com/people/literature-and-arts/music-history-composers-and-performers-biographies/isaac-watts'

6. Marini, Stephen A.(2003).Sacred Song in America: Religion, Music, and Public Culture. Urbana: University of Illinois Press.

7. p 76

8. p71

9. p76

10. http://religiousaffections.org/articles/articles-on-worship/the-watts-controversy/

11. Ibid

12. http://www.gty.org/resources/sermons/TM13-11

13. Source: Published by Hillsong Church, Brian Houston, Vision Sunday 2014 - YouTube,

   www.youtube.com/watch?v=wPnikhaDwDw

   Published 02/02/2014.

Chapter 11–The devil has all the good music?

1. http://canadianchristianity.com/bc/bccn/0709/20angel.html

2. http://www.larrynorman.com/about.html/

3. http://www.cbn.com/cbnmusic/artists/norman_larry.aspx?mobile=false&u=1

4. http://canadianchristianity.com/bc/bccn/0709/20angel.html/

5. https://en.wikipedia.org/wiki/Upon This Rock (LarryNormanalbum)

6. http://canadianchristianity.com/bc/bccn/0709/20angel.html#articletop

7. Ibid

8. http://www.cbn.com/cbnmusic/artists/norman_larry.aspx?mobile=false&u=1

9. Details sourced from an archived article on http://allmusic.com

   http://archive.li/vCxi1

   god gave rock-and-roll-to-you-a-history-of-contemporary-christian-music

   also

   http://www.biography.com/people/amy-grant-207490

10. http://www.wayoflife.org/database/did_luther_use_tavern_music.html

    Quoted in Walter E. Buszin's essay, entitled "Luther on Music," published in the January 1946 issue of the MusicalQuarterly,G. Schirme rpublisher. In the following footnotes, the name W.E. — Buszin iv St L., XXIa, 1574 (W.E. Buszin).

11. http://beggarsallreformation.blogspot.com.au/2014/03/luther-why-should-devil-have-all-good.html

12. http://www.av1611.org/question/cqdevila.html

13. http://www.azquotes.com/author/26216-Fanny_Crosby

14. http://www.lyricsmania.com/why_should_the_devil_have_all_the_good_music_lyrics_larry_norman.html

    Taken from Lyrics Mania website

15. http://youtu.be/TliWDSLrYb8

Chapter 12 -- Righteous Rocker Holy Roller

1. http://www.slate.com/articles/arts/music_box/2007/07/id_like_to_dedicate_this_next_song_to_jesus.html

   http://www.poetpatriot.com/links-jesus-movement.htm#Artists

2. http://classicchristianrockzone.blogspot.com.au/2014/04/agape.html

3. ibid

Lance Goodall

4. http://www.allmusic.com/artist/larry-norman-mn0000132579/biography

   addtl details on wikipedia – People!

5. https://en.wikipedia.org/wiki/Love_Song_(band)

6. https://en.wikipedia.org/wiki/Calvary_Chapel

   and

   https://www.wayoflife.org/database/getty_townend_and_contemporary_hymns.php

7. Ibid

8. http://hubpages.com/religion-philosophy/Pastor-Chuck-Smith-Moved-From-Holey-Tent-to-Mansion-of-Glory

9. http://www.christianpost.com/news/legacy-of-calvary-chapels-pastor-chuck-smith-shared-by-countless-christian-leaders-105895/

10. https://en.wikipedia.org/wiki/Calvary_Chapel

11. https://youtu.be/XoV0p1zI4As

    The kathryn kuhlman show

12. https://www.wayoflife.org/database/calvary_chapel_and_maranatha.php

13. http://hubpages.com/hub/Pastor-Chuck-Smith-Moved-From-Holey- Tent-to-Mansion-of-Glory

14. http://www.network54.com/Forum/419882/thread/1181153070/Calvary+Chapel+Cult+Experience

15. www.wayoflife.org/free_ebooks/downloads/Baptist_Music_Wars_p.php

16. https://www.youtube.com/watch?v=cQHDDtlTbiM

    Calvary Chapel Drum Solo 71

17. Clarke, Gerald (June 24, 2001). "New Lyrics for the Devil's Music".Time.

18. https://en.wikipedia.org/wiki/Church_Growth

19. http://www.wayoflife.org/database/getty_townend_and_contemporary_hymns.php

20. http://canadianchristianity.com/bc/bccn/0709/20angel.html

21. http://www.onlyvisiting.com/larry/interviews/interview3.html

22. https://www.wayoflife.org/database/calvary_chapel_and_maranatha.php

23. http://www.wayoflife.org/database/getty_townend_and_contemporary_hymns.php

24. Ibid

25. https://archive.org/details/JohnToddFormerIlluminatiOccultMemberGivesTestimonyOfInvolvementIn/tape1a.mp3

   -- tape 3b

Chapter 13– Purple Haze

1. ThePurposeDrivenChurchZondervan1995pg281,82

2. http://www.wayoflife.org/database/saddlebackrocks.html

   http://www.oocities.org/fcfc.geo/sundquist4.htm

3. https://www.planetshakers.com/awakening/malaysia-2016/#invitation

   also

   http://www.rockprophecy.com/madison.html/

4. Paul Zimmerman interviewed Jimi for Newsweek in NYC May 1969 * Zimmerman, Paul D. Newsweek, May 26, 1969, p.82.

5. http://www.letusreason.org/popteac25.htm

6. RickWarrenPurposeDrivenChurch.p.243)

Chapter 14 – Love Yourself

1. http://www.atlasobscura.com/places/crystal-cathedral

2. http://www.octhen.com/2010/02/robert-schullers-drive-in-church.html

3. http://www.letusreason.org/Poptea1.htm

4. https://en.wikipedia.org/wiki/Hillsong_Conference_2006

5. http://store.hillsong.com/store /products /teaching/ hillsong-conference/hillsong-conference-2014/

6.   Lynne & Bill Hybels, Rediscovering Church, (Zondervan, Grand Rapids, MI, 1995), p.69

7.   Tim Stafford, A Regular Purpose Driven Guy, Christianity Today, 18.11.02, Vol 46, No. 12, p.4

8.   http://newswithviews.com/PaulProctor/proctor32.htm

9.   ibid

10.   http://www.cfr.org/about/membership/roster.html?letter=W

11.   https://en.wikipedia.org/wiki/Rick_Warren

12.   http://pastors.com/creating-a-culture-of-worship/

13.   http://www.daystar.com/events/hillsong-conference/

14.   http://en.wikipedia.org/wiki/Existentialism

15.   https://coercioncode.com/2014/08/31/the-tragedy-of-religious-error-victoria-osteen-blasphemes/

16.   https://www.youtube.com/watch?v=axxlXy6bLH0

Chapter 15 – It's the Rhythm of the Night

1.   Leonard J. Seidel, God's New Song, p. 69-70

2.   http://heartcheckreality.blogspot.com.au/2013/11/the-dark-truth- behind-rock-and-roll.html

3.   http://www.middletownbiblechurch.org/lochurch/rockmu01.htm

4.   Donald E. Nelson, Explo '72 Biblically Examined, p.27

5.   [79] The Evening Star, Feb. 11, 1993, p. A10

6.   https://en.wikipedia.org/wiki/Drum

7.   http://encyclopedia.jrank.org/DRO_ECG/DRUM_early_forms_drome_or_dromm.html

8.   http://www.1066.co.nz/Mosaic%20DVD/library/Medieval%20Instruments.pdf

     1911 Encyclopedia Britannica

9.   https://www.blueletterbible.org/lang/lexicon/lexicon.cfm?t=kjv&strongs=h8596

10.   http://www.memidex.com/timbrels

11. http://logosresourcepages.org/Music/rock.htm

12. http://biblehub.com/commentaries/pulpit/leviticus/18.htm

13. http://www.keyway.ca/htm2001/20010731.htm

    -Valley of Hinnom

14. (Charles White, The Life and Times of Little Richard, p. 197) – sourced from.internationaldeliveranceministries.org/docs/YC%202009%20Deception%202.pdf

15. https://www.youtube.com/watch?v=WMy1hpJ2hcg

Chapter 16 - Another Jesus, another 'Godspell'

1. https://musicaeadoracao.com.br/recursos/arquivos/ingles/quotes_warren.htm

2. https://www.youtube.com/watch?v=ej0Gd7_LKW8

    Also

    http://www.youtube.com/watch?v=YJdFdvFGV6M&feature=related

Chapter 17 - Celebrity Driven Church

1. https://en.wikipedia.org/wiki/Hillsong_Music_Australia/

2. ibid

3. http://www.charismamag.com/spirit/church-ministry/8469-a-sound-from-down-under?showall=

4. http://www.charismanews.com/world/41646-australia-s-hillsong- church-exports-its-influence-through-praise-and-preaching

5. https://www.youtube.com/watch?v=eVkVidBmpnE

6. http://www.crosswalk.com/11618087/

7. http://onceuponacross.blogspot.com.au/2010/01/false-gospel-of-hillsong-part-1-houston.html

8. https://www.youtube.com/watch?v=FMnAfqM5WaM

9. https://en.wikipedia.org/wiki/Hillsong_United_(band)

10. http://worshipedeth08.blogspot.com.au/2013/01/history-of-hilsong-united-band-formed.html

11. http://www.aibi.ph/articles/cool.htm

   COOL' CHRISTIANITY Relevance or compromise - Ebook by Andrew Strom Page8,9- 11

Chapter 18 - You Cannot Serve God and EMI

1. http://www.todayschristianmusic.com/artists/hillsong/news/emi-cmg-and-hillsong-form-exclusive-alliance-for-north-america-and-latin-america/

2. http://www.metrolyrics.com/break-free-lyrics-hillsong-united.html

Chapter 19 - The Cross and the Phoenix

1. http://www.cbn.com/cbnmusic/news/hillsong-united-returns-to-us- aftermath-tour.aspx

2. https://en.wikipedia.org/wiki/Aftermath_(Hillsong_United_album)

3. http://en.wikipedia.org/wiki/Aftermath

4. http://abcnews.go.com/Entertainment/pitbull-rocks-gma-summer-concert-series/story?id=39586089

5. http://ancienthistory.about.com/cs/grecoromanmyth1/g/phoenix bird.htm

6. http://www.metrolyrics.com/our-god-lyrics-chris-tomlin.html

7. http://andersen.sdu.dk/forskning/motiver/vismotive.html?id=70

8. http://www.metrolyrics.com/aftermath-lyrics-hillsong-united.html

9. http://en.wikipedia.org/wiki/Phoenix (mythology)

10. http://www.bibliotecapleyades.net/sociopolitica/secret_destinyamerica/secret_destinyamerica04.htm

11. http://www.cephasministry.com/nwo_symbols.html

   Also

   http://en.wikipedia.org/wiki/Great_Seal_of_the_ United_States

12. http://en.wikipedia.org/wiki/William_Barton_(heraldist)

13. http://holywar.org/txt/dollar.html

14. http://www.bibliotecapleyades.net/sociopolitica/secret_destinyamerica/secret_destinyamerica.htm

    also

    http://ancienthistory.about.com/cs/grecoromanmyth1/g/phoenixbird.htm

    http://www.ancient-origins.net/myths-legends/ancient-symbolism-magical-phoenix-002020

15. http://hillsongcollected.com/creative/itunes-review-aftermath

16. http://www.spurgeongems.org/vols31-33/chs1849.pdf

Chapter 20 – Hillsong's Tattoo Culture

1. https://en.wikipedia.org/wiki/Guy_Sebastian

2. ibid

3. http://www.news.com.au/entertainment/pop-star-guy-sebastian-reveals-the-heartbreaking-true-stories-behind-his-new-record-madness/news-story/256fc7bdc495c918e9c413eaa551056d

4. https://coercioncode.com/2014/09/22/joel-houston-tattoo-and-hillsongs-tattoo-culture/

    also

    http://www.cwm.org.au/3/13-59/61-tattoos-making-their-mark-part-1/

Chapter 21 - Highway to Hell

1. http://www.christianpost.com/news/perry-noble-megachurch-ac-dc-highway-to-hell-easter-160107/

2. http://www.pajamapages.com/who-knew-you-needed-an-excuse-not-to-play-highway-to-hell/

3. http://www.christianpost.com/news/pastor-perry-noble-of-newspring-church-causes-stir-with-revelation-he-is-taking-anti-depressants-for-mental-anxiety-115231/

4. http://www.christianpost.com/news/perry-noble-opens-up-double-life-daily-drinking-problem-led-firing-from-newspring-church-170954/

5. http://www.charismanews.com/us/58283-pastor-perry-noble-fired- after-16-years-at-newspring-church/

Chapter 22 – Hillsong's Hellraisers

1. http://www.religionfacts.com/persecution-early-church

2. https://en.wikipedia.org/wiki/Constantine_the_Great

3. ibid

4. https://en.wikipedia.org/wiki/Constantine_the_Great

5. ibid

6. http://www.ritchies.net/p2wk1.htm

7. History of the Christian Church, Volume III: - Nicene and Post-Nicene Christianity. A.D. 311-600. By Philip Schaff pg 12 Third Revision 1889 - Sourced from White Horse Media. Schaff, Philip, History of the Christian Church,(Oak Harbor, WA: Logos Research Systems, Inc.) 1997. The material has been carefully compared and corrected according to the Eerdmans reproduction of the 1910 edition by Charles Scribner'ssons,with emendations by The Electronic Bible Society, Dallas, TX, 1998. ---Now In publicdomain

8. http://spectator.org/articles/37691/defending-constantine-and-christendom

9. https://en.wikipedia.org/wiki/History_of_Christianity

10. The Revelation of Jesus Christ; John F. Walvoord; Mood Press1966 page 69

11. ibid

12. History of the Christian Church, Volume III: Nicene and Post-Nicene Christianity. A.D. 311-600. by Philip Schaff - Available through Christian Classics Etheral Library in PDF.

    http://www.ccel.org/ccel/schaff/hcc3.html

    pg.13

13. Ibid – pg 14

    Ibid - Pg 22

14. http://wesley.nnu.edu/john-wesley/the-sermons-of-john-wesley-1872-edition/sermon-89-the-more-excellent-way/

    Alternatively – Search John Wesley Sermons – wesley.nnu.edu/john-wesley – More Excellent Way – Sermon 89.

15. http://www.nbcnews.com/news/investigations/flying-high-exclusive-inside-story-biebers-pot-plane-n22056?cid=par-people-mobile-headlines_20140205

16. http://www.christianpost.com/news/justin-biebers-baptism-story-detailed-by-hillsongs-pastor-carl-lentz-152938/

17. http://www.nydailynews.com/life-style/hillsong-nyc-draws-thousands-young-new-yorkers-spiritual-message-article-1.1880489

18. http://ipost.christianpost.com/post/famous-people-who-attend-justin-biebers-church-hillsong-nyc-photos and

    http://www.harpersbazaar.com/culture/features/news/a11853/hillsong-church/

19. http://www.gq.com.au/success/opinions/hillsong+what+its+really+like+inside+the+pentecostal+megachurch,44047

20. http://global.christianpost.com/news/rapper-actor-ja-rule-talks-jehovah-witness-upbringing-getting-saved-at-hillsong-nyc-and-confusion-over-pastor-mason-bethas-explicit-lyrics-121794/

21. http://www.independent.co.uk/news/people/news/justin-bieber-arrested-on-suspicion-of-dui-and-drag-racing-in-miami-9080201.html

22. http://www.christiantoday.com/article/justin.bieber.worships.seattles.city.church.pastor.judah.smith.nfl.quarterback.russell.wilson/37213.htm?email=1

    Also

    http://www.celebuzz.com/2014-06-20/selena-gomez-is-back-to-cleaning-up-justin-biebers-act-going-to-bible-study/

23. http://worldtruth.tv/monarch-mind-programming-in-plain-sight/ justin'smask

24. http://www.dailymail.co.uk/tvshowbiz/article-3145462/Ignorant- Justin-Bieber-wears-Marilyn-Manson-s-ANTI-CHRIST-t-shirt- Hillsong-Church-conference.html#ixzz3f54LIZ5X

25. http://www.christianpost.com/news/marilyn-manson-justin-bieber-bigger-than-satan-shirt-159767/

26. http://www.thefader.com/2016/10/12/justin-bieber-pacsun-purpose-tour-merch-collection

27. http://www.theopedia.com/Sandemanianism

    Encyclopædia Britannic Eleventh Edition (1911), now in the public domain; s.v. Glasites, or Sandemanians, bracket added.

28. Romans 2:1–3:20 The Righteous Judgment of God D. Martyn Lloyd-Jones Banner of Truth 1989 Chapter1–pg. 11

Chapter 23 - Jesus Christ Superstar

1. http://www.daystar.com/events/hillsong-conference-2014/

   And

   http://astepfwd.com/hillsong-conference-championing-the- cause-of-the-local-church/

2. http://peifreemasonry.com/thomas-fraser-fullerton-pgm/

3. http://www.smh.com.au/good-weekend/inside-the-hillsong-churchs- moneymaking-machine-20151026-gkip53.html

   Annual Report 2014

   http://retro.hillsong.com/assets/Annual-Report.pdf

   http://d9nqqwcssctr8.cloudfront.net/wp-content/uploads/2015/11/15233735/AnnualReport14WEB.pdf

4. http://www.azlyrics.com/lyrics/vanhalen/bestofbothworlds.html

5. http://letusreason.org/Wf36.htm

6. http://store.hillsong.com/

7. http://www.scientology.org/what-is-scientology.html?link=sidewis

8. http://www1.cbn.com/700club/joel-osteen-man-behind-americas-largest-church

9. http://www.spurgeongems.org/vols22-24/chs1342.pdf

   1877 Ups and Downs of Dagon Charles Spurgeon Sermon

10. https://en.wikipedia.org/wiki/Moralistic_therapeutic_deism

11. http://www.dailybread.com.au/5000/200/202/index_charles_finney.html

12. http://www.daystar.com/ondemand/video/?video=3957101671001

    http://www.itsmilkandhoney.com/all-the-reasons-we-loved-colour-conference-2015/

13. http://apprising.org/2011/ 09/ 04/ beth-moore-praises-brother-lawrence-and-obscures-the-reformation/

    And

    http://apprising.org/2012/01/11/beth-moore-the-mystic/

14. https://en.wikipedia.org/wiki/Lectio_Divina

15. https://www.youtube.com/watch?v=BvwKl63sGqM

16. http://apprising.org/2009/12/09/rick-warren-now-openly-promoting-contemplative-spiritualitymysticism/

17. ASummaryofChristianHistory- RobertAndrewBaker,JohnM. Landers p. 274 published by Broadman and HolmanPublishers

Chapter 24 - Church of the Poisoned Mind

1. http://vimeo.com/16946072

2. http://coercioncode.com/2015/12/20/hillsong-carols-2015-silent-night-sordid-night/

3. http://www.reformedreader.org/spurgeon/dgc09.htm

Chapter 25 - Nights on the Broadway

1. https://hillsongchurchwatch.com/tag/the-church-i-see/

2. https://www.youtube.com/watch?v=HYv5X35mgtY

3. http://saddlebackworship.com/academy/

Chapter 26 – All Along The Watchtower

1. https://en.wikipedia.org/wiki/Heavy_metal_music

   And

https://en.wikipedia.org/wiki/Christian_metal

2. http://www.av1611.org/crock/crockex3.html

3. http://www.timetracts.com/Tracts/knowthembytheirfruit.htm

   http://www.av1611.org/question/cqsaved.html

4. https://youtu.be/lp82l9YIy4E

   and https://youtube/PSoIUtxSDaw

5. https://www.youtube.com/watch?v=c9yyR6vMZRQ

6. http://www.planetshakers.com/college/

7. http://www.ridingthebeast.com/numbers/nu777.php

Examples of planetshakers

8. Get up -
   http://www.youtube.com/watch?v=uCiGH8GJVd8&feature

   =related

   http://www.youtube.com/watch?v=NLIzp16H9s&feature =related

9. Dance Now-

   http://www.youtube.com/watch?v=rA cyZpPbSc&NR=1

10. Boom -
    http://www.youtube.com/watch?v=kkvZCLpHyDc&feature=relate
    d

    Jump around -

    http://www.youtube.com/watch?v=IrVeD4LBHhI

11. http://www.theage.com.au/news/national/young-believers-pray-
    and-sway-to-a-
    newbeat/2007/04/07/1175366538300.html?page=fullpage#cont
    entSwap1

12. http://en.wikipedia.org/wiki/ Mortification (band)# cite note-
    Imperiumi-0

13. https://www.youtube.com/watch?v=ElA1E8goqjk

    Also

    https://www.youtube.com/watch?v=0m_ZtwivwQ8

14. http://www.interdisciplinary.net/ci/mmp/mmp1/moberg.pdf

Chapter 27 -- Satan's Saints Rock Rocketown

1. http://www.beliefnet.com/columnists/gospelsoundcheck/?s=rocketown

2. http://www.nashvilledowntown.com/go/rocketown

3. http://www.examiner.com/gospel-music-entertainment-in-nashville/ rocketown-controversy-hardcore-satanic-metal-at-christian-teen- venue-rocketown-halloween-week

4. http://only-with-corroborative-evidence.blogspot.com/2007/07/why- does-michael- w-smiths-rocketown.html).

5. https://aubreeblogpage.wordpress.com/2012/11/08/michael-w-smith-wolves-in-sheeps-clothing/

6. http://www.metrolyrics.com/black-valor-lyrics-the-black-dahlia-murder.html

7. http://www.jesus-is-savior.com/Evils%20in%20America/CCM/michael_smith_phony.htm

8. Ibid

Chapter 28 – Against the Wind

1. Paul S. Jones Chapter 21, Luther and Bar song: The Truth Please: Singing and making music (Phillipsburg, New Jersey P&R Publishing 2006 P. 171 –178)

2. R A Torrey How to Obtain Fullness of Power in Christian Life and Service (Fleming H Revell Company 1897 Chap. 4 The Power Of Prayer, P.81)

Chapter 29 - All You Need is Love

1. https://www.studylight.org/commentaries/guz/exodus-32.html

2. ibid

3. ibid

4. http://www.studylight.org/commentaries/mhm/view.cgi?book=ex&chapter= 032

5. ibid

6. A W Tozer The great god entertainment -extract found in PDF of the best of Tozer – P 71 from the scripture alone.com

7. http://www.biblebb.com/files/spurgeon/amusement.htm

Chapter 30 – I heard through the grapevine

1. The Knowledge of the Holy, James Clarke & Co .Ltd Pg. 95 published 1965 Great Britain

Or see Pg. 114 of The Knowledge of the Holy Authentic Media 2008

2. Precious Remedies Against Satan's Devices: Being a Companion for Christians ... By Thomas Brooks Pg 55

Brian Houston Saddleback

https://hillsongchurchwatch.com/2013/01/20/brian-houston-accused-of-his-continual-avoidance-of-the-subject-of-repentance-part-1/

https://saddleback.com/archive/blog/community-blog/2012/12/18/faux-new-years-party

3. Destined to Reign p.27.

4. http://www.cwm.org.au

Bible Versions: All preaching the same Message?

Written by James P Smith

Published: 17 December 2014

Chapter 31 - Won't Get Fooled Again

1. http://press.princeton.edu/titles/6679.html

2. http://www.christianpost.com/news/andy-stanley-christians-are-now-the-minority-must-adapt-approach-to-sharing-gospel-92232/

3. http://www.dennyburk.com/andy-stanleys-poison-pill-for-the-doctrine-of-scripture/

4. http://hillsong.com/media-releases/hillsong-church-statement-%20by-senior-pastor-brian-houston/Martyn Lloyd-JonesSermon

5. http://www.mljtrust.org/search/?q=once+saved

   One Saved Always Saved? Romans 14 and also the illustration is referenced the book; Preaching And The Emerging Church A Homiletical Analysis And Critique Of A Select Number O fEmerging Church Pastors Mark Driscoll Dan Kimball Brian Mclaren And Doug Pagitt With Contemporary Implications For Evangelical Expository Preaching Publisher: Proquest, Umi Dissertation Publishing (2011) Author John S Bohannon-mentioned on Pg 309 in footnotes Surprised

6. http://www.christianpost.com/news/gay-couple-at-center-of-hillsong-controversy-say-theyve-been-open-and-forthright-about-relationship-from-the-get-go-142563/#bFpZP6tHuAkB2gxJ.99 hillsongs statement

7. http://hillsong.com/collected/blog/2015/08/do-i-love-gay-people/#.Vqa7ifl97IU engaged

8. http://www.christianpost.com/news/hillsongs-brian-houston-corrects-report-that-openly-gay-couple-leads-nyc-church-choir-insists-stance-on-homosexuality-absolutely-has-not-changed-142255/

9. https://www.nytimes.com/2014/10/18/us/megachurch-pastor-signals-shift-in-tone-on-gay-marriage.html?_r=0

10. https://www.youtube.com/watch?v=nf93TDOOreY

    also

    http://www.out.com/entertainment/popnography/2014/08/27/broadway-boyfriends-reed-kelly-josh-canfield-join-survivor

    http://www.playbill.com/article/broadway-boyfriends-of-survivor- get-engaged-on-stage-plus-video-com-340487

11. http://gonola.com/2015/03/24/gonola-interview-grand-marshals-of- new-orleans-pride-festival.html

    and

    Interview

    https://www.youtube.com/watch?v=OiSmkwwSQOM

    Gonola pride statement

12. http://gonola.com/2015/06/04/high-five-to-new-orleans-pride.html

13. The History of Romanism Rev. John Dowling 1845 Edward Walker publisher 114 Fulto n Street New York 4th Book 2Chapter 6Pgs. 110- 111 –Book In public domain

14. http://www.christianpost.com/news/kevin-durant-talks-baptism-at-hillsong-nyc-church-98716/

15. http://www.gq.com/story/inside-hillsong-church-of-justin-bieber-kevin-durant

16. http://hillsongchurchwatch.com/2015/10/26/hillsongs-homophobic- leadership/

17. http://www.abc.net.au/news/2015-11-23/hillsong-leader-ignored- conflict-interest-commission-finds/6964172

18. (Man, the Dwelling Place of God, Chapter 10 The Old Cross and the New pgs. 37,38 originally published 1966-revised 1977 by Zur Ltd - Published by Wing Spread Publishers Camp Hill PA, USA)

Chapter 32 - Strange fire in the nostrils

1. https://www.studylight.org/commentaries/acc.html

2. http://graceonlinelibrary.org/church-ministry/preaching/preaching-that-hinders-revival-by-richard-owen-roberts/

3. http://www.baptistbiblebelievers.com/LinkClick.aspx?fileticket=ZKq2lSFPBx8%3D&tabid=307&mid=1011

4. http://biblehub.com/commentaries/leviticus/10-1.htm

5. ibid

6. http://www.fullbooks.com/Expositions-of-Holy-Scripturex518210.html

Chapter 33 - Jesus is just alright with me

1. Personal Declension and Revival of Religion in the Soul Chapter 1 Incipient Declension pg. 9 Octavius Winslow 1847 – Robert Carter New York --Publisher

Pages 278

Internet Archive

Book contributor Princeton Theological Seminary Library

http://www.gmission.org/study/pdf/Personal_declension_and_rev
ival_of_relig.pdf

2. ibid

3. http://biblehub.com/commentaries/mhcw/leviticus/2.htm

4. https://en.wikipedia.org/wiki/Kyphi

5. https://en.wikipedia.org/wiki/Gold_parting

6. http://www.britannica.com/technology/silver-processing

7. https://en.wikipedia.org/wiki/Cupellation

8. http://www.joethorn.net/blog/2012/10/16/25-marks

Chapter 34 – Knockin' on heaven's Door

1. http://www.charlottemagazine.com/Charlotte-Magazine/ January-
2014/The-Story-of-Elevation-
Church/index.php?cparticle=1&siarticle=0#artanc

2. http://illuminatiwatcher.com/decoding-illuminati-symbolism-
triangles-pyramids-and-the-sun/

3. http://www.muslimsandtheworld.com/triangle-inside-circle-
occult-illuminati-symbol/

4. http://www.crossroad.to/articles2/006/migration-2.htm

5. http://musicians4freedom.com/wp-content/uploads/2013/04/
Triangle-inside-Circle-Occult-Illuminati-Symbol-Muslims-and-the-
World.pdf

6. http://illuminatiwatcher.com/decoding-illuminati-symbolism-
triangles-pyramids-and-the-sun/

7. http://www.masonsmart.com/freemason-symbols.html

8. http://www.masonic-lodge-of-education.com/square-and-
compasses. html#ixzz3L79wXiR1

9. http://illuminatiwatcher.com/decoding-illuminati-symbolism-
triangles-pyramids-and-the-sun/

10. http://www.cuttingedge.org/free16.htm

11. http://illuminatiwatcher.com/decoding-illuminati-symbolism-triangles-pyramids-and-the-sun/

12. http://www.tekgnostics.com/Eye.htm#.VKSvTfmSzZ0

13. http://www.masonic-lodge-of-education.com/masonic-eye.html

14. http://elevationchurch.org/our-code/

15. http://www.whitehavennews.com.au/papal-encyclical-demonstrates-need-to-address-climate-and-energy-as-integrated-priorities/

Chapter 35 - Glorious Ruins

1. http://onlinedigitalpublishing.com/article/Morning Rises/1436067/164571/article.html

2. http://www.christianpost.com/news/hillsong-live-to-release-22nd-live-album-glorious-ruins-96049/

3. https:// brianandbobbie.com/

   Previously on the above site now found at

   https://www.facebook.com/hillsongstockholm/posts/10151602715456764

4. http://themadmanblogger.blogspot.com.au/search?q=ruins

5. The Works of John Howe = The Living Temple

   -- Sourced from US Archive as PDF published 1863 – reference pg 306

6. http://found-in-grace.blogspot.com.au/2013/06/2013-06-02-glorious-ruins-pastor-brian.html

   Hillsong Trailer

7. https://www.youtube.com/watch?v=pMOnz9r48aU/

8. http://www.sdrock.com/messages/2013-06-09/

   http://youtu.be/6upkk311XYQ/

Chapter 36 - Houston we have problem

1. http://hillsongchurchwatch.com/2014/03/17/brian-houston-the-muslim-and-you-we-actually-serve-the-same-god

2. http://coercioncode.com/2013/08/02/desiring-god-or-desiring-influence-part-2/

3. http://www.prophecynewswatch.com/2014/March20/201.html#vrjGXSMOdak5sOKO.99

4. http://www.lighthousetrailsresearch.com/blog/?p=7108/

5. http://www.zenit.org/en/articles/pope-s-address-to-representatives- of-the-churches-ecclesial-communities-and-other-religions

6. http://www.catholicherald.co.uk/news/2013/03/20/full-text-of-pope-franciss-address-to-religious-leader/

7. http://www.wnd.com/2013/11/pope-authentic-islam-opposes-violence/

8. http://www.inquisitr.com/3110802/pope-francis-equates-isis-jihad-with-the-christian-great-commission/

9. http://www.frontpagemag.com/fpm/263709/pope-francis-fool-or-liar-islam-raymond-ibrahim

10. http://www.answering-islam.org/authors/durie/islamic_jesus.html

11. http://www.god.t v/ hil lsong-church /video / brian-houston-hillsong-tv/living-for-the-masters-well-done

Chapter 37 – Would I Lie to You

1. http://www.christianpost.com/news/hillsong-church-pastor-brian- houston-denies-promoting-chrislam-says-sermon-taken-out-of- context-116966/

2. http://www.bible.ca/islam/islam-photos-moon-worship-archealolgy.htm/

And

https://www.biblebelievers.org.au/moongod.htm

3. http://www.religionresearchinstitute.org/Mohammad/ishmael.htm

4. http://ivarfjeld.com/2014/03/18/hillsong-and-brian-houston-join- the-new-age-movement/

5. http://www.cbn.com/spirituallife/OnlineDiscipleship/ UnderstandingIslam/Is the Arab nation descended from Ishmael. aspx

6. http://www.religionresearchinstitute.org/Mohammad/ ishmael.htm

7. ibid

8. http://religionresearchinstitute.org/mohammad/ishmael.htm/

9. http://www.cbn.com/spirituallife/OnlineDiscipleship/ UnderstandingIslam/Is the Arab nation descended from Ishmael. aspx

10. http://www.allaboutreligion.org/five-pillars-of-islam-faq.htm#sthash.

11. http://www.answering-islam.org/Hahn/son.html/

12. http://executableoutlines.com/islam/islam 03.htm http://islam.uga.edu/jesusdif.html

13. http://themostimportantnews.com/archives/islamic-prayers-

to-be-held-at-the-vatican

14. http://themostimportantnews.com/archives/in-new-york-pope-francis-embraced-chrislam-and-laid-a-foundation-for-a-one-world-religion/

15. http://abcnews.go.com/US/read-pope-francis-yorks-st-patricks-cathedral/story?id=34023376

Also

http://www.nowtheendbegins.com/the-shocking-message-pope-francis-preached-at-new-yorks-st-patricks-cathedral/

Chapter 38 -- Eyes Wide Shut

1. http://www.banner.org.uk/misc/vision.html

2. http://w w w.holly woodreporter.com/news /rough-seas-noah-darren-aronofsky-679315

3. ibid

4. http://saturndeathcult.com/crimes-of-the-saturn-death-cult/stanley-kubrick-and-the-saturn-death-cult/

5. http://saturndeathcult.com/crimes-of-the-saturn-death-cult/stanley-kubrick-and-the-saturn-death-cult/

6. https://en.wikipedia.org/wiki/Eyes_Wide_Shut

7. http://www.banner.org.uk/misc/vision.html

Chapter 39 – Another Dark Horse

1. http://www.billboard.com/articles/columns/pop-shop/5915761/katy-perrys-prismatic-tour-coming-to-australia

2. https://en.wikipedia.org/wiki/The_Prismatic_World_Tour

3. http://youtu.be/10rx15v28yk

4. https://www.youtube.com/watch?v=vkFnd3G607I

   and

   https://www.youtube.com/watch?v=TIfPYTW_z6A

5. https://en.wikipedia.org/wiki/56th_Annual_Grammy_Awards

   Also

   http://youtu.be/ZSaxGesjybA

6. http://youtu.be/NYiSpDL3Htk

7. http://www.britannica.com/EBchecked/topic/646097/witches-sabbath

8. http://www.bibliotecapleyades.net/cienciareal/cienciareal20.htm

9. https://en.wikipedia.org/wiki/PRISM_(surveillance_program)

10. http://www.truthnet.org/Zechariah/Chapter6/Zechariah-6.htm

11. http://blogs.wsj.com/economics/2015/01/19/very-rich-get-very-richer-wealthiest-20-hold-94-5-of-worlds-money/

12. https://www.bustle.com/articles/172805-the-lyrics-of-katy-perrys-rio-olympics-song-will-remind-you-of-her-other-inspirational-anthem

13. Ibid

14. http://hillsong.com/network/

Chapter 40 -- Walk like an Egyptian

1. https://en.wikipedia.org – tourism in Egypt

2. http://w w w.hillsong.com/ blogs /collected/2013/may/mount-zion-colour-2013-stage-design

3. Ibid

4. http://www.jesus-is-savior.com/False%20Religions/ Illuminati/ illuminati exposed-part2.htm

5. http://www.granddesignexposed.com/obelisk/meaning.html

6. http://www.ancient-code.com/sacred-allignment-the-constellation-of-orion-and-ancient-egypt/

   And

   http://www.bibliotecapleyades.net/piramides/esp_piramide_8.ht m

7. http://rikijo.blogspot.com.au/2010/07/phase-v-operation-maras-kiss-connecting.html

8. http://w w w.hillsong.com/ blogs /collected/2013/may/mount-zion-colour-2013-stage-design

9. http://coercioncode.com/2015/01/13/hillsong-uniteds-pyramid-scheme-zion-tour-2013/

10. http://rikijo.blogspot.com/2010/07/phase-v-operation-maras-kiss- connecting.html#ixzz3P9CmSHNP

11. http://www.tourplanisrael.com/?CategoryID= 622&ArticleID=325

12. http://www.rense.com/general44/gikdeb.htm

13. Ibid

Chapter 41 --- Bridge Over Troubled Waters

1. http://www.allmusic.com/album/zion-mw0002469943

2. http://hillsong.com/contributor/taya-smith/

3. https://en.m.wikipedia.org/wiki/Oceans_(EP)#cite note-4

   2014 Annual Report

4. http://d9nqqwcssctr8.cloudfront.net/wp-content/uploads/2015/11/15233735/AnnualReport14WEB.pdf

5. Plato,Laws700-701a.citedinWellesz,p.395.

6. http://metroyouthnetwork.com/2013/08/27/the-story-behind-hillsong-uniteds-oceans/

7. http://thomasmarkzuniga.com/2014/02/girl-sings-oceans-hillsong-united/

8. HillsongUnited-Oceans(WhereFeetMayFail)Lyrics|MetroLyrics

9. http://dictionary.reference.com/browse/ocean?s=t

10. http://www.thesaurus.com/browse/the+great+unknown and

http://www.abc.net.au/radionational /programs /futuretense / mapping-the-great-unknown-the-ocean-floor/5731532

11. http://www.billboard.com/articles/news/6274271/hillsong-united-wins-big-at-dove-awards

12. (foreword to Get Up Off Your Knees: Preaching the U2 Catalog). ("Calvin College on U2," Christianity Today, Feb. 2005).

13. (McLarenandCampolo,Adventures inMissingthe Point, 2003,pp. 50, 51)

14. Crystal, David, ed. (1995), "Mystery Religions", Cambridge Encyclopedia of The English Language, Cambridge: Cambridge UP.

15. http://ebookee.org/The-Esoteric-Mystical-and-Occult-Christianity-Books453936.html#4tcyjpxkPTjgJmCQ.99 https://en.wikipedia.org/wiki/Greco-Roman mysteries

16. http://www.huffingtonpost.com/2013/11/05/australia-hillsong-church- influence n 4214660.html

17. Ibid

18. ibid

19. https://en.wikipedia.org/wiki/Religious ecstasy

20. Ibid

21. http://www.stevenhalpern.com/prod/meditation-music/initiation.html

22. http://sofiatopia.org/equiaeon/water.htm

23. www.relevantmagazine.com/culture/music/hillsong-united-0 #Jm6 s2Gfk03HUEAYw.99

24. https://www.youtube.com/watch?v=M-3s78M4jv0-1:02:46

25. https://www.youtube.com/watch?v=M-3s78M4jv0-1:04:00

26. https://coercioncode.com/2016/08/04/hillsongs-young-and-free-youth-revival-or-hexing-the-youth

27. http://www.theforbiddenknowledge.com/symbology/2o5.htm

28. https://en.wikipedia.org/wiki/OctaviusWinslow

29. Personal Declension and Personal Revival in the life of the soul – Octavius Winslow 1847- pg3Preface

Chapter 42 - Dawning of the Age of Aquarius___

1. http://www.nytimes.com/2007/12/29/arts/design/29awak.html?r=1&

2. http://www.starwars.com/video/star-wars-the-force-awakens-official-teaser

3. http://www.tonyrobbins.com/events/unleash-the-power-within/

4. http://www.christianbook.com/life-wide-open-david-jeremiah/9781591452867/pd/452864

5. http://www.elevation-worship.com/

6. http://www.songlyrics.com/hillsong/wake-lyrics/

7. http://www.lucistrust.org:8081/obooks/?q=node/288

8. http://www.conspiracyarchive.com/NewAge/LucisTrust.htm

9. https://www.lucistrust.org/arcane school/talks and articles/ the esoteric meaninglucifer

Chapter 43 - Hillsong and the Coming AntiChrist

1. https://en.wikipedia.org/wiki/Francis_Bacon

2. http://vigilantcitizen.com/musicbusiness/the-hidden-meaning- of-lady-gagas-telephone/

3. http://vigilantcitizen.com/musicbusiness/britney-spears-mind-control-and-hold-it-against-me/

4. http://vigilantcitizen.com/musicbusiness/the-hidden-meaning-of-lady-gagas-telephone/

5. http://youtu.be/-AyJfSrPPU4

6. http://abcnews.go.com/blogs/entertainment/2013/12/beyonce-or- beysus-singers-last-supper-pose/

7. http://coercioncode.com/2014/06/28/beyonces-pastor-defends-her/

8. http://freemantv.com/beyonce-baphomet-sasha-fierce/

9. Ibid

10. http://www.harpersbazaar.com/culture/features/news/a11853/hillsong-church/

11. https://www.youtube.com/watch?v=angFSgO2oZw

Addtl. clips

12. https://www.youtube.com/watch?v=KXjV8f7THP0

13. https://www.youtube.com/watch?v=TPlcYWglh8

14. http://www.lyricsmode.com/lyrics/k/kesha/dancingwith the devil. html/

15. http://illuminatimindcontrol.com/rihanna-the-illuminati-princess-pushing-satanic-agenda/

and

http://beginningandend.com/rhianna-illuminati-princess-tweets-satan/

16. http://www.whitehorsemedia.com/docs/THETWO BABYLONS.pdf - P 14

17. 'The Externalisation of the Hierarchy', Alice Bailey P. 514

Chapter 44 –The Fall of Empires: Faith In Ruins

1. http://www.starpulse.com/news/CaseyJohnson/2010/06/15/ megan fox poses with nude mannequinin

2. http://exposingthematrix.blogspot.com.au/2012 / 03/masonic-checkerboardduality-symbolism.html

http://v igilantcitizen.com/sinistersites/sinister-sites-irs-headquarters-maryland/

3. http://www.themasonictrowel.com/masonictalk/stb/stbs/94-04.htm

4. https://en.wikipedia.org/wiki/Black-and-whitedualism

5. https://www.youtube.com/watch?v=zH1soECEGfM

6. http://www.rainerlinz.net/NMA/articles/altering.html

7. http://www.cuttingedge.org/news/n1487.cfm

8. http://www.breitbart.com/national-security/2016/01/12/
   professional-atheist-dawkins-says-christianity-bulwark-against-
   something-worse/

9. http://www.smh.com.au/entertainment/movies/society-is-past-
   its-use-by-date-20111202-1oajg#ixzz3yRhjKlU2

10. http://tobingrant.religionnews.com/2014/ 01/27/great-decline-
    religion-united-states-one-graph/#sthash.Vy0Bv43t.dpuf

11. http://www.huffingtonpost.com/cari-pattison/what-times-square-
    yoga-ta b7757436.html

12. http://www.spectator.co.uk/2016/ 05/ britain-really-is-ceasing-
    to-be-a-christian-country/

13. https://en.wikipedia.org/wiki/Drops ofJupiter

14. Taken from the lyrics of the song Drops of Jupiter by the band
    Train- released in 2001.

Chapter 45 – Come Together

1. http://www.freerepublic.com/focus/f-religion/1025395/posts

2. http://www.mirror.co.uk/news/world-news/lightning-bolt- hit-
   vatican-not-1705156

3. https://en.wikipedia.org/wiki/Pope Francis

4. http://www.bethelbaptistlondon.com/Replacing%20Hymns%20
   with%20Contemporary%20Praise%20Music.pdf

5. http://rainhadocanto10-evangelicalchristian.blogspot.com.
   au/2011/03/musical-associations-and-ccm-adaptation.html

6. http://www.huffingtonpost.com/2013/11/05/australia-hillsong-
   church-influence_n_4214660.html

7. http://www.wayoflife.org/database/how_contemporary_
   praise_transforms_churches.html and
   http://cbcyouthquakertown.com/music/

8. http://hillsongchurchwatch.com/tag/world-youth-day-2008/Also
   https://las5solas.wordpress.com/tag/symphony-of-scripture/

9. http://www.christiantoday.com/article/darlene.zschech.andrea.bo celli.sing.at.prayer.for.persecuted.church.event.hosted.by.pope. francis/57935.htm

10. http://www.christianpost.com/news/pope-francis-joins-lecrae-hillsong-historic-1-million-strong-together-2016-dc-event-164925/

Poland

11. https://coerc ioncode.com /2016/07/27/kra kow-pola nd- world-youth-day-2016-symbol-of-the-phoenix/

12. https://coercioncode.com/2016/06/11/pope-francis-joins-hillsong- united-and-lacrae-at-together-2016-dc-event/

13. https://watch.pair.com/cult-diakrisis.html

14. http://www.granddesignexposed.com/obelisk/meaning.html

15. http://blogs.weta.org/boundarystones/2013/07/16/mystery-popes-stone

16. http://christiannews.net/2016/06/10/together-2016-organizer-meets- with-pope-francis-to-unite-christians-catholics-on-national-mall/

17. https://foolishnesstotheworld.wordpress.com/2016/06/12/pope-meets-again-with-charismatic-protestants/- MikeBickle

18. http://www.theopedia.com/roman-catholicism

19. http://www.theforbiddenknowledge.com/hardtruth / council_of_trent.htm

20. The History of the church William Jones PDF Vol 2 pg. 19 http:// www.biblerays .com/uploa ds/8/0/4/2/8042023/ history_of_the_church_v2.pdf

21. For its Final Propositions, see http://www.zenit.org/en/articles/final- list-of-propositions-of-the-synod-of- bishops (March2014)

22. See Pope Francis Evangelii Gaudium. The Joy of the Gospel (London, CTS:2013)

23. http://together.ourchurchweb.org.uk/berkshire/docstore/97.pdf

24. http://w2.vatican.va/content/francesco/en/apost_exhortations/ documents/papa-francesco_esortazione-ap_20131124_evangelii-gaudium.html

http://www.understandthetimes.org/audio% 20commentary/ transcripts/rwinterview4.shtml and

25. http://www.understandthetimes.org/comentary/c143rickwarren. shtml

26. https://ezekielcountdown.wordpress.com/2014/ 08/21/is-beth-moores-spiritual-awakening-taking-the-evangelical-church-towards- rome/

27. http://www.chron.com/news/houston-texas/houston/article/Osteen- meets-with-Pope-Francis-at-Vatican-5533805.php

28. http://www.click 2houston.com/news /joel-osteen-talks-with-local-2s-dominique-sachse-about-visit-with-pope-francis/ 26377834

29. http://www.christianpost.com/news/pastor-joel-osteen-mormon-senator-other-us-leaders-meet-with-pope-francis-in-rome- video-121116/

30. http://christiannews.net/2014/06/08/joel-osteen-meets-with-pope- francis-at-vatican-hes-made-the-church-more-inclusive/

31. http://www.deliveredbygrace.com/joel-osteen-does-it-again/

32. http://www.star-telegram.com/news/local/community/fort-worth/ article3863248.html#storylink=cpy

33. http://www.aljazeera.com/news/2016/ 02/pope-meets-russian-orthodox-head-962-year-split-160212202522134.html

34. https://en.wikipedia.org/wiki/Pontifex_Maximus

35. http://w2.vatican.va/content/francesco/en/speeches/2016/june/ documents/papa-francesco_20160625_armenia-incontro-ecumenico. html

36. https://ezekielcountdown.wordpress.com/2014/ 08/21/is-beth-moores-spiritual-awakening-taking-the-evangelical-church-towards- rome/

37. TheHistoryoftheChurch Vol 1pg56PrefaceWilliamJones

http:// www.thechristianidentityforum.net/downloads/History-Church1.pdf

38. Eliphas Leviquote—Dr. Rara Coomaraswamy, The Destruction of the Christian Tradition, p.133.

39. http://www.songfacts.com/detail.php?id=191

40. http://www.popmatters.com/feature/133565-the-sentimental-journey-of-imagine/

Chapter 46 -- We built this city

1. Alice A. Bailey, The Destiny of the Nations, Lucis, 1949, p.152.

2. https://en.wikipedia.org/wiki/Zion_(Hillsong_United_album)

3. ibidWikipedia

4. http://www.theforbiddenknowledge.com/hardtruth/13_33_freemason_sig.htm

5. http://humansarefree.com/2014/10/exposing-shadow-forces-behind-nwo.html

6. http://numerology-school.com/karmic-numbers.html

7. http://www.numerology.com/numerology-numbers/11-master-number

8. ibid

9. http://thegabrielmessages.com/the-1111-gateway-to-unity-consciousness/

10. https://en.wikipedia.org/wiki/Armistice_Day

11. http://numerology-thenumbersandtheirmeanings.blogspot.com.au/2011/05/number-11.html

12. http://www.cuttingedge.org/pages/seminar2/NUMBERS.htm

13. http://www.numerology.com/numerology-numbers/11-master-number

14. Bullinger, E.W. NumberinScripture,KregelPublications, 1967 P.205

15. http://www.sacredpursuit.org/gpage39.html

16. http://amos37.com/abna2/#sthash.Qm2zZlb6.dpuf

17. Ibid

18. http://inthenameofpurpose.org/

    and

    http://www.understandthetimes.org/commentary/c97.shtml

19. Rick Warren, CNN Larry King Live, Aired December 2, 2005, Transcript,

   http://transcripts.cnn.com/TRANSCRIPTS/0512/02/ lkl.01.html.

20. http://666surveillancesystem.com/tomorrowland-paganism-on-steroids-part-1/

21. http://www.contenderministries.org/UN/ciaun.php

22. http://www.catholicherald.co.uk/news/2015/11/30/pope-francis- says-he-is-not-losing-any-sleep-over-vatican-leaks-trial/

23. https://www.yahoo.com/news/pope-says-fundamentalism-disease- religions-041229589.html

24. http://www.israelnationalnews.com/News/News.aspx/181689 #. VA5HbRYXOXx

Chapter 47 - Dancing with the Devil

1. https://coercioncode.com/2016/04/19/hillsong-london-satanic-sanctioned-easter-service/

2. http://www.jewishvirtuallibrary.org/jsource/History/Maccabees. html

3. http://jewishencyclopedia.com/articles/1589-antiochus-iv-epiphanes

4. http://www.cliohres.net/books4/1/02.pdf

5. Ibid

6. http://www.nostos.com/olympics/

7. http://dide.mag.sch.gr/grfa/Olympiaki_paideia/kathigites.pdf

8. https://www.moriel.org/sermons-in-english/5957-hanukkah-part-1. html

9. http://www.cliohres.net/books4/1/02.pdf

10. ibid

11. https://en.wikipedia.org/wiki/Menelaus_(High_Priest)

12. http://www.reformjudaism.org/hanukkah-history/

13. http://www.bibarch.com/chronology/Hellenistic/H-Period.htm

14. http://www.bible-history.com/archaeology/greece/2-antiochus-iv-%20bust-bb.html – copy and paste to search engine

15. https://www.moriel.org/sermons-in-english/5957-hanukkah-part-1. html

16. http://www.reformjudaism.org/hanukkah-history

17. http://www.jewishvirtuallibrary.org/jsource/History/Maccabees.html

18. http://jewishencyclopedia.com/articles/1589-antiochus-iv-epiphanes

19. https://www.moriel.org/sermons-in-english/5957-hanukkah-part-1. html

20. https://www.christiancourier.com/articles/1191-daniels-prophecy-of-antiochus-epiphanes

21. https://www.moriel.org/sermons-in-english/5957-hanukkah-part-1. html

22. ibid

23. https://www.youtube.com/watch?v=zwg2GPF8Aw8

Chapter 48 –Hillsong or Hellsong

No Endnotes or footnotes

Chapter 49 - Epilogue

1. http://www.piratechristian.com/berean-examiner/2015/08/03/update-hillsong-issues-statement-8-months-after-worship-leader-announces-his-upcoming-homosexual-marriage/

2. http://www.playbill.com/article/broadway-boyfriends-of-survivor-get-engaged-on-stage-plus-video-com-340487

3. http://www.christianpost.com/news/hillsongs-brian-houston-corrects-report-that-openly-gay-couple-leads-nyc-church-choir-insists-stance-on-homosexuality-absolutely-has-not-changed-142255/

4. "I'd Rather Have Jesus" is from the album A Beautiful Life: Songs of Inspiration. Written by Rhea Miller/George Beverly Shea.

27884484R00253

Printed in Poland
by Amazon Fulfillment
Poland Sp. z o.o., Wrocław